THE BASEBALL
HALL OF SHAME™

THE BASEBALL HALL OF SHAME™

THE BEST OF BLOOPERSTOWN

BRUCE NASH and ALLAN ZULLO

LYONS PRESS
Guilford, Connecticut
An imprint of Globe Pequot Press

Lyons Press is an imprint of Globe Pequot Press.

Project editor: Meredith Dias
Layout: Mary Ballachino

Library of Congress Cataloging-in-Publication Data

Nash, Bruce M.
The baseball hall of shame / Bruce Nash and Allan Zullo.
  p. cm.
ISBN 978-0-7627-7845-4
1. Baseball—United States—Humor. I. Zullo, Allan. II. Title.
GV863.A1N36 2012
796.357—dc23

                              2011040064

Printed in the United States of America

10 9 8 7 6 5 4 3 2 1

To my true blue Dodger pals Waylon Sall, William Kramer,
and Jonathan Kramer, for inspiring me to bring back these zany
Baseball Hall of Shame™ stories for a whole new generation of readers.
—BRUCE NASH

To my son-in-law Mike Gorospe, who plays baseball the way he
lives his life—with passion, joy, honor, and grit.
—ALLAN ZULLO

CONTENTS

ACKNOWLEDGMENTS

We are especially grateful to those former players who shared a few laughs with us as they recounted the inglorious but funny moments that earned them a place in The Baseball Hall of Shame™.

For their research efforts, we wish to thank Jess Davis, Dylan King, Karen Nusbaum, and Emily Butali. In addition, we offer our gratitude to John Horne, of the National Baseball Library, for all of his excellent research; to our editor, Keith Wallman, for his unflagging enthusiasm and support; to our project editor, Meredith Dias, for her diligence and professionalism; and to our agent, Doug Grad, for his passion and belief in this book from the beginning.

We also send a special shout-out to Jack Davis, one of America's most famous cartoonists and illustrators, whose artwork has graced all the Hall of Shame books. At the age of 86, Jack came out of semi-retirement to create the hilarious cover for this book. We are honored to have such a remarkable talent—a member of the Comic Book Hall of Fame and the Society of Illustrators Hall of Fame—on our team.

Finally, we wish to acknowledge the "curator" for our previous Hall of Shame books, the late Bernie Ward. He was instrumental in uncovering many of the vintage stories that appear in this book. Bernie will always be part of The Baseball Hall of Shame™.

FROM COOPERSTOWN TO BLOOPERSTOWN

In baseball, there is just no end to shame.

We're not talking about steroid use and performance-enhancing drugs, player suspensions and superstar confessions, congressional hearings and federal trials. No, the shame we're talking about is the flip side of Major League Baseball—the bloopers, blunders, and bone-headed plays that make us laugh.

In our *Baseball Hall of Shame*™ series, published between 1985 and 1992, we chronicled more than 100 years of baseball goofs and gaffes. As historians of the offbeat side of sports, we paid homage to the Major Leagues' zaniest characters, funniest plays, and head-scratchingest moments. For example, in true Hall of Shame fashion, Chicago Cubs outfielder Lou "The Mad Russian" Novikoff insisted that his wife taunt him from the stands because it made him a better hitter. Another classic Hall of Shamer was New York Yankees outfielder and famed trencher man Ping Bodie, who took on Percy the ostrich in the heavyweight spaghetti-eating championship of the world and beat the bird in the 11th round. Then, there's Philadelphia Phillies batter Richie Ashburn, who hit a screaming foul ball into the stands that smacked a grand-mother in the face and then, as she was being carried out on a stretcher, whacked another foul ball that struck her again! And don't forget pitcher Burleigh Grimes. He was so furious at Goose Goslin for getting a hit off him that three innings later he threw a beanball at Goslin—while Goose was still standing in the on-deck circle!

Although we stopped writing the Hall of Shame series to pursue separate interests, our love for baseball—especially the game's wacky side—never waned. Much to our delight, the national pastime has continued to provide fans with a never-ending supply of embarrassingly nutty moments. Whether he's an All-Star or a journeyman, every ball-player is capable on any given day of a goofy misplay.

Over the years, we have, in our own individual ways, shared many of our favorite Hall of Shame stories with a whole new generation. Bruce has been regaling young fans at Dodger Stadium with classic accounts of shame. Allan has, too, with his grandchildren, nieces, and nephews, and with kids playing Cal Ripken Baseball in Tallahassee, Florida, and Asheville, North Carolina.

So it was only a matter of time before we decided to return with another irreverent volume that not only picks up where we left off 20 years ago but also celebrates the national pastime's all-time craziest moments: *The Baseball Hall of Shame™: The Best of Blooperstown*.

If our selection process seems totally subjective to you, that's because it is. However, we did have certain standards that all inductees had to meet. For each incident, we asked ourselves such questions as: Is it true? Does it make us laugh? Is it so outrageous that we shake our heads in disbelief? Does it make a good yarn? If the answer was yes to all those questions, then the incident had an excellent chance of making the cut.

We were after the "wow!" factor. Like, "Are you kidding me? That really happened? Oh, wow!" As a result, you won't find a whole lot of statistics highlighting the worst in batting, fielding, and pitching. You can go to a record book or encyclopedia for that kind of information. What we tried to chronicle was the human element behind those stats— the unintended, hilarious, red-faced moments when a player, manager, coach, or fan screwed up in a funny way or did something else that would make you laugh.

We also favored little-known stories over the widely-known ones. That's why you won't read about Eddie Gaedel. As most every fan knows, St. Louis Browns owner Bill Veeck sent the 3-foot-7 little person up to bat in a 1951 game for laughs, and Gaedel walked in his only plate appearance. But you *will* read about Kitty Burke, the brassy nightclub singer who caused an uproar when she "pinch-hit" during a 1935 game between the Cincinnati Reds and St. Louis Cardinals.

Among the criteria for induction into *The Baseball Hall of Shame™: The Best of Blooperstown* was that the shame-worthy incident had to occur during a Major League game or happen to a Major League player.

It broke our hearts to reject some great stories, but we had to because they took place in the minors. Take for instance, Clarence "Climax" Blethen, who kept his false teeth in his back pocket when he played for the Knoxville Smokies in 1933. Once, while sliding into second, he felt his choppers clamp down on his butt. In every way possible, Blethen was nipped at second. We learned of a prank pulled by fun-loving jokester Casey Stengel when he was an outfielder for the Montgomery (Alabama) Rebels in 1912. During a game, he hid in an underground irrigation box in left field. Minutes later, when a batter hit a fly ball to left, Stengel reached out from the box and made the catch.

We fans can debate in ballparks, sports bars, and man caves all the merits and demerits of those who may deserve induction into the hallowed halls of Blooperstown as well as Cooperstown. But there's one thing we can all agree on: As long as there is baseball, there will always be zany moments—because fame *and* shame are part of the game.

OPENING DAZE

For the Most Embarrassing Opening Day Debacles of All Time, The Baseball Hall of Shame™ Inducts:

FRANKIE ZAK
Shortstop · Pittsburgh, NL · April 17, 1945

No one wanted to be in Frankie Zak's shoes after his untied shoelaces cost his team an Opening Day victory.

Playing against the Reds in Cincinnati, the Pittsburgh Pirates were leading 1–0 in the top of the fifth inning when Zak, the Pirates shortstop, beat out a bunt, putting runners on first and second. Moments later, just as Reds pitcher Bucky Walters went into his stretch, Zak noticed that his shoe was untied and called for time. First base umpire Ziggy Sears waved his arms in an attempt to halt play, but his signal wasn't seen by Walters, plate umpire George Barr, or batter Jim Russell.

Walters threw the pitch and Russell clouted it into the right field bleachers for what he thought was a three-run homer. "I was feeling pretty damn good about it," Russell recalled. "But when I got to first base, Ziggy was holding up his hands and shaking his head and telling me to go back to the plate. I said, 'What the hell is wrong?' And he said, 'I called time, Jim. The homer doesn't count.'

"I hollered and [Pirates manager] Frankie Frisch argued, but there was nothing we could do about it. Through it all, Zak just stood on first shaking his head in shame."

Once Zak tied his shoe, Russell returned to the plate, but he couldn't duplicate his feat, although he did hit a single to drive in the only Pirates run of the inning. That was little consolation for Pittsburgh. Scoring only one fifth-inning run instead of three—thanks to Zak's untied shoe—the Pirates ended up losing 7–6 in 11 innings.

"I'll always remember we lost a game that we should have won on that homer," Russell said. "Zak kept apologizing so I couldn't get too mad at him."

The same couldn't be said for their manager. The next day, Frisch walked over to Zak's locker and handed him a package. "What's this?" asked the surprised shortstop.

"Buckle-up shoes," Frisch replied with a scowl. "I don't want to see you out there calling time to tie your damn shoes anymore."

EBBETS FIELD OPENING CEREMONIES
April 9, 1913

From the day of its birth, there was little doubt that Ebbets Field—home of the Brooklyn Dodgers (then known as the Superbas)—would be the scene of some of the daffiest moments in baseball history.

The crowd at the first Opening Day ceremonies of Charles Ebbets's new playground was treated to a preview of the Flatbush Follies that would be on display there off and on for nearly half a century.

Thousands of fans started lining up at dawn to get seats. They waited and waited and waited. That's because the ballpark's superintendent had forgotten the key to the front gate. An official rushed home for a spare key while the throng continued to hang on.

Once the gates swung open, the fans poured into the ballpark, ogling and admiring all the features. But the builder had neglected one thing—there was no press box. So the grousing sportswriters had to cover the big event from the grandstand.

Finally, the band struck up patriotic songs and the dignitaries and players started their march to center field for the flag-raising ceremony. But Charles Ebbets suddenly disrupted the procession by dropping to his knees behind second base to search in the grass for the 15 cents that he had dropped. Hot dog magnate Harry Stevens, who was walking with him, kindly offered to help Ebbets search for the coins. But Ebbets, a penny-pincher, waved him off in alarm, saying, "No, I don't want you to help me. You might find them."

Ebbets eventually rejoined the procession as it arrived at its destination. Bursting with pride, the owner turned to an aide and said, "The flag, please."

With his face turning red, the aide replied, "Sorry, Charlie, we forgot the flag."

KIRK GIBSON
Right Fielder · Detroit, AL · April 9, 1981

In the most humiliating game of his storied career, Kirk Gibson got bonked on the head *twice* with fly balls. And it happened on, of all days, the first Opening Day that he played in front of the hometown crowd.

Gibson, who made his Major League debut at the end of the 1979 season, had experienced his first Opening Day in 1980, but that had been on the road. Not until 1981 did he play a season opener at home.

"I was really looking forward to Opening Day," Gibson recalled. "It's like a holiday in Detroit. Everybody takes off work and goes to the game. You can't get another person in the stadium, and everybody there expects the Tigers to win."

Throughout spring training, the 23-year-old outfielder had been working out in left and center field in preparation for the coming season.

"I walked into the clubhouse, knowing I was going to start in my first Opening Day game [in Detroit]," he recalled. "I figured I would be playing either left or center field. When I looked at the lineup card, I couldn't believe it. There was a nine beside my name. I had to play right field.

"'Oh, God,' I thought. 'It's an afternoon game, there's not a cloud in the sky, and Tiger Stadium is one of the worst places in the early spring to play right field in the day.' I went to [manager] Sparky Anderson and said, 'I think you've made a mistake in the lineup.' And Sparky said, 'No, I didn't. I know you can play right field.' Having the big ego that I do, I said, 'Sure I can.'"

But it just wasn't Gibson's day in the sun.

The first ball hit to him came in the second inning on a deep fly swatted by the Toronto Blue Jays' Willie Upshaw. Gibson misplayed it off his head for what the official scorer charitably ruled a standup triple.

"I kept going back, back, back until I was against the wall," Gibson recalled. "I lost it in the sun, and the ball whacked right off the side of my head and bounced back toward the infield. I was so embarrassed. I began to hear some boos."

In the next inning, with Toronto's Lloyd Moseby on third and one out, John Mayberry hit a soft shallow line drive to right. Gibson broke late, then charged the ball and caught it off his shoe tops. Moseby tagged up and sprinted for home. Gibson would have had a play at the plate, but as he got in position to throw, he dropped the ball.

"They really started to boo me—even when I came to bat," recalled Gibson, who grounded into a force-out at second base during his next at-bat. "When I returned to the outfield, I kept thinking, 'Oh, man, don't hit another one out here to me.'"

No ball came near him in the fourth. But leading off the top of the fifth, Ernie Whitt hit a high fly to right. Gibson didn't drift over toward the ball; he staggered. Squeamish fans turned their heads away, not wanting to see how he'd butcher the play.

"The ball was right dead in the middle of the sun, and I wasn't real good at using my glasses at the time," said Gibson. "But I had my glasses down and I saw it, and then I thought I saw it, and then I didn't." The next thing he knew the ball bounced off his right ear, and Whitt ended up on third for a three-base error on Gibson. "I got booed unmercifully by 51,000 people, and I felt so humiliated," he said. "I'd never been booed like that in my whole life." A sacrifice fly drove Whitt home for an unearned run, giving the Blue Jays a 2–1 lead.

In the top of the sixth, Toronto's Barry Bonnell lofted a fly to right. While fans held their breath, Gibson caught the ball to the mocking cheers of the unforgiving Detroit faithful.

After the game, which the Tigers won 6–2, Gibson told reporters: "I had some tough times, but we won anyway. I'll learn from my mistakes. I'll improve. I fielded that last ball hit to me without any trouble. See? I'm getting better already."

POLO GROUNDS FANS
New York, NL · April 11, 1907

The fans in the Polo Grounds got the shame, but the weatherman got the blame for the New York Giants' forfeit of their Opening Day game to the Philadelphia Phillies—because of a wild snowball fight.

Despite an unusually heavy April snowfall, the field had been cleared to play ball on a day that was more suited for pigskin. The game was a bummer for Giants fans because Philadelphia grabbed an early 3–0 lead and held it through eight innings while New York could muster only one hit.

The cold, uncomfortable fans grew progressively more restless. Given the conditions and the tempting piles of snow that had been scraped off the seats, the outcome was inevitable. The only surprise was that the game went into the ninth inning before the first snowball sailed through the air.

Of course, one good snowball deserves another, and within minutes it looked like another blizzard had hit the Polo Grounds. The air turned white as the fans bombarded one another. Naturally, with such inviting and convenient targets down below, their attention soon turned to the Giants, the Phillies, and, with happy revenge in their hearts, to the umpires.

Snowballs rained down on the field. The players couldn't tell the snowballs from the baseballs and took refuge in the dugouts. When it was obvious that the man-made snowstorm was not going to let up, umpire Bill Klem ordered the game forfeited to the Phillies . . . and that's snow joke.

FRANKLIN D. ROOSEVELT
President · United States of America · April 16, 1940

One of the duties Franklin D. Roosevelt enjoyed most as President of the United States was throwing out the ceremonial first ball on Opening Day.

After eight years as chief executive, he had plenty of experience doing the honors. Nevertheless, Roosevelt threw the wildest first ball in Major League history.

On that fateful crisp April afternoon, the president stood up in the bunting-covered first row at Griffith Stadium in Washington, D.C., to carry out the happy springtime ritual initiated 30 years earlier by President William Howard Taft. (On Opening Day, 1910, umpire Billy Evans walked over to the president's box and, on the spur of the moment, asked Taft if he would like to toss out the first ball. He gladly accepted, and a tradition was born.)

Like the five presidents before him, Roosevelt was right-handed. Like the five presidents before him, he didn't have much of a throwing arm. Unlike the five presidents before him, Roosevelt flung a mortifying first ball.

As the players from the Washington Senators and Boston Red Sox gathered on the field in front of the president, FDR cocked his arm and threw such a wild ball that it smashed into *Washington Post* photographer Irving Schlossenberg's camera, and broke it.

In his letter of apology to the photographer, Roosevelt jokingly wrote that he declined to pay the damages because Schlossenberg had taken such poor photos while covering the White House.

FDR flinging a wild pitch

ALLIE REYNOLDS
Pitcher · New York, AL · April 19, 1948

After belting the first and only home run of his long career, New York Yankees pitcher Allie Reynolds had to be coaxed to circle the bases—because he refused to believe he had hit a round-tripper.

The case of the bewildered batter unfolded on Opening Day 1948 at Griffith Stadium, the Washington Senators' home park. What made the incident all the more mortifying was that Reynolds embarrassed himself in front of President Harry Truman, Commissioner A. B. "Happy" Chandler, and a TV network audience. (The game was one of Major League Baseball's first telecasts.)

In the first inning, the Yankees exploded for four quick runs and had two runners on base when Reynolds, the ninth man to bat in the frame, stepped to the plate. The New York pitching ace was hardly a threat with the lumber. All he had to show for 13 years in the bigs was a less than threatening .163 lifetime batting average.

But on this day, Reynolds teed off on an Early Wynn fastball and sent it soaring. Running to first base with his head down, Reynolds never saw what everyone else in the stadium did—that the ball landed in the left field bleachers.

"I hit it pretty hard, so I figured it was two bases for sure, and maybe three," Reynolds recalled. "I was the last person in the ballpark who expected it to go over the fence. So when I rounded second base, I saw the third base coach with his arms up. It looked to me like he wanted me to stop."

Instead of going into the standard home run trot, Reynolds screeched to a halt, pivoted and slid back into second base in a cloud of dust. "I tore a hole out there getting stopped, and it was so big you could have buried a Mack truck in it," Reynolds recalled.

Not realizing he had whacked a homer, he remained on second and ignored the pleas from the Yankees dugout to circle the bases. Even Senators second baseman Al Kozar urged him to finish the trot. "Since television started, all you guys want to be actors," Kozar told Reynolds. Pointing to the bleachers, he added, "The ball is outta here."

Reynolds shook his head. "I'm not leaving," he told Kozar. "I've seen you guys talk people off bases before."

Neither Kozar nor shortstop Mark Christman could convince Reynolds to abandon his safe perch. Even when the umpire waved him on, Reynolds refused to budge. Finally, Yankees manager Bucky Harris convinced him that he had indeed hit a home run and that it was safe to leave second base.

"After they talked me off second, I finally got to do my home run trot, even if it was only halfway," Reynolds recalled. "Everyone in the place got a big laugh out of it—my teammates, the fans, even President Truman. He was laughing harder than anybody.

"I'll never forget that home run. First of all, it was the only one I ever hit in the big leagues. And second, after I hit it, I had to go and embarrass myself like that in front of the President of the United States."

KEVIN MILLAR
Right Fielder · Florida, NL · April 2, 2002

Hoping to get an edge on Opening Day, Florida Marlins right fielder Kevin Millar doused his bat with a secret elixir—doe urine.

How the pee from a lady deer would help him hit better is anyone's guess, and most anyone could have told him what he discovered after the season opener. It doesn't work.

During the offseason in Beaumont, Texas, where he made his home, Millar was hunting with friends who suggested he put some doe urine on himself to attract the bucks.

But the Los Angeles–born Millar, who was an inexperienced hunter, didn't know he was supposed to put only a drop on his shoes. Instead, he poured it all over himself.

"I was putting it on like it was Calvin Klein cologne," he later told the *Miami Herald*.

His hunting buddies roared with laughter, and Millar realized he wasn't cut out to be much of a hunter. "If I shot a deer, I'd be down on the ground, telling him I was sorry," Millar told the *Sun-Sentinel*.

Millar figured that if doe urine could attract deer, then maybe it could attract hits. So he promised his Texas hunting pals that he would sprinkle it on his bat for the season opener. Sure enough, he brought a bottle of the doe pee with him to Montreal (no word on how he explained the urine to customs officials or got it past airport security workers) for the Opening Day game against the Expos.

He told reporters that if he got some hits, he would continue to use the urine on his bat. If he went hitless, well, at least he would have kept his promise to his hunting buddies.

Unfortunately for Millar, the idea of a bat aided by doe urine proved to be a pisser. He went 0-for-3, including a strikeout, in a 7–6 Marlins defeat.

After the game, Millar told reporters that he might have applied too much deer pee to his bat. He admitted the odor got to him as the game went on because the urine had seeped into his batting gloves and made his hands smell.

"You go up to wipe your nose, you know, and it smelled so bad," he told the *Miami Herald*. "Maybe I put too much on."

GEORGE MYATT
Third Baseman · Washington, AL · April 16, 1946

Washington Senators third baseman George Myatt was so pumped about the 1946 Opening Day game that he never got the chance to play—because he was so pumped.

After batting .296 in the previous season, Myatt was looking forward to another great year and couldn't wait to get back on the field. When he was penciled in the starting lineup as the leadoff hitter, he could barely contain his enthusiasm. And that posed a problem.

After President Harry Truman threw out the first ball at Griffith Stadium for the game against the Boston Red Sox, the spirited infielder was bursting with anticipation. To the roar of the crowd, Myatt led his teammates up the steps of the dugout. But Myatt was so excited that he didn't watch where he was going and tripped over his own feet.

As his teammates watched in shock, he sprawled backward down the steps, fracturing a bone in his ankle.

The woebegone third sacker was put out of action and replaced by Sherry Robertson—the first substitute in an Opening Day game that hadn't even started yet. Myatt never fully recovered and played in only 48 games over the next two years before calling it quits.

NEW YORK GIANTS HITTERS
April 15, 1909; April 14, 1910; April 12, 1911

When it came to Opening Day, no team did a worse job of supporting its starting pitcher than the New York Giants.

For three years in a row, Giants hurler Red Ames was given the honor of taking the mound for the club's season opener. For three years in a row, he performed brilliantly. And for three years in a row, the rest of the Giants didn't.

On Opening Day in 1909, the right-handed curveball artist, who in the six previous years with New York had compiled a respectable 57-40 record, was masterful against the Brooklyn Dodgers (then known as the Superbas). In fact, Ames held his opponents hitless for nine innings at the Polo Grounds. Unfortunately for him, his teammates couldn't muster a single run against Brooklyn's Irvin "Kaiser" Wilhelm.

So, although Ames pitched nine innings of no-hit ball, he had to keep on pitching thanks to his teammates' cold bats. With one out in the 10th inning, he gave up his first hit, a single to Whitey Alperman. Still, Ames pitched with all his heart and shut out Brooklyn through 12 innings. And how did his teammates respond to his masterpiece? They failed to score. In the 13th inning, Ames finally petered out, surrendering three runs to lose the game, 3–0.

In the 1910 opener, Ames once again twirled a sparkling gem, this time holding the Boston Braves (then known as the Doves) hitless for seven innings. He clung to a 2–1 lead with two outs in the ninth and the bases empty. But before he could get that final out, he gave up a walk and two singles that produced the tying run. For the second year in a row, Ames had to go into extra innings in the season opener. He eventually lost in the 11th inning on a Giants error.

On Opening Day in 1911, the Giants gave Ames less support than a deadbeat dad. The hurler didn't give up a hit through six innings against the Philadelphia Phillies and kept them scoreless through eight. But the New York batters had collected only two hits of their own against Philadelphia's Earl Moore. With two out in the ninth, Ames surrendered a two-run double for the only runs of the game, losing his third straight Opening Day heartbreaker.

It was a portent of things to come. By August of that year, Ames had a 5-9 record. In four of those losses, the Giants had scored two runs or less. After a 2–0 loss to the Phillies on August 12, an article in the *New York Times* said, "Ames stacks up against the toughest luck of any pitcher in the big show . . . Won't someone please send Mr. Ames the left hind foot of a churchyard rabbit . . . and some old rusty horseshoes?"

Ames never started another Opening Day game for the Giants.

WELCOME TO THE BIGS!

For the Most Inauspicious Major League Debuts of All Time, The Baseball Hall of Shame™ Inducts:

BILLY HERMAN
Second Baseman · Chicago, NL · August 29, 1931

Billy Herman can't remember a whole lot about his big league debut, even though it was a memorable one.

Thrilled at getting a chance to break into the starting Chicago Cubs lineup, Herman was determined to show he belonged. In his first at-bat in the Majors, he singled off Cincinnati Reds hurler Si Johnson, much to the delight of the Wrigley Field crowd.

In his next at-bat, Herman, his confidence growing, dug into the batter's box. On Johnson's first pitch, the rookie took a tremendous swing and fouled the ball straight down. It hit the ground in back of the plate and, with wicked reverse English, bounced straight up, smacking Herman in the back of the head.

So a sterling career that spanned two decades highlighted by a .304 lifetime batting average started out in the most forgettable— for him, at least—way possible. Billy Herman was carried off the field on a stretcher—knocked out cold by his own foul ball.

DOE BOYLAND
Pinch Hitter · Pittsburgh, NL · September 4, 1978

In his first Major League at-bat, Pittsburgh Pirates rookie Doe Boyland struck out—while sitting on the bench.

In the seventh inning of a home game against the New York Mets, Pittsburgh manager Chuck Tanner sent Boyland in to pinch-hit for pitcher Ed Whitson. The count was 1-and-2 on Boyland when Mets right-handed pitcher Skip Lockwood had to leave the game because he hurt his arm.

New York switched to southpaw Kevin Kobel, so Tanner, going by the book, lifted the left-handed-swinging Boyland and put in right-handed batter Rennie Stennett to pinch-hit for the pinch hitter.

While Boyland watched helplessly from the bench, Stennett struck out on Kobel's first pitch. Under the scoring rules, the strikeout was charged to Boyland for his inauspicious debut.

DOC HAMANN
Pitcher · Cleveland, AL · September 21, 1922

Cleveland Indians rookie reliever Doc Hamann was so nervous when he was thrust into his first and only Major League game that he never got a single batter out.

With the Indians trailing the visiting Boston Red Sox 9–5, Hamann entered the game in the top of the ninth inning. Unfortunately, he couldn't find the strike zone with a road map.

Shaking like a motherless pup, the 22-year-old hurler walked the first two batters he faced, Johnny Mitchell and Ed Chaplin. Then Hamann beaned the next batter, pitcher Jack Quinn, to load the bases.

Hamann became more frazzled and walked Mike Menosky, forcing in a run. The young pitcher finally got the ball over the plate, only to watch Elmer Miller blast it for a bases-clearing triple. After giving up a run-scoring single to George Burns, the rattled rookie uncorked a wild pitch and then yielded another RBI single to Del Pratt, which made the score 15–5.

Cleveland manager Tris Speaker had seen more than enough. He mercifully yanked Hamann, who never played in the Majors again. The stats for his entire pitching career: three hits, three walks, six runs, one wild pitch, and one hit batsman . . . and an ERA of infinity.

Although he pitched in only one game, Hamann left a dubious mark in Major League history: the most batters faced in a career without getting anyone out.

THE WHITE SOX'S BERMUDA SHORTS
August 8, 1976

Chicago White Sox owner Bill Veeck, who was always dreaming up wacky schemes to attract fans, figured that if he couldn't field a winning team he could at least present a fashionable one.

So in the middle of the summer of 1976, he introduced Bermuda shorts to the Major Leagues. He helped create the bizarre outfits—navy blue shorts with white shirts, wide collars, and blue lettering—"to showcase our wares." The only thing showcased were a lot of knobby knees and red faces.

Before the Bermudas' debut, the *Chicago Tribune* asked the players for their opinion on the fashion statement they would soon be making. The reaction was mixed. Second baseman Jack Brohamer claimed, "I'm not going to wear short pants unless they let me wear a halter top, too." Third baseman Kevin Bell said, "I've got to go out and get a tan. I'm all white." Designated hitter Lamar Johnson loved the idea because, "I got the nicest thighs you ever saw. I can't wait." But outfielder Buddy Bradford countered, "Not me. They'll have to force me to get into them." Pitcher Ken Brett wasn't quite so adamant, saying, "I'll get into them, but I may not get out of the dugout." Fellow hurler Dave Hamilton saw the good and the bad in wearing shorts. "I don't have nice legs—they're bird legs," he said. "I don't think I'll look too good in them. But maybe when the batters see me they'll get all distracted."

Legs go, White Sox!   MANNY MILLAN/*SPORTS ILLUSTRATED*/GETTY IMAGES

In the first game of a doubleheader against the visiting Kansas City Royals, the White Sox took the field in their Little Lord Fauntleroy shorts. Chicago won the game 5–2, some say because the Royals collapsed in hysterics at the sight. "You guys are the sweetest team we've seen yet," cackled Royals first baseman John Mayberry. He shouted to White Sox speedster Ralph Garr (shown in the photo above with coach Minnie Minoso), "Hey, Ralph, if you get to first base I'm going to kiss you!" (Mayberry didn't keep his word.) Another Royals player said White Sox pitcher Clay Carroll looked like "a pilgrim going out to shoot a wild turkey."

Between games of the twin-bill, the players stripped off their Bermudas and put on grown-up pants. Manager Paul Richards said they changed because it was getting too chilly for shorts. More likely, it was the players' low tolerance for humiliation. Besides, they didn't like the wolf whistles.

The White Sox wore the Bermuda shorts two more times during the season before they were abandoned for good. Years later former Chicago hurler Goose Gossage told the *Sacramento Bee:* "They were ugly. And I'll tell you, we played exactly like we looked. But what are you going to do? Go on strike? That was the circus atmosphere that Bill Veeck created there."

JOHN FRANCIS "PHENOMENAL" SMITH
Pitcher · Brooklyn, AA · June 17, 1885

For sheer shame, nothing will ever match "Phenomenal" Smith's pitching debut with Brooklyn. He was slaughtered 18–5 in a scandalous loss that was—yet wasn't—his fault.

The utter disgrace of this game cannot be fully understood by reading the box score, which shows that of the 18 runs scored against him, only 11 were earned.

The seed of ignobility was planted by John Francis Smith himself. The 5-foot-6-inch, 20-year-old lefty possessed an enormous ego and gave himself the nickname Phenomenal. After playing in six games the previous year with two other teams, he joined Brooklyn (then known as the Trolley Dodgers of the American Association). The cocky pitcher told his new club that he was so good that he could win even if the players didn't play well. Such brashness did not endear him to his teammates. In fact, they downright hated him. And they took him up on his boast that he could win without their support.

Making his debut for Brooklyn at home against St. Louis, Phenomenal quickly discovered that his fellow players made no effort to conceal their antipathy toward him. They were determined to see him lose—and lose big—which he did. He pitched the entire game, giving up 12 hits, issuing six walks and striking out two. Other than third baseman Bill McClellan, who played to win despite his dislike for Smith, the infielders intentionally dropped pop-ups, let grounders skip through their legs, and threw wildly as they racked up 14 errors. Their misplays were so blatant that the players were roundly booed by the 1,600 disgusted spectators at Washington Park.

The next day, the *Brooklyn Eagle* condemned "the disgusting rottenness which prevailed in the ranks of the team." The paper blasted the conspirators for not having "brains enough to properly conceal their little game." The *Eagle* declared, "They so plainly exposed their hands in their crooked work that the occupants of the grandstand saw it, and it aroused their just indignation to such an extent that they hissed the wretched muffing work of the [Brooklyn players]."

Shortstop Germany Smith was the most flagrant fumbler, committing seven errors, while catcher Jackie Hayes made two miscues and was charged with five passed balls. The official box score does not reflect the easy fly balls and grounders that the Brooklyn fielders let go untouched for base hits.

"It's an outrage!" stormed Charlie Byrne, president of the Brooklyn club, after the debacle. "The way my men treat this new player is a disgrace, and I will take steps to punish them for it." He did, too, by fining each of the guilty players. He made one other move to ensure team harmony—he reluctantly released Phenomenal Smith after his Brooklyn debut.

PAT TABLER
Second Baseman · Chicago, NL · August 21, 1981

The only thing Pat Tabler needed to make his Major League debut complete was a deep dark hole to crawl into and hide.

"They don't have any holes in the middle of the infield at Wrigley Field, but I sure was looking for one," recalled Tabler. "It was the most embarrassing predicament I'd ever been in. I just wanted to disappear. I even prayed for a tornado to come down and get me out of there."

The Chicago Cubs front office had touted Tabler as "the second baseman of the future." But in his first game, which was against the visiting San Francisco Giants, the rookie looked like just another member of the same old sorry Cubs.

"When I started the game, I was so excited I couldn't concentrate," Tabler recalled. "I had to keep pinching myself to realize I was really playing in Wrigley Field. I even got a hit [a single] my first time up in the big leagues, and I thought, 'Oh, wow! This is awesome!' I was just going through the motions because I was practically in shock. I didn't know the number of outs, the inning, or even the score."

And that was the problem.

In the top of the eighth inning with the score tied 3–3, the Giants loaded the bases with one out. Pinch hitter Jim Wohlford then tapped a made-to-order double-play ball to shortstop Ivan De Jesus. It should have been a textbook twin killing, but apparently Tabler hadn't read the book.

De Jesus scooped up the ball and tossed it to Tabler, who stepped on the bag for the force-out at second. But he didn't pivot and throw to first to record his first Major League double play. Instead, Tabler kept the ball and ran toward the Cubs third base dugout—while the lead runner scampered across the plate with what proved to be the winning run.

"I knew I had screwed up when [Cubs third baseman] Kenny Reitz came running at me, screaming, 'No! No! No!'" said Tabler. "Then it hit me. There were only two outs! I started to throw to first, pretending that I really knew what I was doing, but it was much too late. I felt like I'd been caught naked out there in front of all those people. The only bright spot was that it wasn't on national television."

Because of that gift run, the Cubs lost 4–3. "When I came into the clubhouse, all the writers were there in front of my locker waiting for me," said Tabler. "I knew then that I really was in the big leagues."

Tabler went on to play 12 years in the bigs, mostly as an outfielder or first baseman. After his debut season, he played only seven games at second base for the rest of his career. Apparently, they'd seen enough of him at that position.

FRANK VERDI
Shortstop · New York, AL · May 10, 1953

JOHN LINDSEY
Pinch Hitter · Los Angeles, NL · September 8, 2010

Frank Verdi said his first at-bat in the Major Leagues was "like your first date—it's something you can never forget." Only in his case, and that of John Lindsey, it was like getting stood up.

After languishing in the New York Yankees' farm system for seven years, Verdi finally made the big club. He sat on the bench until that memorable Sunday in 1953 at Boston's Fenway Park when he filled in at shortstop for Phil Rizzuto, who had been taken out in the sixth inning for a pinch hitter.

In the top of the seventh, Verdi was all set to make his long-awaited debut at the plate. The Yankees had rallied to take a 5–3 lead and had the bases loaded with two out. What a great moment for Verdi. All the years of toiling in the minors—the sweaty bus rides, the two-bit towns, the fleabag hotels—were about to pay off. Here was his golden opportunity to knock in some important runs in his first big league at-bat.

Verdi stepped into the batter's box, anxious to take his cuts. But then he heard Red Sox pitching coach Bill McKechnie shout, "Time!" McKechnie sent pitcher Ellis Kinder to the showers and brought in reliever Ken Holcombe. After the new pitcher completed his warm-up tosses, Verdi stepped back into the batter's box.

Once again, he heard, "Time!" It was Yankees manager Casey Stengel, who was sending Bill Renna to pinch-hit for Verdi, even though both were right-handed batters. Renna grounded out to third to end the inning.

As for Verdi, that was his debut in the bigs. It was also his finale. Verdi was sent back to the minors, never to return.

John Lindsey can certainly identify with Verdi. At least Verdi actually got to play an inning in the field in his first game. In Lindsey's debut, he officially played in a game that he never played in.

After spending 16 grueling, drawn-out years in the minor leagues, Lindsey was rewarded for his persistence and determination when the Los Angeles Dodgers, at long last, called him up for the final month of the 2010 season.

On September 8, the Dodgers were trailing the home team San Diego Padres 4–0 in the top of the eighth, but had runners on first and second with one out. That's when the rookie, who was now 33 and older than most of his fellow Dodgers, was told by manager Joe Torre to pinch-hit for left fielder Scott Podsednik. The years of waiting were over for Lindsey. The moment had arrived—the one he had dreamed of since he was drafted in the 13th round by the Colorado Rockies in 1995 after graduating from Hattiesburg (Mississippi) High.

What a thrill it was to hear his name announced as he stepped into the batter's box to face southpaw reliever Joe Thatcher. What a disappointment it was when the Padres brought in right-handed reliever Luke Gregerson and Torre countered by sending up lefty Andre Ethier to pinch-hit for Lindsey.

Back in the dugout, Lindsey watched Ethier hit into an inning-ending double play. The Dodgers lost 4–0. After the game, Torre handed Lindsey the lineup card and said, "Now you're in the record books."

"What?" Lindsey replied. "For not playing in the game?"

His teammates put a good spin on his debut. Recalled Lindsey, "Somebody said, 'You're so good, you can get in a game without having to hit.' Somebody else said, 'You must be good. They'd rather face Ethier than face you.'"

Lindsey had to wait one more day before he had the chance to actually hit the ball. In the top of the seventh inning of a 3–2 loss to the Houston Astros, he pinch-hit for hurler Ted Lilly and flied out to deep center field. Three days later, he got his first big league hit—a pinch-hit line drive single in a 7–4 loss to the Astros.

When ESPN.com columnist Jayson Stark asked him which game he counts as his true debut, Lindsey replied, "I count the official one. To me, it was still a special moment. I can always say that I was so intimidating they brought a right-hander in because they didn't want to face me."

AL GRUNWALD
Pitcher · Pittsburgh, NL · April 18, 1955

It's one thing to hit for the cycle. It's quite another to *be* hit for the cycle, which is what happened to Pittsburgh Pirates southpaw Al Grunwald in his first Major League game.

He was summoned to the mound in the fourth inning against the home New York Giants at the Polo Grounds. The Giants had scored two runs in the frame and were leading 5–0 with runners on second and third and one out.

Willie Mays welcomed Grunwald to the show by whacking a 400-foot blast to right-center for a two-run triple. After Hank Thompson grounded out, Monte Irvin belted a 390-foot shot off the left field fence for a run-scoring double. Then Don Mueller drilled a single, driving in another run.

The rookie hurler was still reeling from those hits when Whitey Lockman stepped to the plate and clouted the ball 410 feet into the upper deck for a two-run homer.

As easy as one, two, three, four, the Giants had hit for the cycle in Grunwald's first Major League inning. Pirates manager Fred Haney wielded his hook and rescued the young pitcher from further trouble as the Giants scored eight runs in the frame and coasted to an easy 12–3 victory.

Grunwald made pitching appearances in just eight games before hanging up his glove without ever recording a win. But he'll always have the historic mark of being hit for the cycle in his debut inning.

BATTY BATTERS

For the Wackiest Plate Appearances of All Time,
The Baseball Hall of Shame™ Inducts:

TONY HORTON
First Baseman · Cleveland, AL · June 24, 1970

Cleveland Indians batter Tony Horton was so fooled on a pitch that he wound up literally crawling back to the dugout in shame.

In the top of the ninth inning of a 7–2 Cleveland victory over the Yankees in New York, Horton faced reliever Steve Hamilton. On occasion, Hamilton liked to toss a high-arching slow pitch that he fondly called his "folly floater." Three weeks earlier, he had thrown one to Horton in Cleveland, and the first baseman singled. Afterward, Horton asked Hamilton if he would throw it again sometime because the slugger was sure he could clobber the peculiar pitch for a homer.

So when Horton stepped into the batter's box against Hamilton, he asked for the floater. The hurler nodded. The tantalizingly slow ball crossed the plate, but Horton was too eager and fouled it off. He begged for a second chance and Hamilton, being an accommodating fellow, tossed another tempting slow pitch.

"I never thought he'd throw two in a row," Horton recalled. The powerfully built home run hitter took a mighty cut . . . and fouled out to the catcher.

Horton's crawl of shame   ERNIE SISTO/THE *NEW YORK TIMES*/REDUX

Horton was so mortified that he threw his cap and bat into the air. Then, to the amusement of fans and players alike, he dropped to his knees and crawled back to the dugout. Everyone erupted in laughter, including Indians manager Alvin Dark.

The fans cheered with delight, causing Hamilton to remark after the game, "That's the biggest ovation I ever got in fourteen years as a pro athlete."

HAL CHASE
First Baseman · New York, Chicago, AL;
Cincinnati, New York, NL · 1905–1919

Hal Chase had one of baseball's weirdest habits—he chewed on his bats.
And it led to one of baseball's weirdest injuries.

Chase had an inexplicable craving for wood. He would simply pick
up a bat—any bat—and chew on the handle. Teammates figured he bit
bats because he wanted to test the quality of the wood. Others said he
enjoyed the taste of the lumber. Chase himself never explained why he
did it.

It looked like his days of bat-biting might end when, as a New York
Yankee, he chewed on a handle and wound up with a painful sliver of
wood in his tongue. The splinter was embedded so deeply that the chagrined player needed a doctor to extract it.

When New York sportswriters heard the story, they were skeptical
at first, until one of them confronted the team bat boy. "Yes, sir, it's true,"
said the bat boy. "Almost every bat we have around our bench has got
Mr. Chase's teeth marks on it. He just sorta gnaws on them."

"Can you tell anything about a bat by biting it?" the sportswriter
asked.

"Mr. Chase never lets anybody know what he finds out by biting the
bat," said the bat boy.

Whatever it was that compelled Chase to bite bats was apparently
pretty powerful. He continued chewing on bats long after he had the
splinter removed from his tongue, even when he played for the Chicago
White Sox, Cincinnati Reds, and New York Giants at the end of his
career, which lasted until 1919. But gnawing on the lumber—despite
the danger—seemed to work for him. Chase had a lifetime batting average of .291.

MINNIE MINOSO
Left Fielder · Cleveland, AL · July 17, 1959

The most pitiful thing that can happen to a batter is to be called out on strikes. Well, not quite. Minnie Minoso found an even more ignoble way to get rung up. He got called out on strikes without ever setting foot in the batter's box.

Minoso's moment of infamy came during a turbulent rhubarb in the top of the eighth inning of an 8–7 Cleveland Indians victory over the host Boston Red Sox. Cleveland manager Joe Gordon vehemently protested after second base umpire Jim Honochick called Indians runner Vic Power out for interference. Failing to change the arbiter's mind, Gordon took up his battle with plate umpire Frank Umont.

Gordon's bellyaching got him nowhere—except booted out of the game. Furious over the ejection, Gordon ran over to his third base coach, Jo-Jo White, and told him to carry on the good fight with Umont. White tried, but the umpire declared the case closed and shooed the coach away. Then the ump ordered the next batter, who was Minoso, to step up to the plate.

But because the Indians were still in an uproar and continued to squawk over the interference call, Minoso refused to budge from his spot near the on-deck circle. Again, Umont motioned for Minoso to get into the batter's box. Again, Minoso stayed put.

Umont wasn't going to stand for any more grandstanding by Minoso, so the ump ordered Bosox hurler Leo Kiely to pitch to an empty batter's box. Kiely delivered three straight strikes, and Umont declared Minoso out.

Only then did Minoso spring into action. First, he hurled his bat at the umpire's feet. Then he charged after Umont as though he were going to tear him to pieces. It took a platoon of umpires and players to restrain the infuriated player. Teammate Rocky Colavito literally dragged him away.

Minoso was not only called out on strikes while away from the batter's box, he was also thumbed out of the game.

RANDALL SIMON
First Baseman · Pittsburgh, NL · July 9, 2003

Randall Simon was known as a batter who would swing at most anything. But his reputation got roasted when he took a cut at a giant sausage.

The incident, dubbed throughout the baseball world as Sausagegate, happened at Miller Park during the famed Sausage Race held at the end of the sixth inning of every Milwaukee Brewers home game. Employees of the team don 7-foot-tall foam costumes representing various sausages of the local Klement's Sausage Company. There's Bratwurst, Polish Sausage, Italian Sausage, Hotdog, and Chorizo (which was added to the race three years after Sausagegate.) The giant sausages start the race between the dugout and the baseline near third base and sprint around home plate and continue toward the finish line beyond first base.

On the night of July 9, 2003, the 22,000 fans at Miller Park were looking forward to the Sausage Race as the Brewers and Pittsburgh Pirates finished six innings tied 1–1. Simon, who was not in the starting lineup for the Pirates, grabbed a bat and stood at the top of the steps of the visitor's first base dugout to watch the wiener race. After a horse-racing fanfare, the four giant sausages were off. It was close from the start, and they were link and link until the final turn when Italian Sausage edged into the lead followed by Hotdog, Polish Sausage, and Bratwurst.

But then, as they sprinted by the Pirates' dugout, Simon took a playful swing at Italian Sausage's oversized head, knocking the giant encased minced meat to the ground. Hotdog then tripped and fell over Italian Sausage. Hotdog recovered and helped Italian Sausage up, and the two finished the race behind Polish Sausage and Bratwurst.

Simon thought his batting performance was funny. But it was no laughing matter.

Mandy Block, 19, who was inside the Italian Sausage costume, and Veronica Piech, who was inside Hotdog, both received medical treatment for minor scrapes and cuts. Then the sheriff's deputies got involved and interviewed Simon. The next day, after he appeared in the

Simon taking his cut at a sausage

Milwaukee County District Attorney's Office, he was cited for disorderly conduct and fined $432.

Simon said he was just playing around when he swatted at Italian Sausage with the bat. "I thought at the moment they [the giant sausages] were trying to play with us," he told reporters later. "They were running right next to the players. I'm a fun player, and I've never hurt anyone in my life."

Mandy said she saw Simon holding the bat as she neared him. "I thought he was just going to fake me out," she said. The blow to the costume's head didn't hurt Mandy because the bat hit the costume above her real head. "I don't think he did it intentionally, like to hurt me. I think he was doing it as a joke."

All she wanted was an apology and the offending bat autographed by Simon—both of which the player gave her.

But Italian Sausage was much more forgiving than Major League Baseball. Simon was suspended for three games and fined $2,000.

Later that season, Simon was traded to the Chicago Cubs for reasons unrelated to Sausagegate. When he returned to Milwaukee with the Cubs, his teammates playfully held him back during the Sausage Race while manager Dusty Baker guarded the bat rack.

In an act of forgiveness, Simon bought Italian sausages for a randomly chosen section of the crowd.

The incident had a lasting impact on Milwaukee fans. Many still wear T-shirts and display other memorabilia with the slogan "Don't whack our wiener!"

MARIO MENDOZA
Infielder · Pittsburgh, NL; Seattle, Texas, AL · 1974–1982

Fair or not, Mario Mendoza unwittingly gave the game a batting statistic that bears his name—the Mendoza Line.

No player ever wants to sink below that line, the figurative boundary between batting averages above and below .200.

It used to be that when a player was batting under .200, he was called a "banjo hitter," "ukulele hitter," "Punch and Judy hitter," or "buttercup hitter." A player with a batting average so low he couldn't hit his weight was known as an "out man." If he did well during morning BP but not in a game, he was labeled a "ten o'clock hitter." In more recent times, a hitter "on the interstate" meant that his batting average looked like an interstate sign; for example, .195 resembles I95 on a scoreboard.

But it wasn't until 1980 that the standard for batting futility was so clearly defined with the Mendoza Line, named after a slick-fielding, weak-hitting journeyman infielder.

Mendoza, who had great hands and a quick release, played for the Pittsburgh Pirates from 1974 through 1978 in a reserve role. During his five years with the team, he batted as high as .221 for a season and as low as .180.

He spent his next two years with the Seattle Mariners, and it was during this time that his legacy—or at least the Mendoza Line—was born. As the starting shortstop in 1979, Mendoza hit a paltry .198 for the season, prompting his teammates to rib him about his hitting prowess.

According to a 1990 *Sports Illustrated* article, Mendoza believed that Mariners outfielder Tom Paciorek invented the term. Paciorek denied it and claimed that it was Seattle first baseman Bruce Bochte who came up with the idea for the Mendoza Line.

Regardless of who deserves the credit, the term hadn't received any widespread play until 1980 when Kansas City Royals star George Brett was flirting with a .400 season. (He finished with .390.) Referring to the weekly list of players' batting averages, Brett told the press at the time, "The first thing I look for in the Sunday papers is who is below the Mendoza Line."

The name began to take hold in baseball circles, but it didn't become firmly entrenched in the minds of fans throughout the country until ESPN anchorman Chris Berman began using the term on *SportsCenter*.

According to Mendoza's friend, Mexican sportscaster Oscar Soria, "Mario said that when Chris Berman mentioned it and people started to laugh, he was angry. But now he enjoys the fame of the phrase 'Mendoza Line.'"

NORM CASH
First Baseman · Detroit, AL · July 15, 1973

Having no luck hitting against fire-balling Nolan Ryan, Norm Cash chucked his bat and came to the plate wielding a table leg.

Ryan was pitching for the California Angels against the home Detroit Tigers, and he was on top of his game, much like he was exactly two months earlier when he twirled a no-hitter against the Kansas City Royals. Now he was gunning for his second no-no as he mowed down batter after batter in Detroit.

Cash struck out the first two times he faced Ryan, who ultimately fanned 17 batters. In his third plate appearance, Cash at least made contact, grounding out to the second baseman.

Going into the bottom of the ninth, the Tigers trailed 6–0 and had yet to get a hit off Ryan. Mickey Stanley led off the frame by grounding out to Rudy Meoli at shortstop. Then Gates Brown hit a soft liner that Meoli caught.

The Tigers were down to their last out. It was up to Cash, who had been handcuffed all day by Ryan, to break up the hurler's no-hit bid.

Figuring his bat hadn't helped him at all, Cash went into the Detroit clubhouse, grabbed the sawed-off leg of an old table, and sauntered to the plate with the leg on his shoulder.

After a good laugh, plate umpire Ron Luciano ordered Cash to get a real bat. Cash protested, "But, Ron, I've got as much chance with this as I do with a bat."

Cash reluctantly retrieved a bat, but it didn't do any good. He popped out to Meoli as Ryan recorded his second no-no of the year. On his way back to the dugout, Cash turned to Luciano and said, "See, I told you so."

Cash wasn't the first hitter to wield a wacky bat. In a 1929 game, Rabbit Maranville, of the Boston Braves, came to the plate with a tennis racquet, hoping to snap a personal batting slump against Dazzy Vance.

Like Cash, Maranville had no success in convincing the umpire to let him use his zany club. And like Cash, Maranville returned with legal lumber and promptly made an out.

LEN KOENECKE
Center Fielder · Brooklyn, NL · August 31, 1934

In one of the silliest cases of absentmindedness by a batter, Len Koenecke laid down a bunt—and then forgot to run.

Koenecke showed he could handle the bat in his first full season with the Brooklyn Dodgers by batting .320 and belting a team-leading 14 home runs in 1934. But bunting was another matter.

He forgot what to do during the second inning of a game against the visiting New York Giants. After Dodgers batter Sam Leslie beat out a single, Brooklyn manager Casey Stengel flashed the bunt sign to Koenecke as he stepped into the batter's box. Koenecke squared around and bunted the ball about 3 feet in front of the plate. Giants catcher Gus Mancuso sprang out of his crouch and pounced on the ball.

Thinking he had a good chance to nail Leslie at second, Mancuso fired the ball to shortstop Travis Jackson, who was covering the bag. But the ball sailed over Jackson's head, so Leslie headed for third.

Meanwhile, back at home plate, Mancuso heard someone behind him cheering for the sprinting Leslie. The catcher turned around and, to his surprise, saw Koenecke still standing at the plate, acting as excited over the play as any of the paying customers in Ebbets Field. Koenecke was jumping up and down, rooting for his Dodger teammate to make third on the overthrow.

Stengel couldn't believe his eyes. He began screaming his head off at the forgetful Koenecke. "Go to first, you idiot!" Stengel yelled. "Go to first!"

By this time, Giants center fielder Hank Leiber had run down the ball and heaved it to Johnny Vergez at third base. But Leslie beat the throw.

With the runner safe at third—and with Stengel raising a dust storm outside the dugout—Koenecke suddenly woke up and realized he was supposed to be running, not watching. He still had a bunt to beat out. So finally he took off for first. But Vergez threw him out by 60 feet.

The embarrassed Dodger hustled off the field and right into the dugout where he got a tongue lashing from Stengel that he never forgot.

KITTY BURKE
Nightclub Singer · July 31, 1935

It's pretty obvious that no Major Leaguer would be caught dead wearing a dress to the plate. But one batter wore one, and turned the at-bat into an outrageous farce that left fans hooting and hollering.

Nightclub singer Kitty Burke hit a ball thrown by St. Louis Cardinals hurler Daffy Dean, becoming the only woman ever to bat during a Major League game. Her at-bat did nothing to advance baseball's sexism barrier, but did much to advance baseball's legacy of craziness.

Kitty's infamous plate appearance occurred during a night game between the world champion Cardinals and the hometown Cincinnati Reds at Crosley Field, which two months earlier had been the site of the first Major League game under the lights. The game in which Kitty made her one and only appearance was played in a carnival atmosphere because night baseball was such a novelty. At the time, Crosley Field had a seating capacity of 26,000, but the game was oversold. As a result, more than 10,000 fans were herded onto the field to watch from a roped off area in foul territory that stretched from behind home plate and down the foul lines to the outfield fences.

Kitty, a blonde blues singer and Cincinnati rooter, was among the fans on the field. She was standing only 10 feet away from home plate when the Cardinals' Joe "Ducky" Medwick stepped to the plate in the eighth inning with St. Louis ahead 2–1. Kitty disliked the cocky player, especially since he had scored on his previous at-bat.

"You can't hit a lick!" she shouted at him. "You couldn't even hit the ball with an ironing board!"

Medwick fired back, "You couldn't hit if you were swinging an elephant!"

In the bottom of the eighth, Kitty was still fuming mad over Medwick's retort. So when the Reds' Babe Herman headed toward the batter's box, Kitty decided to take action.

"Hey, Babe!" she hollered. "Lend me your bat."

Herman decided to play along, so he called time and offered his bat to the lady. "Go ahead," he said.

Wearing a dress and high heels, Kitty marched up to Herman, took his bat and then stepped into the batter's box while the crowd roared with laughter. Among the spectators was baseball commissioner Kenesaw Mountain Landis. Neither he nor plate umpire Bill Stewart tried to stop the determined woman.

Kitty showing off her batting form

After taking a few practice swings, Kitty shouted to Dean, "Hey, you hick. Throw me a pitch!"

Dean stood on the mound, unsure what to do. By now the crowd was in hysterics and shouting at Dean to throw the ball. Finally, Stewart yelled, "Play ball!"

Rather than fire a fastball, Dean lobbed the ball underhanded. Kitty swung and hit a slow dribbler back to the pitcher. He fielded her tap and ungallantly threw her out. Kitty then ran back into the cheering crowd and into baseball history.

But you won't find her name in any record book. Her appearance at the plate didn't count, even though St. Louis manager Frankie Frisch made a half-hearted argument that Cincinnati should be charged with an out.

Kitty parlayed her at-bat into an act that she took on the burlesque circuit, billing herself as the only woman ever to bat in a Major League game.

After the contest, which the Reds won 4–3 in 10 innings, Herman told reporters, "That's the first time a broad ever pinch-hit for me."

"SILENT JOHN" TITUS
Right Fielder · Philadelphia, NL · September 26, 1905

Philadelphia Phillies right fielder "Silent John" Titus holds the unofficial record for the longest delay of a game by a batter while looking for the smallest piece of lumber.

Titus, a lifetime .282 hitter, attributed much of his success at the plate to lucky toothpicks. He always kept one clenched between his teeth when he batted. "Without my bitin' on that ol' toothpick, I ain't able to hit nothin' past the pitcher," he once said.

Rival pitchers came to hate the sight of that ever present toothpick, none more so than Sandy McDougal, a rookie pitcher for the St. Louis Cardinals. During a 9–2 loss to the Phillies, McDougal fired a ball straight at Titus's mouth, trying to knock his toothpick right down his throat. Titus ducked safely out of the way. But to his dismay, he lost his toothpick.

Calling time, he frantically got down on all fours and searched for the sliver, but couldn't find it. After a delay of nearly four minutes, the umpire ordered Titus to get up and bat. Instead, Titus rushed over to the Phillies dugout and begged his teammates for a toothpick. But nobody had one.

At that point, Titus knew he was a doomed man. He slowly trudged back to the plate . . . and struck out.

RUN FOR YOUR LIVES!

For the Most Outrageous Baserunning Boners of
All Time, The Baseball Hall of Shame™ Inducts:

MARV THRONEBERRY
First Baseman · New York, NL · June 17, 1962

Marvelous Marv Throneberry endeared himself to New York Mets fans with his self-effacing humor regarding his shortcomings as a fielder. But on this day, he showed the world that his baserunning skills were just as ridiculous.

At the Polo Grounds, the host New York Mets were trailing the Chicago Cubs 4–1 in the bottom of the first inning with one out and runners on first and second when Throneberry came up to bat. He whacked the ball into the deepest part of right field and, with his head down, chugged around first. Gathering all the steam of a hamstrung moose, the 6-foot-1, 190-pound Throneberry passed second and rambled to third. There he stood, huffing and puffing, reveling in the cheers from fans who rarely saw him run the bases. Stumble over them, yes, but seldom run them. The runners in front of him scored, making it a 4–3 game.

As the applause began to fade, Cubs first baseman Ernie Banks strolled over to first base umpire Dusty Boggess and said,

Not so Marvelous Marv

"He didn't touch first, you know." Banks called for the ball and stepped on the bag. Boggess then called Throneberry out.

Mets manager Casey Stengel stormed out of the dugout to protest the call. As he began arguing, second base umpire Stan Landes walked over and said, "Don't bother, Casey. He missed second base too."

Stengel glowered at Landes and then stared at Throneberry, who was still perched on the bag across the diamond. Exasperated, Stengel told the umpires, "Well, I know he touched third because he's standing on it."

Instead of having the tying run on third with one out, the Mets had no one on base and two outs. That was particularly galling for Stengel because the next batter, Charlie Neal, walloped a game-tying home run, prompting the manager to burst out of the dugout. As Neal rounded the bases, Stengel pointed to each base, making sure that Neal didn't commit the same baserunning blunder as Marvelous Marv.

Throneberry's run that wasn't hurt the Mets; they lost 8–7.

JIMMY ST. VRAIN
Pitcher · Chicago, NL · April 27, 1902

Jimmy St. Vrain lasted only 12 games in the Majors, but not before leaving a legacy of baserunning folly that you might see only in T-Ball.

The 18-year-old rookie had a problem finding first base. This was understandable considering he seldom made it to first, batting a weak .097 for the year.

A lefty on the mound, he batted right-handed. But that wasn't working out for him. So, after St. Vrain struck out twice during a home game against the Pittsburgh Pirates, Chicago manager Frank Selee suggested the young hurler bat left-handed.

St. Vrain agreed to try, and on his next at-bat, he stood on the opposite side of the plate from where he was used to swinging. Wonder of wonders, he hit the ball. Okay, so it was a dribbler that went only as far as shortstop Honus Wagner, who was already playing in on the grass. That mattered little to the exuberant St. Vrain. He had made contact with the ball. In his excitement, he dropped the bat and took off on a dead run—toward third base!

Wagner fielded the ball and then stood for a moment holding it in stunned disbelief while watching St. Vrain race up the third base line. Wagner didn't know where to throw the ball. To first for the out . . . or to third for the tag?

Meanwhile, St. Vrain's incredulous teammates were yelling at the wayward runner to turn around. He finally did, but by then Wagner had fired the ball to first. It was probably the only time a batter was thrown out by more than 90 feet.

GATES BROWN
Pinch Hitter · Detroit, AL · June 9, 1968

Detroit Tigers slugger Gates Brown gave the most outrageous exhibition of hot-dogging on the basepaths that baseball has ever seen.

In a home game against the Cleveland Indians, Brown was sitting on the bench, watching a pitchers' duel between Luis Tiant and Denny McLain. Late in the game, Brown, a 220-pounder whose love for baseball was exceeded only by his love for food, managed to get someone to sneak him two hot dogs. Sitting in the far corner of the dugout, Brown slapped mustard and ketchup on the dogs and planned to eat them on the sly. He knew Tigers manager Mayo Smith, who was always hounding him to lose weight, would be furious if he saw a player eating in the dugout during a game. But Brown was starving.

With Cleveland ahead 2–0 in the bottom of the eighth inning, the Tigers had two outs and nobody on base. At the time, Brown was the league's best pinch hitter—he went 18 for 39 for the year—and usually was called on to hit when there were runners in scoring position. Figuring he wouldn't be summoned in the current situation, he took a bite out of the first hot dog. Suddenly, from the other end of the dugout, he heard Smith say, "Gates, get your bat and hit."

Brown was not prepared to play. His belt was unbuckled, his shoes were untied, and he was holding a hot dog in each hand. By turning his back to Smith, Brown was able to hide his dilemma from the manager. But because Smith was still staring at him, Brown couldn't dump the hot dogs without getting into trouble. So he did the only thing he could do—stuff them in his jersey. Then he tied his shoes, buckled his belt, grabbed a bat, and headed for the batter's box.

"I always wanted to get a hit every time I went up to the plate," Brown recalled. "But this was one time I didn't want to get a hit. I'll be damned if I didn't smack one in the gap and I had to slide into second—headfirst no less. I was safe with a double. But when I stood up, I had mustard and ketchup and smashed hotdogs and buns all over me."

The front of Brown's white jersey looked like a painter's drop cloth of reds and yellows. "The fielders took one look at me, turned their backs, and damned near busted a gut laughing," Brown said. "My teammates in the dugout went crazy. That had to be my most embarrassing moment in baseball."

Brown was left stranded at second when the next batter, Dick McAuliffe, struck out. "I was pissed off," recalled Brown. But it wasn't because his double was wasted. "I messed up my hot dogs and I couldn't eat them."

In addition to the mustard and ketchup that stained his uniform, Brown had plenty of Mayo with his hot dogs. "When I returned to the dugout, Smith said, 'What the hell were you doing eating on the bench in the first place?'" Brown recalled. "I decided to tell him the truth. I said, 'I was hungry. Besides, where else can you eat a hot dog and have the best seat in the house?'"

The manager fined him $100.

COAKER TRIPLETT
Left Fielder · Philadelphia, NL · July 11, 1943

Coaker Triplett wanted to show his new team how to play like a confident winner. Instead, he looked like a baserunning fool.

He tried to steal an occupied base. But it got much worse than that. On the play, he forced his teammate off the bag for an out. Then Triplett stomped off the base in disgust over his own blunder and was tagged out too.

Triplett's baserunning debacle occurred a few weeks after he had been traded by the speed-happy world champion St. Louis Cardinals to the lackluster, cellar-dwelling Philadelphia Phillies.

He quickly discovered that his new teammates were so used to losing—they had finished in last place five years in a row—that they played with the vigor of tired old grandpas on a hot summer day. He figured the only way to inspire the Phillies on the basepaths was to set an example for them. He set an example, all right—a shameful one.

In a game against the visiting Cincinnati Reds, the Phillies were losing 7–1 when they mounted a feeble rally. With one out, Ron Northey
and Triplett walked and Jimmy Wasdell dropped a single into right field
to load the bases.

To Triplett this was the perfect opportunity to make something
happen, to play his old Cardinals' way. Inching off second, Triplett set
his sights on a stolen base. On the next pitch, he broke for third. He
slid safely in a cloud of dust, only to find Northey standing on the bag
with his mouth open in surprise. Triplett had just assumed Northey had
scored on the previous play. Incredibly, Triplett never bothered to notice
that third was still occupied.

"Get the hell off the bag!" Triplett screamed.

Even though Northey had possession of the base, he obediently
sprinted for home. But Reds catcher Al "Moose" Lakeman was holding
the ball and easily tagged him out.

Shamefaced over his own goof, Triplett stomped off the bag, kicking
the dirt and cursing his fate. Here he was, wearing the goat horns in front
of his new teammates and a Shibe Park crowd that would boo a baby.

As Triplett continued to berate himself, Reds third baseman Steve
Mesner—keeping a straight face—quietly signaled for the ball. When he
got it, he walked over to the fuming Triplett and put the tag on him for
a double play that ended the inning and quashed the rally.

RONNY CEDENO
Pinch Runner · Chicago, NL · April 20, 2007

LEE LACY
Outfielder · Pittsburgh, NL · July 24, 1979

Ronny Cedeno and Lee Lacy hold a dubious dishonor. Each was a runner on first who managed to get thrown out at second—on a walk.

In a 2007 game, Cedeno was a pinch runner on first, representing the
tying run for the Chicago Cubs in the bottom of the ninth inning with

one out and the visiting St. Louis Cardinals ahead 2–1. The next batter, Jacque Jones, ran the count full. On the 3-2 pitch, Cedeno broke for second, drawing a throw from catcher Yadier Molina as Jones took ball four.

Because Cedeno was running hard on the pitch, he slid past second base. Cards shortstop David Eckstein took Molina's throw and tagged the runner out (shown in photo). Cedeno claimed the ball was dead because of the walk, but St. Louis manager Tony LaRussa knew better. The umpires agreed with LaRussa.

"The call there was ball four and the runner is entitled to second base, but that's it," explained crew chief Larry Young after the game. "He over-slid the bag and was tagged out."

So instead of having the potential tying and winning runs on first and second and one out, the Cubs had a runner on first and two out. The next batter, pinch hitter Matt Murton, then popped out to Eckstein to end another Cubs game that was tarnished by a crazy gaffe.

Cedeno out on a walk

ASSOCIATED PRESS

Twenty-eight years earlier, Pittsburgh Pirate Lee Lacy committed the same mistake because he didn't keep his eyes and ears open.

In the bottom of the fourth inning, the visiting Cincinnati Reds were leading the Pirates 4–3. But Pittsburgh was threatening with Lacy on first and Phil Garner on third, two out, and batter Omar Moreno at the plate with a 3-1 count.

When Reds pitcher Fred Norman delivered the next pitch, Lacy broke for second in an attempted steal. The pitch was called ball four by plate umpire Dave Pallone, but catcher Johnny Bench instinctively fired the ball to shortstop Dave Concepcion. Lacy was called out at second by umpire Dick Stello. In reality, Lacy was safe because Moreno, who was still in the batter's box, had walked.

But Lacy failed to check the call of the home plate umpire. Thinking he had been thrown out, Lacy left the bag at second and began trotting toward the dugout. However, when he saw Moreno head to first, Lacy tried to scramble back to second base. But Concepcion made the tag—again. And Stello called Lacy out—again.

The play triggered one of baseball's longest arguments in decades—34 minutes. Lacy and Pittsburgh manager Chuck Tanner claimed Stello misled the runner when the ump called him out on the attempted steal. The umps eventually ruled that because Moreno had walked, Lacy initially was safe at second rather than caught stealing. But they also ruled he was out when he was subsequently tagged by Concepcion. Tanner announced he was playing the game (won by the Reds 6–5) under protest.

National League president Chub Feeney turned down the protest, saying, "Lacy left second base on his own volition and should have been aware of the possibilities of Moreno receiving a base on balls."

WILLIE STARGELL
First Baseman · Pittsburgh, NL · September 19, 1978

Willie Stargell couldn't believe his eyes. Pittsburgh Pirates manager Chuck Tanner had given him the steal sign.

For Pops, whose legs could hardly shift from neutral to first gear, stolen bases were about as common as an eclipse of the sun. In the previous 10 years, he had swiped a whopping six bases. But on this particular day, after teammate Dave Parker blasted a homer to break an 11–11 tie in the top of the 11th inning against the Chicago Cubs at Wrigley Field, Stargell thought, "Who am I to argue with Tanner?"

So Stargell lumbered toward second in one of the most ridiculous base-stealing attempts ever seen in the Majors.

The paunchy 38-year-old veteran ran as fast as he could, which meant his shadow was beating him to the bag. When Stargell was about two-thirds of the way to second base, he began a slide that made him look more like a beached whale than a ballplayer.

He came to a dead stop about 10 feet short of the bag. Closing in on the prone runner, Cubs second baseman Manny Trillo was about to make an easy tag. Stargell, who thought much quicker than he ran, decided there was only one possible way out of this predicament. He stood up, formed a T with his hands, and shouted, "Time out!" The only "out" the umpire called was Stargell.

Pops returned to the dugout, where his teammates were rollicking with laughter.

After they regained their composure, they asked Stargell why he slid so soon. "I was given some bad information," he answered with a straight face. "I was told the bases were only 70 feet apart."

He never stole a base the rest of his Hall of Fame career.

DAZZY VANCE
Pitcher

CHICK FEWSTER
Second Baseman

BABE HERMAN
First Baseman
Brooklyn, NL · August 15, 1926

August 15, 1926, was a landmark day in baseball history. Three Brooklyn runners held an impromptu meeting at third base during a game—while the ball was in play.

In a pitching duel at Ebbets Field, the visiting Boston Braves were winning 1–0 going into the bottom of the seventh inning. Otto Miller, Brooklyn's regular third base coach, lamented to manager Wilbert Robinson, "God, I'm getting tired walking out there and back. Nothing ever happens at third base when we're at bat."

Hearing the coach's complaint, catcher Mickey O'Neil jumped up and told Miller, "Sit still, Otto. I'll handle it this inning." O'Neil figured a change in the coaching box might bring the team some luck. Oh, it did all right—bad luck.

The Dodgers (known as the Robins back then) mounted a rally and tied the game. Then, with one out, they loaded the bases with Hank DeBerry on third, Dazzy Vance on second, and Chick Fewster on first. That brought up Babe Herman, who blasted a drive to deep right field. DeBerry scored. But Vance was worried the ball might be caught, so he waited on second until he saw the ball ricochet off the wall before he started plodding toward third. By then Fewster, who could tell from his vantage point that it was an extra base hit all the way, tore around second and was breathing down Vance's neck. Meanwhile, Herman knew he had a sure double and decided on the fly to stretch it into a triple. So with his head down and his arms pumping, he galloped past second and sprinted for third.

O'Neil saw disaster looming and yelled at Herman, "Back! Back!" But Vance, who was headed toward home plate, thought the coach was talking to him. So he hurried back to third, arriving just in time to meet Fewster who had advanced from second. A split-second later, Herman chugged into third to make it three on a bag.

Fewster figured he was out and trotted off toward the dugout. Meanwhile, the relay throw had reached Braves third baseman Eddie Taylor, who was as confused as the rest, so he tagged everyone in the neighborhood. Then for good measure, second baseman Doc Gautreau snatched the ball, chased down Fewster near the dugout and tagged him too.

When it was finally sorted out, the umpires ruled Vance was safe at third because he got there first. Fewster was out because he had been tagged and Herman was out for passing him on the basepath.

Incredibly, Herman had doubled into a double play!

Robinson, disgusted by one of the greatest baserunning blunders in baseball history, growled, "That's the first time those guys got together on anything all season."

And it was the last time O'Neil coached at third.

JOSE LOPEZ
Second Baseman

ADRIAN BELTRE
Third Baseman

RAUL IBANEZ
Left Fielder
Seattle, AL · September 2, 2006

It had never been done before, but somehow the Seattle Mariners managed to run themselves into a triple play without hitting the ball.

In the first inning of an away game against the Tampa Bay Devil Rays, Mariners leadoff hitter Ichiro Suzuki beat out an infield single. Jose Lopez walked and Adrian Beltre slapped a run-scoring single. Seattle was poised for a big inning with Beltre on first and Lopez on third, no outs, and cleanup hitter Raul Ibanez at the plate.

But then the Mariners' fortunes sank like the *Titanic*. Ibanez struck out looking on a full count for the first out. Seeing Beltre trying to swipe second base, Rays catcher Dioner Navarro looked Lopez back to third and then fired a perfect peg to second where speedy shortstop Ben Zobrist caught the throw. Beltre could tell he was a dead duck, so he put on the skids and tried to retreat toward first. Zobrist ran him down and tagged him for the second out. Meanwhile, Lopez, thinking that Zobrist was too distracted by Beltre to pay attention to third base, broke for the plate. Bad decision. Zobrist wheeled around and fired the ball to Navarro, who easily tagged Lopez for the third out to complete the stunning 2-6-2 triple play.

In a few seconds—and without a batted ball—Seattle went from runners at the corners and no outs to *inning over*. Nothing had ever taken the sails out of a potential Mariners rally like this one had.

"You have to get rid of that absolute hollow feeling in the pit of your stomach," Seattle manager Mike Hargrove said after the game. "That takes a couple of innings. It was one of those things that everything had to be right for it to be pulled off—and it did, and we gave away an inning."

A 2-6-2 triple play had never happened before, according to the Society for American Baseball Research. From the year 1900 to the day of the game, there had been 524 triple plays in the Majors, but this one was unique.

"Oh, man, that was the first triple play I've ever seen," said Tampa Bay's starting pitcher J. P. Howell after the game. "I was trying to throw a strike. I was wrapped up in that so badly that I just watched the ball fly around like a snowball fight. But it was fun, man. I needed that."

It couldn't have come as a complete shock to the Mariners. They had hit into a triple play just three months earlier—one of nine in the team's relatively short history.

"It definitely was a weird play," Ibanez said. "It's embarrassing. The Rays pulled off the triple play, but we battled back and won the game. And that's the important thing."

Even though Tampa Bay lost 4–3, Navarro found a silver lining in the defeat. He told reporters, "I'm looking forward to seeing myself on ESPN tonight."

OLLIE O'MARA
Shortstop · Brooklyn, NL · September 5, 1916

Somewhere between home plate and first base, Ollie O'Mara lost his mind.

In a 5–2 win over the home team New York Giants, the Brooklyn Dodgers (then known as the Robins) had runners Hi Myers on first base and Jack Coombs on second when O'Mara stepped to the plate with orders to bunt. O'Mara dropped a slow roller down the third base line. Catcher Bill Rariden grabbed the ball, but threw wildly to third, trying to catch Coombs coming from second. Almost immediately, Rariden shouted, "Foul ball!" He hoped to wipe out his error by tricking home plate umpire Bill Klem into thinking the ball hadn't been fair.

O'Mara, who had started for first, turned around and headed back toward the batter's box after he heard someone shout that his bunt rolled foul.

But Klem yelled, "Fair ball!"

O'Mara, oblivious to the errant throw, bellowed back, "Foul ball!"

Klem insisted otherwise and thundered, "Fair ball!"

Meanwhile, Giants left fielder George Burns was chasing the ball, which had bounded all the way to the wall. As O'Mara continued to argue with the umpire, four Dodgers jumped out of the dugout, raced up to O'Mara, and exhorted him to start running. But the hardheaded O'Mara refused to listen to them and remained at the plate.

As the debate raged on, baserunners Coombs and Myers scored, while Burns tracked down the ball. In desperation, the Brooklyn strong-arm squad grabbed O'Mara and hustled him down the first base line as he kicked, punched, and screamed at his teammates.

It was all to no avail. The protesting O'Mara and his escorts were thrown out at first base by 10 feet.

GENE FREESE
Second Baseman · Pittsburgh, NL · May 28, 1955

Who doesn't know that the most infamous baserunning boner in Major League history was committed by Fred Merkle, the guy who forgot to touch second base, negating a crucial game-winning hit in a tight pennant race?

Well, apparently, Gene Freese didn't know, or else he forgot, because he duplicated the classic blunder nearly a half century later.

All ballplayers should know about Fred Merkle, the rookie for the New York Giants. In the bottom of the ninth inning of a 1–1 game against the visiting Chicago Cubs on September 23, 1908, the Giants' Moose McCormick was on third and Merkle on first with two outs. The next batter, Al Bridwell, lined a base hit up the middle, scoring McCormick with the apparent winning run. Merkle was about 15 feet from second base when, in celebration, he veered off to the clubhouse while thousands of deliriously happy Polo Grounds fans swarmed the field. Cubs second baseman Johnny Evers retrieved the ball, stepped on second, and summoned home plate umpire Hank O'Day. The ump agreed that Merkle had failed to touch second and called him out on a force play. Because the umpires couldn't clear the crowd from the field, O'Day declared the game a tie, a decision that was later upheld on appeal. As luck would have it, the Cubs and Giants ended the season tied in the standings, forcing them to play the makeup game at the Polo Grounds. The Cubs won 4–2 to capture the pennant. For the rest of his playing career, Merkle was saddled with the nickname Bonehead.

For 47 years no player dared commit such an astounding blunder . . . that is, until Gene Freese did it, reversing an apparent Pirates victory.

"People called me Merkle after my boner," recalled Freese. "But, hell, he cost them the pennant. All I did was move my team from 31 games out to 32."

Freese's baserunning bungle happened during a home game against the Philadelphia Phillies. In the bottom of the 10th inning of a 4–4 deadlock, the last-place Pirates had a golden opportunity to break out of their slump, having lost 13 of their last 14 games. They had Tom Saffell aboard on third and Freese on first with two outs. Batter Ramon Mejias then punched a single to center that scored Saffell for what the Pirates and their 3,082 fans thought was a 5–4 win.

Freese started toward second, but he was so elated over their rare victory that he turned around and went back toward first to shake hands with Mejias. Then Freese ran into the dugout.

Phillies center fielder Richie Ashburn spotted the gaffe and, having scooped up Mejias's hit, fired the ball to shortstop Roy Smalley, who then stepped on second base for a force-out.

Freese's brother Bud, who played third base in the game, saw what happened. "Bud came off the bench and tried to drag me back onto the field," Gene recalled. "I pulled away from him and ran into the clubhouse. But nobody followed me. I thought, 'Gee, that's a hell of a victory celebration.'"

The umpires, who had started off the field, were surrounded by Phillies who claimed they had made a force-out at second, ending the inning and nullifying the run. The umps agreed and ordered the Pirates to take the field for the top of the 11th inning. But first the diamond had to be cleared of hundreds of victory-starved fans who had run onto the field, thinking the game was over.

Given a reprieve, the Phillies promptly tallied four runs to win 8–4.

"That was probably my shortest winning streak ever—a few minutes—but my whole career was like that," Freese recalled. "[Manager] Fred Haney jumped all over me and said that since I was a rookie, a boneheaded play like that would stick with me for the rest of my life. I told him I doubted it. You have to be good before people remember how bad you are."

JEFF KENT
Second Baseman

J. D. DREW
Right Fielder

Los Angeles, NL · October 4, 2006

In the most shameful baserunning fiasco in playoff history, Los Angeles Dodgers runners Jeff Kent and J. D. Drew were tagged out in bang-bang succession at home plate on the same play.

Kent and Drew hit singles to lead off the top of the second inning of Game 1 of the National League Division Series against the New York Mets. Russell Martin then clubbed a liner that caromed off the base of the right field wall . . . and that's when the fun began.

Kent had tagged up at second, waiting to see if the ball would be caught, while Drew had gone slightly more than halfway between first and second. When the ball landed safely, both runners took off. But because Kent got such a late jump, Drew was practically nipping at his teammate's heels.

Dodgers third base coach Rich Donnelly waved them both around third. Mets right fielder Shawn Green pegged the ball to second baseman Jose Valentin, who fired a perfect throw to catcher Paul Lo Duca, nailing Kent as he dived headfirst for the plate.

Stuck in no man's land between home and third, Drew decided to try his luck at scoring because Lo Duca was spun around on the play at the plate and didn't realize at first that another Dodger was foolish enough to head for home. When Lo Duca struggled to his feet and turned his head, he saw Drew bearing down on him. The catcher then tagged out Drew, who also tried a headfirst dive. It was your typical 9-4-2-2 double play—on a base hit, no less.

After the game Donnelly told the press that he had no choice but to send the runners. "If I hold Kent, we've got two guys at third base," he explained. "I was hoping they'd throw the ball away. I didn't really want to send Jeff, but J. D. was right behind him, and I thought, one's going to be out and one's going to be safe."

It never occurred to him that both might be out.

Double trouble for the boys in blue   NEW YORK DAILY NEWS/GETTY IMAGES

After the game, Dodgers manager Grady Little sighed and tried to make light of the double play at home, saying, "We know about traffic jams [in L.A.]. We certainly had one again right there."

Lo Duca called the play "bizarre," adding, "It was one of those I'd like to see again, because I'm still not sure exactly what happened."

Said Valentin, "I couldn't believe we got them both. We got two for the price of one."

Mets manager Willie Randolph had seen this play before when he played for the New York Yankees in a game against the Chicago White Sox on August 2, 1985. Yankees runners Bobby Meacham and Dale Berra were both tagged out at home on a double by Rickey Henderson.

New York manager Billy Martin was so furious at Berra, who was the trailing runner, that Martin benched him on the spot. The Yankees ruined a scoring threat and lost 6–5.

Recalled Randolph, "I remember very vividly [third base coach] Gene Michael throwing his hands up like, 'What the hell's going on?' I remember how funny that play was when I first saw it. This one [with the Dodgers] was even more humorous to me."

It wasn't quite so funny for the Dodgers. The baserunning bungle proved costly, as the Mets won 6–5 and went on to sweep the series, three games to none.

RICKEY HENDERSON
Left Fielder · Oakland, AL · July 25, 1982

Oakland Athletics star Rickey Henderson—the greatest base stealer in baseball history and one of the game's most daring and exciting players—once was called out while advancing from first to third on a ground-rule double!

Anyone, even your kid sister, can safely stroll from first to third on a ground-rule double. But Henderson found an embarrassing way to mess up the easiest baserunning play in baseball.

In the top of the fifth inning of a 6–2 loss to the Baltimore Orioles, the A's were losing 3–0 with Henderson on first base and Dwayne Murphy at the plate and one out. On the pitch to Murphy, Henderson took off for second and slid into the base headfirst before realizing that Murphy had looped a fly ball to left field.

Believing that Murphy's ball might be caught, Henderson got up and retreated toward first. But the ball landed safely and then bounced into the seats for a ground-rule double. So Henderson jogged across the infield to third base. But he forgot to retouch second base.

Orioles second baseman Rich Dauer alertly spotted the infraction and called for the ball. Pitcher Dennis Martinez tossed it to Dauer, who stepped on the bag, and umpire Nick Bremigan called Henderson out.

A's manager Billy Martin rushed out of the dugout to argue. Bremigan cited the rule, which says that a runner must retouch a base once he relinquishes it. Martin claimed the ball was dead once it was ruled a ground-rule double. He lost his case and Murphy lost his double. Murphy was sent back to first and credited with hitting a pitcher-to-second force-out.

Henderson's gaffe cost Oakland a run because Dan Meyer followed the controversial play with a two-run homer—a blast that would have been a game-tying three-run shot if Henderson hadn't screwed up. Several Oakland players waved towels from the dugout and heckled Bremigan after the round-tripper. The A's should have directed their anger at one of their own—Rickey Henderson, who seemed to forget that in baseball, the shortest route between two points is not necessarily a straight line.

THE BLIGHTS
OF SPRING

For the Zaniest Spring Training Shenanigans of
All Time, The Baseball Hall of Shame™ Inducts:

GEORGE HARPER
Outfielder · Cincinnati, NL · March, 1922

George Harper shamed the name of hitters everywhere when he slunk back to the dugout even though he hadn't finished taking his turn at bat.

After four years in the minors, Harper was called up by the Cincinnati Reds for spring training in 1922. When Cincinnati met the Washington Senators in Tampa for an exhibition game, it was the first up-close-and-personal look many of the Reds had at fireballing pitcher Walter Johnson. Even though he was near the end of his career, Johnson had a fastball that was still a fearsome pitch for the fainthearted at the plate. Harper was among the faintest of the faint.

The first time he went up to hit against Johnson, Harper didn't even get the bat off his shoulder. The ball whizzed by him as umpire Bill Klem barked "Strike one!" Harper stepped out of the batter's box, shook his head in astonishment at the velocity of the Big Train and then moved back into his stance. Harper had hardly planted his feet when another pitch zipped past him, and Klem hollered "Strike two!"

That was enough for Harper. He turned and began walking away.

"Wait," Klem said. "You still have another strike left."

"I don't want it," the white-faced Harper answered. He then kept heading straight for the safety of the dugout.

LONNY FREY
Second Baseman · Cincinnati, NL · April 12, 1942

Lonny Frey was a bit too patriotic during the last spring training game of 1942.

Playing at home against the Detroit Tigers, the Cincinnati Reds took to the field for the start of the exhibition game. The players paused for the playing of "The Star-Spangled Banner," but the public address system malfunctioned so the game began without honoring the flag.

Tigers leadoff batter Jimmy Bloodworth then swatted an easy grounder toward Frey at second. Just as Frey bent over to field the ball, the maintenance guy got the public address system to work. Suddenly, the loudspeakers blared, "Oh, say, can you see . . ."

At the sound of the national anthem, Frey dutifully stopped, doffed his cap, and stood at attention, allowing the ground ball to bounce right past him for a single.

"When the anthem started playing, I stopped running down toward first," recalled Bloodworth. "But then I figured I'd better run it out. If Lonny hadn't been so patriotic, I wouldn't have had a hit."

WILBERT "UNCLE ROBBIE" ROBINSON
Manager · Brooklyn, NL · March 13, 1915

Brooklyn manager Wilbert Robinson tried catching a baseball dropped from an airplane and ended up catching a lot of good-natured flak instead.

During spring training in 1915, "Uncle Robbie" was listening to several of his players marvel over the feat achieved a few years earlier by Washington Senators catcher Gabby Street. In 1908, Street, on his 13th try, caught a ball dropped from the observation level of the Washington Monument—a distance of 500 feet.

Robinson, a former catcher with the old Baltimore Orioles, took this as a personal challenge. "Hell, that's nothing," the roly-poly, 52-year-old skipper told his players. "I can catch a ball dropped even higher from an airplane."

Team trainer Jack Coombs, a wizard with figures, calculated the velocity and force of a baseball dropped from the height of nearly 600 feet. He said it seemed a little dangerous, but Robinson scoffed at him. Uncle Robbie—as the Brooklyn manager was fondly called—was determined to be the first to accomplish this feat for the aviation and baseball worlds.

Coombs climbed into a biplane in the lone seat behind pioneer woman flyer Ruth Law. But there was a slight snag in the plans. She confessed to Coombs that she had forgotten the baseball back in her hotel room and as a substitute handed him a grapefruit from the lunch of one of her crew members. Whether out of concern for Robinson's safety or out of a lust for laughs, Coombs decided not to tell Robinson.

The plane took off and circled above the team's training camp in Daytona Beach, Florida, at an altitude higher than the Washington Monument. When the signal was given, Coombs dropped the grapefruit.

Robinson saw the "ball" leave the plane and waved players and spectators away like an outfielder, shouting, "I got it! I got it!" The plummeting sphere looked bigger and bigger to him as it sped earthward. Still thinking it was a baseball, Robinson bravely camped under the grapefruit, poised to make the historic catch.

The grapefruit slammed into his glove with a loud splat as seeds, juice, and pieces of fruit exploded and splattered all over him. The impact tore the glove off his hand and flipped him right over on his back. Feeling the warm grapefruit juice, Robinson thought he was covered in his own blood and called for help. The players rushed to his aid, but once they saw that he wasn't hurt, they burst out laughing.

Robinson, however, didn't think it was all that funny. He was fuming because he had risked his life and limb over a lousy grapefruit instead of an official baseball.

"I'd have caught it," he said, "except for that damn cloudburst of grapefruit juice."

PING BODIE VS. PERCY THE OSTRICH
April 3, 1919

Ping Bodie, the 5-foot, 8-inch, 195-pound New York Yankee, handled a knife and fork with the same skill as a bat and ball. The pudgy outfielder covered more ground at the dining table than Joe DiMaggio ever did in center field.

Bodie's most ludicrous gastronomical feat occurred in 1919 at the Yankees' spring training camp in Jacksonville, Florida, when he challenged an ostrich named Percy to the heavyweight pasta-eating championship of the world. As one of the first Italian-Americans to play in the Majors, Bodie (who was born Francesco Stephano Pezzolo) loved his spaghetti.

In front of a packed local hall known as the South Side Pavilion, Yankees co-owner Til Huston introduced his trencherman to the cheering crowd. Bodie bowed gracefully after stepping into the boxing ring where the eating event was about to take place. Truck Hannah, the team's 190-pound catcher and fellow gorger, acted as Bodie's second.

The ostrich, sponsored by the Jacksonville Chamber of Commerce, was led in by Brooklyn manager Wilbert Robinson, himself a legendary greedy-gut who consented to act as Percy's second.

Bodie scowled defiantly at his feathered opponent while the ostrich sharpened his beak on the canvas and then playfully poked Robinson in his jelly belly.

The match, which was not advertised for fear of arousing the wrath of animal lovers, would determine whether Percy or Bodie could eat

The champ: Ping Bodie   NATIONAL BASEBALL HALL OF FAME LIBRARY

the most bowls of spaghetti. The following is an actual round-by-round, firsthand account:

Round 1

Both pasta bowls were cleaned within seconds after the bell rang. Bodie was a trifle disconcerted by a sprig of spaghetti that eluded his fork, so he grasped it between his thumb and forefinger and flung it in his mouth with a flourish.

Round 2

Once again Bodie polished off his bowl in less than a minute while Percy seemed to tarry a bit. Experts began to figure that the ostrich—billed as the world's greatest eater—had met his match at last. Members of the Chamber of Commerce, who had wagered heavily on the contest, began to look for a chance to hedge their bets.

Round 3

Percy came back strong and gobbled his third bowl of spaghetti with such gusto that he accidentally swallowed Robinson's pocket watch and chain when the manager was timing him. The smile of confidence remained on Bodie's face as his teammates shouted, "Stay with him, Ping!" Bodie sneered at the ostrich when they went to their respective corners at the end of the round.

Round 4

The ostrich began displaying signs of discomfort. Percy's sides had begun to swell visibly while Bodie showed not an ounce of trouble. Both contestants finished their fourth bowl.

Round 5

The ostrich came out of his corner looking a bit weary. Bodie's smile widened, and he refused the napkin offered by his solicitous second. It took a bit longer but both competitors ate their pasta.

Round 6

It was obvious that Percy was tiring. Many women at ringside started for the door because they couldn't stomach seeing the poor bird topple over. But the ostrich rallied and matched Bodie by finishing the sixth bowl.

Round 7

Even strong men began to edge back from the ring, fearing that at any time Percy would explode. Somehow, though, the ostrich downed the pasta to keep up with Bodie.

The chump: The Ostrich   PAUL BRUINS/FLICKR/GETTY IMAGES

Round 8

It was plain to all the remaining spectators that Bodie was nowhere close to quitting after eating his eighth bowl of spaghetti while Percy was weakening considerably. But the feathered eating machine refused to give up.

Round 9

At the start of the round, even hardened eaters were demanding that Robinson throw in the napkin. "Do you want your bird killed?" a spectator hollered. Robinson retorted, "He won't quit while he's on his feet." And so the competitors slurped up the ninth bowl of pasta.

Round 10

The ostrich staggered out of his corner with his beak sagging. There seemed no room left in his stomach for even one strand of spaghetti. Bodie just grinned while consuming the 10th bowl. Now unsteady on his feet, Percy barely managed to finish his portion.

Round 11

The ostrich staggered out from his corner. His eyes were bloodshot and his sides were heaving as he toed his pasta bowl. Everyone knew he was a beaten bird. Bodie was almost finished with his bowl when Percy dropped to his knees. The timekeeper began to count. Bodie wolfed down the last morsel and stepped back to survey his fallen opponent. When the timekeeper counted to ten, the ostrich keeled over, never to rise again.

Bodie was then declared the undisputed spaghetti-eating champion of the world.

DIZZY DEAN
Pitcher · St. Louis, NL · March, 1934

Nobody detested batters more than pitcher Dizzy Dean. Show him a guy with a bat in his hand and Dean would foam at the mouth. And pity the poor batter who dared dig in against him. Dean would yell, "Are you all done? You comfortable? Well, send for the groundskeeper and get a shovel 'cause that's where they're gonna bury you!" The hitter would then be diving in the dirt with the next pitch.

As one of the crazier members of the St. Louis Cardinals' Gashouse Gang, Dean served notice even in spring training that he would take personal offense at any team who got the better of him. During an exhibition game in Miami, Dean felt extremely offended when the New York Giants scored seven runs off him in one inning.

Stomping and snarling on the mound, Dean went to work to get even. He reportedly plunked the next seven batters in a row—one for each run scored on him. Finally the umpire stopped the mayhem by ordering Cardinals manager Frankie Frisch to get "that maniac" off the mound. It was, after all, only spring training.

TUG MCGRAW
Pitcher · New York, NL · April, 1968

Hurler Tug McGraw got himself into deep doo doo after taking his dog along to training camp.

It probably wasn't the smartest thing for McGraw to do, considering he shuttled between the New York Mets and the minors in his three previous seasons and sported a 4-19 career record at the time.

The pitcher's pet, a mid-sized mutt named Pucci, put him in the doghouse the night before the final cut at the Mets' camp in St. Petersburg, Florida, in 1968. That evening, McGraw opened his motel room door to let in some air—and what happened next shouldn't happen to a dog.

"Pucci wandered out," McGraw recalled. "She trotted down the outdoor corridor to the room where [teammates] Dick Selma and Danny Frisella were living. They were having a party at the time . . . so they sort of boozed up old Pucci, feeding her a few nips."

The liquor must have upset her stomach, because she dumped a load right in front of coach Joe "Piggy" Pignatano's room. "Then Piggy came out of his room in his bare feet to see what the commotion was about, and naturally he stepped smack into Pucci's deposit," recalled McGraw. "Man, he put up a frightening clamor, complete with cussing and howling the way only a coach can."

Just twelve hours later, McGraw was on his way back to the Mets' farm team in Jacksonville, Florida, accompanied by his hungover boozehound.

MEL HALL

Left Fielder · Cleveland, AL · March 16, 1986

Cleveland Indians left fielder Mel Hall became so caught up in a spring training game that he hung his head—and uniform—in shame.

In the bottom of the fourth inning at Phoenix (Arizona) Municipal Stadium, Oakland Athletics batter Carney Lansford hit a looping line drive over third base. Hall chased the ball into foul territory near a restraining fence that separated the bleachers from the field.

Suddenly, Hall stopped dead in his tracks as though he had been caught in a stop-action video replay. The fence had snared the long-sleeved T-shirt under his jersey. Hall couldn't move and was forced to watch helplessly as the ball bounced away from him.

Shortstop Julio Franco raced to retrieve the ball, but when he realized that Hall was hung up, Franco began laughing. Meanwhile, Lansford circled the bases for an inside-the-park home run.

Hall was still trying to free himself when his manager, Pat Corrales, began arguing with umpire Don Denkinger. Mused Oakland manager Jackie Moore, "This is the first time I can remember a discussion about whether a player, rather than a ball, was in play."

After Hall unsnagged himself, teammate Joe Carter had a suggestion: "Mel needs a tear-away jersey."

MICKEY MANTLE

Center Fielder · New York, AL · March 11, 1951

Everybody raved about Mickey Mantle, the new kid with blazing speed and a thundering bat. But the raves turned to raspberries when the much-ballyhooed rookie zeroed in on the first fly ball hit to him in his first spring training game—and got smacked right between the eyes.

Mantle had arrived at the New York Yankees' temporary spring training camp in Phoenix in 1951 as the heir apparent to Hall of Famer Joe DiMaggio. Brought up as a shortstop, Mantle was immediately

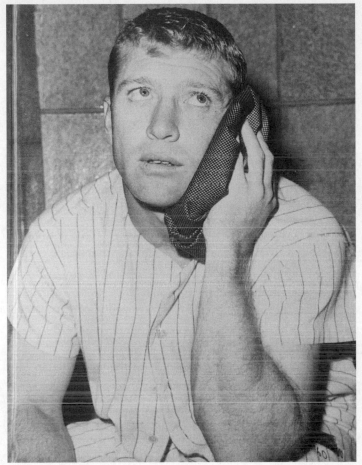

Mickey, a head-liner from the start   © BETTMANN/CORBIS

shifted to the outfield by manager Casey Stengel, who was impressed with the rookie's speed and powerful arm.

Former Yankees outfielder Tommy "Old Reliable" Henrich was assigned the job of teaching Mantle the tricks and treacheries of the outfield. Henrich had his work cut out for him.

"I stood out there with him day after day," Henrich recalled. "Mickey had a tough time making the adjustment from shortstop to the outfield because there were so many things he had to learn that were unnatural for him.

"We must have hit hundreds of fly balls to him while I tried to teach him the finer points of playing the outfield. I had to teach him how to use sunglasses. Knowing when to flip them down as the ball comes out of the shadows can be pretty tricky. Mickey had never used them before, and I thought he never would get the hang of them. Finally, I figured he had it nailed down."

Not quite.

The first spring training game was against the Cleveland Indians, and Stengel started the excited rookie in center field. In his autobiography, *The Mick*, Mantle recalled what happened next:

"Practice makes perfect, right? My first game as a Yankee. And Cleveland shortstop Ray Boone hit a line drive straight at me. I ran in a few steps and flipped my sunglasses down. *Bam!* Nothing but blackness. The ball caught me square on the forehead."

Left fielder Gene Woodling dashed over, grabbed the ball and threw it in. He then ran to Mantle's side and, with great concern in his voice, asked not about Mantle's head, but, "Did the glasses break?"

Meanwhile in the Yankees dugout, Henrich threw his hands up in despair. "Oh, no, back to the drawing board," he moaned.

Trainer Gus Mauch ran out to the injured rookie, applied cold compresses to the rising knot on Mantle's forehead, and led him off the field. As he staggered into the dugout, Mantle looked over at his new teammates. "Everybody was laughing," he recalled. "After that, I had nowhere to go except up."

RIPPER COLLINS
Pinch Hitter · St. Louis, NL · March, 1933

St. Louis Cardinals first baseman Ripper Collins was looking to have a little fun during an exhibition game. But it was no laughing matter to the umpire.

Collins was called on to pinch-hit during a 1933 exhibition game. Before leaving the dugout, he secretly tucked a ball under his left armpit where nobody could see it, including plate umpire Bill Klem. On the first pitch, Collins dragged a bunt down the first base line and at the same time let the ball drop from under his arm.

"The pitcher ran over to get the ball that I had bunted and the catcher picked up the one I had dropped," Collins recalled. "Neither one threw, they were so surprised.

"Klem threw me out of the game. He told me, 'There will be none of that, young man. This is serious business, even in an exhibition game.'

"For a minute, though, it was fun."

JACK GRANEY
Pitcher · Cleveland, AL · February, 1908

As a rookie hurler up from the minors, Jack Graney wanted to make a lasting first impression in spring training. Boy, did he ever. Unfortunately, the impression he made was from a pitch that beaned the manager.

Graney was a young pitching sensation in his hometown of St. Thomas, Ontario, and in the minors in Pennsylvania. In 1908, the Cleveland Indians (then known as the Naps) invited him to spring training for a tryout. To see what the 22-year-old southpaw could do, player-manager Nap Lajoie had Graney throw batting practice.

Most of Graney's pitches sailed everywhere but over the plate. Nevertheless, he kept firing away, hoping that eventually he'd master his control problems. Then Lajoie stepped in to hit against the wild prospect.

"When Lajoie came up to the plate, I wanted to give it everything I had because he was the manager of the team and one of baseball's greatest hitters," recalled Graney. "I was pretty cocky and had a crazy idea I could strike out Lajoie. That's all I could think about, the boys back in St. Thomas sitting around the coal stove talking about how Jack Graney struck out the great Lajoie. I reared back and threw the fastest ball I'd ever pitched."

The ball hit Lajoie on the side of the head above the ear and careened into the stands. "He went down like a load of bricks," Graney recalled. "Instead of striking him out, I knocked him out."

Later that evening, Graney was summoned to Lajoie's room. The rookie walked in and saw the manager holding an ice bag to his head. "I started to tell him I was sorry, but he stopped me," Graney recalled. "He said, 'They tell me the place for wild men is out west. So you're going west, kid, so far west that if you went any farther your hat would float.'"

It was a ticket to Portland, Oregon, home of the minor league Beavers of the Pacific Coast League.

Graney returned to Cleveland in 1910 and played 13 seasons for the team—as an outfielder.

MICKEY HATCHER
Infielder · Minnesota, AL · March 17, 1986

Minnesota Twins infielder Mickey Hatcher attempted to bring a little levity to an exhibition game, and he damn near died trying.

Because it was St. Patrick's Day, the Minnesota Twins' happy-go-lucky 31-year-old utility infielder felt an obligation to celebrate the holiday in the most colorful way he could. He sneaked into the maintenance room next to the dugout of Tinker Field, the team's spring training home in Orlando, and found a can of green paint that had been earmarked for sprucing up the outfield walls.

Hatcher had a better use for it—he would paint himself green. He took the can into the clubhouse restroom and, dipping a towel in the paint, covered his face, neck, and arms in bright green. When he went into the clubhouse, his teammates roared with laughter.

But third baseman Gary Gaetti wasn't laughing. In all seriousness, Gaetti told him, "Hey, Hatch. You're going to suffocate. Your skin's got to breathe, man."

Hatcher sloughed off the warning and replied, "If I get dizzy, I'll take myself out." He donned his uniform and went onto the field for some pregame fun. Waving a green paintbrush like a symphony conductor's baton, Hatcher led early-arriving fans in an Irish ditty.

Recalled teammate Bert Blyleven, "He didn't realize that the paint was enamel. It was a hot March day and everyone was laughing. Well, the game started, and Mickey was sitting next to me on the bench, and all of a sudden he told me 'Bert, I'm having trouble breathing.' His pores had closed and the paint was going into his system. We had to take him out of there and back into the clubhouse and douse him with rubbing alcohol to get the paint off of him. Luckily, he ended up being okay."

The only thing Hatcher's teammates worried about was what he'd do if he decided to paint the town red.

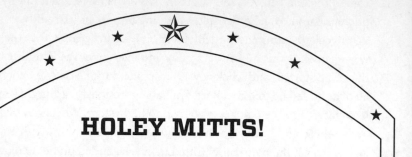

HOLEY MITTS!

For the Goofiest Fielding Fiascoes of All Time,
The Baseball Hall of Shame™ Inducts:

DUTCH LEONARD
Pitcher · Washington, AL · August 1, 1945

Washington Senators pitcher Dutch Leonard was robbed of a fielding assist by his baggy pants, causing him to curse the sons of britches.

Leonard was hurling a shutout against the visiting Philadelphia Athletics in the eighth inning when A's batter Irv Hall lined a knuckleball right back to the mound. The ball smacked into Leonard's stomach, and he doubled over, holding his glove in front of his belt. Leonard, who wasn't hurt, thought he had trapped the ball between his belly and his mitt. But when he straightened up to throw Hall out at first, the pitcher was shocked that the ball wasn't in his glove. Frantically, he searched the mound and the infield. Nothing.

Where could it be? Suddenly, Leonard felt something weird inside his pants. It was the ball! Somehow, when he doubled over, the ball rolled down his shirt, through his loosely-belted waist, and into his left pant leg. By the time Leonard removed the ball from his pants, Hall was already perched on first, laughing uncontrollably along with the rest of the players and fans.

According to the rule book, it is not a catch if the fielder uses his "cap, protector, pocket or any other part of his uniform in getting possession."

After the game, which Leonard won 2–1, he always buckled his belt a notch tighter.

LARRY BIITTNER
Right Fielder · Chicago, NL · September 26, 1979

A "hat trick" spurs accolades in hockey, but Larry Biittner discovered that it triggers embarrassment in baseball.

After the Chicago Cubs lost 8–3 to the visiting New York Mets, the players and 5,827 fans couldn't stop talking about the play Biittner made in the fourth inning. New York's Bruce Boisclair hit a sinking liner to right field. Biittner charged in and made a spectacular lunging dive at the hard-hit ball. Unfortunately, he trapped it. Scrambling to his feet so quickly that his cap flew off, Biittner knew the only way to hold the runner to a single was to fire the ball to second base in a hurry. But the ball wasn't in his glove and he couldn't find it anywhere.

Launching a frantic search, Biittner checked the warning track behind him, peered at the right field bullpen, looked toward the infield, and glanced at center fielder Jerry Martin. No ball. Out of sheer frustration, Biittner even scanned the sky to see if a nasty seagull had swooped down and snatched the ball and carried it away.

Finally, the perplexed outfielder picked up his hat in disgust. To his utter amazement, he found the ball. It was hidden under his cap the whole time!

While the spectators and players were cracking up, Boisclair was streaking for third base. Somehow Biittner managed to overcome his chagrin and throw out the Mets runner at third.

After the game, Biittner was asked when he knew the ball was covered by his hat. He replied, "When I couldn't find it anywhere else."

LENNIE MERULLO
Shortstop · Chicago, NL · September 13, 1942

No infielder ever played a shakier inning than Lennie Merullo.

The Chicago Cub turned the shortstop position into a disaster area during the second inning of a game against the Boston Braves at Braves Field. Every time he touched the ball, he booted it—on four consecutive plays. But at least he had an excuse.

Shortly before Merullo took the field, his wife, Mary Jean, had presented him with their first-born child. Obviously, Merullo's mind was at the hospital and not in the game.

So when Clyde Kluttz tapped an easy grounder to the shortstop, Merullo muffed it for error No. 1. Ducky Detweiler then stroked a single to right field as Kluttz raced to third. When Detweiler broke for second base on the throw-in from right fielder Bill Nicholson, Merullo attempted to cut off the peg, but he dropped the ball for error No. 2. That put runners on second and third, compliments of the nervous new daddy.

After the next batter struck out, Tommy Holmes sent another grounder to Merullo, who once again bobbled the ball for error No. 3 as Kluttz scored. An ignoble record was within Merullo's grasp, even if the balls hit to him in the inning weren't.

With runners on the corners, Al "Skippy" Roberge dinked a roller to the Cubs' fumble-fingered shortstop. This time, Merullo gloved the ball without mishap, but just as he started to throw to second for the force-out, the ball squirted out of his hand and bounced off his head. The fourth—and record-setting—error was his. The second unearned run of the inning scored, but luckily for the Cubs, they won anyway, 12–8.

Teammate Lou Stringer, who played second base that day, knew exactly how Merullo felt. A year earlier, Stringer had set the record for most errors (four) by a shortstop on Opening Day, but at least he did it over the span of nine innings.

If ever a player had an excuse for screwing up, though, it was Merullo. He just couldn't concentrate on baseball because he was so excited, nervous, and proud to be the father of a healthy seven-pound, four-ounce son. After the game, the baby, who was named Lennie Jr., was given a nickname in honor of Daddy's unforgettable day: Boots.

TOMMY JOHN
Pitcher · New York, AL · July 27, 1988

New York Yankees hurler Tommy John committed not one, not two, but *three* errors on *one* play!

"I've made errors before," said the veteran lefty, "but these seemed like a lifetime's worth with one ball."

In a game against the Milwaukee Brewers, John's control on the mound was masterful. But in the field he fell apart at the seams like a dime-store baseball, and tied a dubious record that hadn't been equaled in 90 years.

With one out in the top of the fourth inning and the Yankees ahead 4–0, John walked Jim Gantner. The next batter, Jeffrey Leonard, tapped a little dribbler to the mound that John should have easily fielded for a routine out. But John bobbled the ball for his first error.

Gantner had already reached second and Leonard was almost at first when John—a pitcher who built his career on pinpoint control—reared back and heaved the ball past first baseman Don Mattingly and into right field for another error.

Gantner rounded third and headed for home on the overthrow while Leonard galloped to second. Right fielder Dave Winfield scooped up the errant throw and was on line to gun down Gantner at the plate. But John unthinkingly cut off the relay. He then guaranteed himself a place in history when he whirled and threw a perfect strike into the Brewers dugout for his third error of the play. Gantner scored, and Leonard, who now had reached third, was waved home by the umpire for the second run.

The embarrassed pitcher, who had rushed to cover home after his third miscue, muttered to plate umpire Rick Reed, "I think I just lost a Gold Glove on that play."

It was the most deplorable fielding disaster by a pitcher since the three errors made by Cy Seymour of the New York Giants way back in 1898. But John's bungles were more shameful because his triple misplay came on one batted ball. Seymour needed a whole inning to rack up his trio of errors.

When the 45-year-old John—the oldest player in the Majors in 1988—learned he had tied Seymour's record, he cracked, "I think I pitched against him in the Eastern League."

Reliving the historic moment years later, John said, "I should have eaten the ball, but I thought I could get him [Leonard] with a good throw to first. That was a mistake. Instead, I threw it into right field. That was a mistake. Then I cut the ball off. That was a mistake. Then I threw the ball to their trainer in the dugout. That was another mistake. I did things like that every once in a while to keep the team loose."

John, who won the game 16–3, had an explanation for his multi-blunder play: "There was a thunderstorm coming and there were a lot of negative ions in the air, and since I was wearing a metal cup, it just glitched my mind."

RICHIE ASHBURN
Center Fielder

ELIO CHACON
Shortstop

FRANK THOMAS
Left Fielder
New York, NL · April 25, 1962

Closing out a great career with the worst team in modern history, New York Mets outfielder Richie Ashburn desperately tried to save his hide from collisions with his teammates.

He wasn't always successful.

The veteran center fielder often dodged disaster in the form of energetic shortstop Elio Chacon. While chasing short fly balls, the two often came perilously close to crashing into each other.

"Elio was always running into people," Ashburn recalled. "He never actually hit me, but he came so close often enough that I knew it would just be a matter of time before he nailed me. Every time I went after a short fly, I had to keep one eye on the ball and one on Elio."

The problem was that they weren't communicating. In fact, they weren't even speaking the same language. Chacon, a native of Caracas, Venezuela, spoke no English. And Ashburn, a native of Tilden, Nebraska, spoke no Spanish. Whenever Ashburn ran in on a short fly, he yelled, "I got it! I got it!" Meanwhile, Chacon was dashing out, shouting the same thing in Spanish, so the Mets sounded like they were baseball's version of the Tower of Babel.

Ashburn feared he'd never make it through that dismal season and ease gracefully into retirement without being maimed for life. So he took his worries to Joe Christopher, his fellow outfielder, who spoke both English and Spanish.

"Instead of calling 'I got it' in English, say it in Spanish," suggested Christopher. "Just shout, '*Yo lo tengo.*' Elio will understand you. I'll explain it to Elio so he knows what's going on."

Before the next game, Ashburn approached Chacon and said, "*Yo lo tengo.*"

"*Si, si!*" replied a beaming Chacon. "*Yo lo tengo.*"

In the third inning, the Cincinnati Reds put runners on first and third with two outs. Batter Leo Cardenas then lofted a short fly ball to shallow left-center field.

Ashburn sprinted in for the catch, yelling at the top of his voice, "*Yo lo tengo! Yo lo tengo!*" Chacon, who had scampered after the ball, pulled up and motioned for Ashburn to take it.

No longer fearing a collision, Ashburn reached out to make the easy catch—and was flattened by 6-foot, 3-inch, 200-pound Frank Thomas, the Mets' hard-charging left fielder. Thomas was never told the meaning of "*Yo lo tengo.*"

EDDIE JOOST
Shortstop · Philadelphia, AL · September 11, 1948

SHEA HILLENBRAND
Third Baseman · Boston, AL · March 15, 2003

JEFF FULCHINO
Pitcher · Houston, NL · July 28, 2009

It's one thing to lose the ball in the sun. It's quite another to lose the ball in your shirt.

Philadelphia Athletics shortstop Eddie Joost suffered that fate in a 1948 game against the Boston Red Sox at Fenway Park. In the bottom of the fourth inning, Boston's Ted Williams was on second base with Billy Goodman at the plate.

Goodman rapped a sharp hopper past A's pitcher Bill McCahan. Joost raced over to make the play and as he bent down for the ball, he came up empty-handed. The ball had disappeared. "Nobody could figure out what had happened," Joost recalled. "McCahan was waiting for me to make the throw to first. When he didn't see anything happening, he ran over to me, waving his arms and yelling, 'Where the hell did it go?'"

It took a few seconds for Joost to find the answer. Incredibly, the ball had bounced off the heel of his glove, rolled up his sleeve, and ended up in the back of his shirt.

Meanwhile, Goodman had made it safely to first and was credited with a hit, while Williams reached third. The two runners, along with everyone else in Fenway, then watched Joost dance up and down like a man with an army of ants in his shirt. He scratched and clawed at his back, but the ball was still just a fingernail out of reach. In desperation, he started unbuttoning his jersey, but that was too slow. So he ripped the shirttail out of his pants. Finally, the ball fell to the ground.

The entire park erupted in laughter. Williams, who could have easily scored from third during Joost's wild search for the ball, had doubled over in hysterics and was too weak to run.

"I picked up the ball and ran over to third base," Joost recalled. "I shook the ball in Ted's face and yelled at him, 'Okay, damn you. You can run now.' But he was laughing so hard he couldn't have run if he wanted to. Everybody was laughing. Even me.

"You know, that never would have happened if we had worn those nice-fitting double-knits that they wear today."

Oh yeah? Tell that to Boston Red Sox third baseman Shea Hillenbrand or Houston Astros reliever Jeff Fulchino.

In a 2003 spring training game, it looked like Hillenbrand had a trick up his sleeve after Tampa Bay Devil Rays catcher Toby Hall chopped a grounder to him. The ball glanced off the heel of Hillenbrand's glove, knocked one of the buttons off his shirt, and disappeared inside the opening. He found it lodged underneath his jersey resting by his stomach.

In a questionable call, the umpires ruled the play dead and awarded Hall second base. The official scorer gave Hillenbrand an error. The play led to three unearned runs off Pedro Martinez—the only runs the Devil Rays scored in a 3–2 victory.

Later in the clubhouse, Hillenbrand told reporters, "It was kind of funny. I was listening to the [radio] commentary in here and they were saying I was penalized for sloppy dressing and not wearing my uniform right."

Afterward, the *Boston Globe* reported that Martinez accused Hillenbrand of "cuddling the ball." Hillenbrand vehemently denied the charge claiming, "Hey, I'm a happily married man."

Six years later, Houston's Jeff Fulchino found himself up shirt creek. In the bottom of the fifth inning of a 2009 game at Wrigley Field, Chicago Cubs leadoff hitter Kosuke Fukudome bounced a ball up the middle to Fulchino. The ball ricocheted off the pitcher's glove—and right into his jersey. As Fukudome raced toward first base, Fulchino dug his hand into his shirt, but couldn't fish out the ball because it had wound its way around to his side. Not quite sure what to do, he threw his hands in the air, giving the same signal that outfielders make at Wrigley when a ball is lost in the ivy-covered walls. Fukudome was credited with a base hit and later scored in the inning.

Fulchino, shirt out of luck

After the game, which the Astros won 11–6, Fulchino said, "I thought I had knocked it down. I looked down and I was like, 'Where is it?' Then I felt it right over here to my side and I was like, 'You gotta be kidding me.'

"It [the ball] cracked the button on my shirt and when it ricocheted off . . ." He stopped in mid-sentence and shook his head before adding, "I don't know how it got in there."

Teammate Geoff Blum told ESPN.com, "I thought he just absorbed it, maybe swallowed it or something." Asked if Fulchino should have just fired the shirt to first base, Blum replied, "Hell, no. That's the last thing we wanted to do. The wind was blowing out. It could have been ugly."

HANK GOWDY
Catcher · New York, NL · October 10, 1924

With the gracefulness Hank Gowdy showed in the seventh and final game of the 1924 World Series, the New York Giants catcher would probably have tripped over his own shadow. His clumsiness opened the door for the Washington Senators to win the world championship.

Gowdy was behind the plate in the bottom of the 12th inning of a 3–3 tie. With no one on base and one out, up to bat for the Senators stepped weak-hitting catcher Muddy Ruel, who had managed to get only two hits in 21 trips to the plate during the Series.

Ruel lifted a high lazy foul behind the dish for what appeared to be an easy out. Like a good catcher, Gowdy threw his mask off and went after the pop-up. But unlike a good catcher, he threw his mask right in his path.

As he circled under the foul, Gowdy stepped on his mask—and got his foot stuck in it. Keeping his eye on the ball, he desperately tried to shake off the discarded hardware. By now, the ball was descending and Gowdy was panicking. As if he was doing a poor imitation of Long John Silver, Gowdy hobbled on his mask and stumbled. The ball nicked his glove and dropped beside him for an error.

Given a new lease on life, Ruel rapped a double down the left field line. He stayed at second on an error by shortstop Travis Jackson, who bobbled pitcher Walter Johnson's grounder. Earl McNeely then swatted a double, and Ruel raced home with the winning (and unearned) run for Washington—and the championship.

BOB TILLMAN
Catcher · Boston, AL · May 12, 1967

Boston Red Sox catcher Bob Tillman spent hours practicing throws to second base so he could shoot down thieving runners. He didn't mow down that many base stealers, but he did manage once to bean his own pitcher.

In a tight game at Fenway Park, Boston reliever John Wyatt came in to pitch in the eighth inning against the visiting Detroit Tigers. Boston fans gave him an ovation because he had yet to be scored on in eight appearances that year.

With one out, he walked Al Kaline, who then broke for second base two pitches later. Tillman cut loose with a strong throw as Wyatt ducked and turned toward second to see how good his catcher's marksmanship was. The hurler painfully learned his batterymate was no sharpshooter.

The throw struck Wyatt smack in the back of his head with such force that the ball bounced all the way to the on-deck circle on the first base side of the field. As wide-eyed fans watched in fascinated horror, Wyatt staggered around on the mound. By the time Tillman retrieved the ball, Kaline had reached third base.

Tillman got an error and Wyatt got a headache. But after being examined by the trainer, the plucky pitcher stayed in the game. The next batter, Willie Horton, hit a sacrifice fly to right field, which allowed Kaline to tag up and score the first run of the year off Wyatt. The run was not only unearned but also crucial, because the Red Sox lost 5–4.

DAVE ENGLE
Catcher · Minnesota, AL · May 15, 1984

Minnesota Twins catcher Dave Engle caught what he thought was a nifty shutout. But he left his position a wee bit too soon—and caught hell.

With one out in the top of the ninth inning and the Twins ahead 1–0, the Toronto Blue Jays had runners on first and second. Pinch hitter

Rick Leach then hit what appeared to be a game-ending double-play grounder to shortstop Houston Jimenez, who flipped to second baseman Tim Teufel for the second out. But first baseman Kent Hrbek dropped Teufel's relay throw that would have ended the game.

Blue Jays runner Mitch Webster steamed from second base around third and headed for home. Hrbek recovered in time and fired the ball to the plate. But no one was there to catch it.

Where was Engle? Thinking the game was over, he was on his way to the mound to congratulate relief pitcher Ron Davis. Prematurely.

Because the catcher had deserted his post, Hrbek's throw sailed to the backstop, allowing the tying run to score. The official scorer charged Hrbek with his second error of the play, although Engle admitted that, as the catcher who left home early, he shared some of the blame. Instead of getting shut out, Toronto used its second chance to put the game away in the 10th inning and win 5–2.

"I went out to congratulate Ron and took my eye off the umpire," Engle said after the game. "Then I heard everybody screaming and I couldn't figure out what it was all about. I turned around and saw the ball was going back toward home plate."

Engle was in no mood to hear Blue Jays catcher Buck Martinez's assessment of the botched play: "You just can't take anything for granted in this game. Sooner or later it will catch up with you, and you'll get embarrassed."

KIP SELBACH
Left Fielder · Baltimore, AL · August 19, 1902
Left Fielder · Washington, AL · June 23, 1904

As an outfielder, there was no one quite like Kip Selbach. The record book attests to that.

Selbach is the only player in Major League history to have two shameful records for outfielders—the most errors in an inning and in a game.

He was an excellent hitter, batting .293 in 13 seasons. But at 5 feet 7 inches and 190 pounds, the short, squat player didn't look like an outfielder. And sometimes he didn't play like one either. He first bumbled his way into the annals of baseball as a Baltimore Oriole when he committed *five* errors in one game while impersonating a left fielder against the visiting St. Louis Browns in 1902. Three times an easy fly ball fell into his glove and three times he dropped it. Two times a routine single bounded straight toward him and two times it rolled right between his legs.

Selbach's fielding in the game became such a travesty that the Baltimore fans cheered derisively and shouted bawdy advice whenever a ball was hit to left field. There wasn't much else they could do while they watched his botchery hand the Browns an 11–4 victory.

Having established his ignominious fielding record in Baltimore, Selbach secured a new mark as a Washington Senator in 1904.

In the top of the eighth inning of a 2–2 game, the New York Yankees had a runner on first when a single was hit to left field. Selbach scooped up the ball, but heaved it so wildly over the third baseman's head that both the batter and the runner scored. Later in the same inning, Selbach misplayed another single, allowing the batter to reach second and a third Yankee to score from first.

Perhaps sensing immortality, Selbach seized the moment in the same inning by dropping a routine fly for two more unearned runs. All told, Selbach's record-tying three outfield errors in one inning gave the Yankees five unearned runs in the frame, enough for a 7–4 New York win.

Just days after Selbach's fielding debacle, the Senators dumped him.

PRANKS A LOT!

For the Wildest Practical Jokes of All Time,
The Baseball Hall of Shame™ Inducts:

BRETT MYERS
Pitcher · Philadelphia, NL · February 16, 2008

One of the most elaborate pranks in baseball history had young Philadelphia Phillies hurler Kyle Kendrick convinced that he had been traded to a Japanese team and would have to catch an early-morning flight to his new country.

The devious practical joke was masterminded by veteran pitcher Brett Myers, who pulled it off with the help of several accomplices, including manager Charlie Manuel, assistant general manager Ruben Amaro Jr., traveling secretary Mike Copenbarger, and even the TV crew from Comcast Sportsnet.

Under the ruse of a TV show featuring a day in the life of a Major League manager, the spring training prank was filmed over the span of several hours in the Phillies clubhouse. Wearing a microphone, Manuel called Kendrick into his office before morning workouts. With Amaro by his side, Manuel dropped the bombshell announcement that the 23-year-old hurler, who was beginning his second year in the bigs, had been traded to the Yomiuri Giants of Japan's Central League.

With the camera rolling, Kendrick sat dumbfounded as Manuel and Amaro went over his travel itinerary with him, telling him he had to catch a 7:00 a.m. flight the next morning for Japan. They even produced documents for him to sign before sending him out into the clubhouse to pack. After the stunned hurler left the manager's office, he bumped into Myers. When Kendrick said he had been traded to Japan, Myers kept a straight face while offering him best wishes.

Rather than fess up that it was all a hoax, Myers and the others kept stringing Kendrick along for much of the day. The film crew followed him as teammates came up to say goodbye and good luck. Later that afternoon, Amaro had reporters gather around him and Kendrick, who still looked totally shell-shocked. Then Amaro informed the press that Kendrick had been officially traded to the Yomiuri Giants in exchange for Kobayashi Iwamura. Kendrick didn't know there was no such player. The made-up name was a combination of competitive eating champ Kobayashi and Tampa Bay Rays outfielder Akinori Iwamura.

When a reporter asked Kendrick for a reaction, the pitcher stared blankly into the camera for several seconds before uttering, "I don't know. Uh, do they have good food in Japan?"

Seconds later, Myers walked over to Kendrick and said, "Do you know what I say? You just got *punked!*" And with that pronouncement, all the players in the clubhouse broke up laughing.

Kendrick just shook his head and smiled. He was so relieved that he wasn't on his way to the land of sushi that he didn't get mad at Myers. "I'm so happy to be staying in Philadelphia," he told reporters. When asked how he would get even with Myers, Kendrick replied, "I don't know. I don't think there's anything I can do to top that."

JACKIE PRICE
Coach · Cleveland, AL · March 26, 1947

If a movie were made about the most memorable prank pulled by Jackie Price, it would probably be called *Snakes on a Train*.

Price was 33 years old when he broke into the Majors with the Cleveland Indians toward the end of the 1946 season. He played in seven games and collected three hits. But team owner Bill Veeck liked him because of his ability to entertain the fans.

Price had honed his special routines and tricks by performing for fans before games in the Pacific Coast League, where he played for several years. In his most famous feat, Price would hang upside down strapped by his ankles to a specially constructed 10-foot-high bar and take batting practice. Batting upside down either left-handed or right-handed, Price could hit fastballs and curveballs. (In fact, he seemed to hit better upside down during BP than he did standing upright in real games.) He could also catch and throw while standing on his head.

He did some amazing feats while upright too. With two balls in one hand, he would throw a fastball to one catcher and a curveball to another catcher all in the same motion. He would shoot a baseball out of a pneumatic tube like a mortar round high in the air, hop into a Jeep to chase after it, and then reach out and catch the ball backhanded. In another feat, he would throw three baseballs with one hand in one motion to three different players stationed around the infield.

Despite his amazing abilities with a baseball, Price just wasn't good enough to make it as a Major Leaguer and was released after his cup of coffee in the bigs. However, Veeck recognized that Price could still be an entertaining pregame draw for fans, so the owner signed him as a coach. Player-manager Lou Boudreau was none too pleased by the move; he thought that Price, who loved to pull jokes and goof around, would be a distraction to the players.

And, besides, not everyone on the team liked the 20 snakes that Price brought with him on road games. The snakes were not only his pets, but also his props. Part of his routine involved hitting and catching with the serpents draped all over him.

On March 26, 1947, the team was on a train in California heading for a spring training game. With a pair of 5-foot-long boa constrictors around his waist, Price sat in the dining car talking to newly acquired second baseman Joe Gordon, a guy who shared Price's sense of humor.

Price's upside-down world   NATIONAL BASEBALL HALL OF FAME LIBRARY

Gordon thought it would be hilarious if Price released the snakes in the dining car. So, goaded on by Gordon, Price did just that.

Also in the car at the time was a group of women bowlers on their way back from a tournament. When they saw the snakes, the women began screaming and leaping onto tables and fleeing from the dining car. The chaos and commotion forced the conductor to stop the train.

It didn't take him long to figure out who was responsible. Grabbing Price with both hands, the conductor demanded to know his name.

Price answered, "Lou Boudreau, and would you kindly remove your hands from me."

At the next station, two policemen came aboard and marched over to Boudreau, who was playing cards with some of the players in another car. The cops threatened to throw him off the train and have him arrested.

"For what?" asked Boudreau, who was totally confounded by the unfolding scene.

"Letting snakes loose in the dining car," a policeman said.

As soon as Boudreau heard the word "snakes," he knew who the prankster was. After convincing the police he was not the culprit, an irate Boudreau decided to save the cops the trouble of kicking Price and his reptiles off the train. Boudreau did it for them. Then, in a wire to Veeck, Boudreau announced he had sent Price and his snakes home for good. It was the last time Price appeared with the Cleveland Indians.

GEORGE MULLIN
Pitcher · Detroit, AL · 1907

Detroit Tigers second baseman Germany Schaefer was arrested and locked up in jail for doing nothing more than executing to perfection the hidden-ball trick.

He had teammate George Mullin to blame for the unexpected incarceration.

Schaefer was obsessed with pulling the trick on unwary runners at second base, and he became very adept at it. He couldn't wait to try it during the 1907 offseason when the Tigers went to Cuba on a barnstorming trip to play Havana's best teams.

In one of the games, the score was tied in the bottom of the ninth with the winning run on second for the Cuban team. Mullin, the Detroit pitcher, called time and summoned Schaefer to the mound. "See if you can get that guy on second," Mullin whispered as he secretly slipped the ball to Schaefer. The second sacker slyly hid the ball in his glove and trotted back to his position.

As Mullin stepped back on the mound, time was called back in, and the runner edged off second base. Then, Schaefer slapped on the tag.

"You're out!" yelled the American umpire. The Cuban fans were outraged and stormed onto the field, wanting to tear the flesh off Schaefer and the arbiter. Police rushed in and managed to protect the player and ump from the wild crowd.

After a few tense minutes, the cops restored order. But then they grabbed Schaefer, announced he was under arrest, and hauled him off to jail. Despite his pleas of innocence, the shocked player spent the night in a dirty cell.

The next morning, he was brought in front of a judge who snorted that the player's hidden-ball play was a "shabby trick." Schaefer began to quake, wondering if he would be tried and convicted on the spot. The judge then leaned over the bench and growled, "I ought to keep you in jail for a week." Schaefer gulped. But after a stern lecture about fair play, the judge told the shaken Schaefer he was free to go.

Not until Schaefer returned home after the barnstorming trip did he learn that he had been set up by none other than George Mullin, a notorious practical joker. Shortly after the team had arrived in Cuba, the hurler had bribed the police to "arrest" Schaefer the first time he pulled the hidden-ball trick.

Everything went according to plan—except Mullin hadn't counted on the fans rioting. As for Schaefer, the old hidden-ball trick no longer seemed as much fun anymore.

RABBIT MARANVILLE
Shortstop · Boston, NL · 1920

Rabbit Maranville was a 5-foot, 5-inch Hall of Fame shortstop who had a huge appetite for the ludicrous. He acted on every zany impulse, from diving fully clothed into a hotel goldfish pond to filling up a hotel closet with pigeons.

As a master prankster, he had teammates entertained . . . and often enraged, which is what happened when he played one of his signature practical jokes in 1920.

In a hotel room filled with fellow players, he started a playful wrestling match with big and brawny Boston Braves teammate Jack Scott. "Stay away from me, Rabbit," warned the 6-foot, 3-inch, 200-pound pitcher. "I don't want to wrestle you because I might hurt you."

Maranville responded by charging Scott, who reluctantly applied a headlock that sent the fun-loving imp slumping to the floor in a dead faint. Scott, a religious man, was upset and said, "Lord, forgive me. I sure didn't want to hurt that boy." Then he left the room.

When Maranville recovered, he conjured up a cruel trick. He smeared talcum powder on his face and arms and stretched out in bed like a corpse. Then he sent an accomplice to tell Scott, "You killed Rabbit. He's dead!" Aghast, Scott raced into the room, fell to his knees in front of Maranville's "lifeless" body, and prayed fervently for a miracle to restore the little shortstop to life. "Lord, you know I didn't mean that boy any harm," he wailed. "Please put the breath of life back into the Rabbit. Please, Lord, have mercy on me—and him—and let the little Rabbit live!"

The distraught Scott went down to the lobby, sat in a chair and waited for what he was sure would be the police coming to arrest him on a murder rap. He was still there early the next morning when Maranville, the picture of health, strolled blithely by and chirped, "Hello, Jack. My, you're up early."

When Scott recovered from the shock and realized he had been duped, he charged after Maranville. This time, Scott really did want to kill him.

Maranville, that Rascally Rabbit   NATIONAL BASEBALL HALL OF FAME LIBRARY

BILL CASTRO   JERRY AUGUSTINE

REGGIE CLEVELAND   BOB GALASSO
Pitchers · Milwaukee, AL · 1979

During an afternoon game on a hot summer day, Milwaukee Brewers relief pitcher Bob McClure had to relieve himself, so he went into the bullpen bathroom at County Stadium.

He entered the bathroom unaware that he was about to become the victim of a prank. The flagpole at the ballpark was directly above the bathroom, and the pole's cord hung just above the door. With McClure inside, relievers Bill Castro, Jerry Augustine, Reggie Cleveland, and Bob Galasso pulled the cord down and wrapped it around the doorknob.

When McClure tried to leave, the door wouldn't budge. He pushed and pushed, but he still couldn't get it open.

Sweating and screaming, kicking and cursing, McClure demanded to be set free. But his fellow hurlers didn't take him out of the outhouse oven until he was well done.

"I swear it was 115 degrees inside, like a hot box," McClure recalled. "I was in there for fifteen minutes, yanking so hard on the door the flagpole almost bent in half. It looked like I had a big old bass on the end of that pole."

MOE DRABOWSKY
Pitcher · Kansas City, AL · October 6, 1969

Moe Drabowsky never set the world on fire as a pitcher, but he did give the gutsiest hotfoot ever.

He came chillingly close to sending baseball commissioner Bowie Kuhn's shoes up in flames.

The fun-loving relief pitcher was in the stands at Minnesota's Metropolitan Stadium to watch his former team, the Baltimore Orioles, complete a three-game sweep of the Twins in the American League

Championship Series. Drabowsky, who had been traded to the Kansas City Royals at the end of the 1968 season, walked into the winners' clubhouse to extend congratulations to his old buddies.

That's when he spotted Commissioner Kuhn—the perfect target for a prank, at least in Drabowsky's warped mind. While Kuhn was happily occupied with the trophy presentation, mischievous Moe crawled up behind him and sprayed lighter fluid on the floor around the commissioner's shiny patent leather shoes. Then Drabowsky set it on fire.

Players snickered but Kuhn was unaware at first that he had been hot-footed. He finally paid attention when the blaze spread to his new shoes. The commissioner leaped like a pivot man on a double play and quickly stomped out the flames before any damage was done.

Marveled Drabowsky, "He must have jumped 4 or 6 feet. Yow! What a scream he gave out. The best part was he never figured out who did it."

DAVID ORTIZ
Designated Hitter · Minnesota, Boston, AL · 1997–present

TORII HUNTER
Outfielder · Minnesota, Anaheim, AL · 1997–present

COREY KOSKIE
Infielder-Outfielder · Minnesota, Toronto, AL; Milwaukee, NL · 1998–2006

David Ortiz found himself in a rather sticky situation as a payback for his pranks.

When Big Papi was the designated hitter for the Minnesota Twins, he liked to play practical jokes on his teammates, especially center fielder Torii Hunter and third baseman Corey Koskie.

As the DH, Papi had time to kill while Hunter and Koskie were out in the field, so he would sneak off into the clubhouse and ravage their clothes. One of his favorite practical jokes was to go into their lockers and cut the toes off their socks so when they put them on after the game, their feet would go right through the mutilated socks. Another time, he put Koskie's street clothes in the freezer. After the game, Koskie found his duds frozen stiff.

But then it was payback time. Koskie smeared peanut butter in Ortiz's underwear while Big Papi was taking a shower. "So David got out of the shower and he's talking and laughing," Hunter told ESPN.com. "Everybody's talking to him but we knew that peanut butter was in his underwear. Then he put his pants on, put his shirt on, put his shoes on, walked out about 10 yards and then felt something funny and started getting upset and screaming at everybody, 'Who put peanut butter in my underwear?'" Ortiz confirmed the story on HBO's *Costas Now*. He told Bob Costas, "I was feeling funny. I walked back in, and it was either people on the ground laughing or people running. But I was going to kill somebody."

Rather than commit murder, Ortiz got even. He lubricated Koskie's underwear with Icy Hot just before a road trip.

When Ortiz was traded to the Boston Red Sox in 2003, he kept up his joking ways, often slamming a shaving cream pie in the face of a teammate. In 2006, he poured a pitcher of milk over teammate Coco Crisp during a photo shoot.

Even though Ortiz was with Boston, he and his former Twins comrades continued to prank each other. After a spring training game between the Twins and Red Sox in 2003, Ortiz went into the clubhouse to change into his street clothes. When he arrived in front of his locker, he discovered his clothes had been stolen. In their place was an orange jumpsuit, the kind worn by work-release prisoners at the local county jail.

Big Papi put it on and walked out of the ballpark to meet with fans. "It was hilarious," recalled Hunter, who took full responsibility for the swapped attire. "He was signing autographs and he was cracking up. He was good with it. He had fun with it."

The first time that he returned to Minnesota as a Boston Red Sox player, Ortiz decided to leave a calling card for Koskie. During the

Big Papi: A little milk with your Coco Crisp?

game, Ortiz sneaked out of the visitor's clubhouse in the Metrodome and walked down a hallway to the Twins locker room. There, he stuffed Koskie's street shoes full of juice and peanut butter. They were the only shoes that Koskie had brought to the ballpark.

WILL MCENANEY
Pitcher

MIKE MCENANEY
Will's Brother

Pittsburgh, NL · September 17, 1978

Will McEnaney double-crossed his manager.

Throughout a game against the visiting Montreal Expos, Pittsburgh Pirates skipper Chuck Tanner thought he could see his left-handed reliever sitting in the bullpen. Actually, Will was relaxing in the clubhouse watching a football game the entire time. Then who was that in his uniform? Will's twin, Mike.

"We planned it all out," the prankish Will recalled. "We're identical twins, and we used to do things like this all the time when we were growing up. We switched classes, girlfriends, and Little League uniforms, but never got caught."

Will concocted the scheme because he wanted to watch the football game between the Pittsburgh Steelers and Cincinnati Bengals on TV. But the gridiron battle was slated to start at the same time as the baseball game.

In a stroke of luck, Mike paid Will a visit to the Three Rivers Stadium clubhouse before the game and mentioned that he'd never been in the dugout or bullpen during an actual Major League contest.

"You will today," said Will, handing his uniform to his twin. "This is the perfect opportunity. Now I can watch the football game."

Mike was leery and said, "I don't think we can get away with this."

"Sure we can," declared Will. "No one is going to find out. Go out to the bullpen for about five or six innings and then come back and I'll take your place."

"What if Tanner calls on me—I mean you—to pitch?"

"If they ask you to warm up, just tell them you have to go to the bathroom first. Then hustle back here to the clubhouse and we'll change. But don't worry. Tanner and I aren't getting along at all, so I really don't expect to be called."

Satisfied but still somewhat nervous, Mike donned his brother's uniform and pretended to be a Pirate.

The Brothers McEnaney got away with their scam. Will watched most of the football game and Mike got to sit in the bullpen in uniform during a Major League contest.

Recalled Mike, "Kids kept leaning over the railing of the bullpen, yelling, 'Hey, Will, give us your autograph.' So I did. I wonder how much a Will McEnaney autograph signed by Mike McEnaney is worth?"

KEN GRIFFEY JR.
Center Fielder · Seattle, AL · April 15, 1995

Seattle Mariners manager Lou Piniella had a cow over a bet he won with his star player, Ken Griffey Jr. No, really, he had a cow—a live one.

The two had made a wager during the early days of training camp at the Mariners' facility in Peoria, Arizona, when the season was delayed because of a players' strike.

"It was batting practice, and I had three swings left," Griffey recalled. "Lou bet me a steak dinner that I couldn't hit a home run to each field on those three swings. I hit one to right and I hit one to center, but I missed the one to left. So I paid up."

Griffey gave him a steak so rare, it mooed. When Piniella arrived in his office, he found a 1,200-pound Hereford inside. "When he walked in, there was the cow and some other stuff the cow had left after lifting its tail, plus he had slobbered everywhere," said Griffey. "Lou got sick."

Piniella took the practical joke with a smile. "It's a long summer," he told reporters at the time. "We just might keep the cow around and let him loose in center field during a game."

Griffey told the press, "When did I think it up? As soon as I lost the bet."

Years later, Piniella recalled, "The cow mooed a couple times and did a couple other things, and we got it out of there. It was okay as a joke, but it smelled like cow [dung] in my office for a week."

The cow escapade inspired a commercial that Griffey did for the Seattle Mariners during spring training the following year. In the spot, he's inside Piniella's office when he cracks open the door and talks to the camera: "Last year, I bet Lou that I would hit the next ball out in batting practice. I lost, so I had a live cow delivered to his office. This year we went with the rack of lamb. Boy, I hope he's hungry."

The next shot is from inside Piniella's office. It's crammed with eight bleating sheep.

TED LYONS
Pitcher · Chicago, AL · 1925

A future Hall of Famer stuck it to another future Hall of Famer in a classic prank that left the victim hopping mad.

Chicago White Sox second baseman and manager Eddie Collins had a habit of sticking a piece of chewing gum on the button atop his cap as he went up to bat. Whenever he got two strikes against him, he would pluck the gum off his cap and chew it like crazy.

One day in 1925, White Sox pitcher Ted Lyons surreptitiously sprinkled red pepper on Collins's gum while it was still perched on top of his cap. When the count went to 0-and-2, the unsuspecting Collins tore the gum off his cap and started chewing like he always did in that situation. All of a sudden, he let out a whoop and spat out the gum. Then he struck out on the next pitch.

Back in the dugout, the furious Collins announced to his players, "I'll fine the joker a million bucks if I ever find him!"

SNOOZE PLAYS

*For the Most Mind-boggling Mental Miscues of
All Time, The Baseball Hall of Shame™ Inducts:*

JOE DIMAGGIO
Center Fielder · New York, AL · July 30, 1951

In all his 13 years in baseball, Joe DiMaggio never suffered a mental lapse on the field—except once.

Through his first 1,713 regular season games, 45 World Series contests, and 10 All-Star games, the Yankee Clipper had never been known to throw to the wrong base, try for an extra base without a good chance of reaching safely, or to be guilty of daydreaming out in the field. But DiMaggio, the thinking man's ballplayer, whom teammates and fans always counted on for his rock-solid dependability, committed an embarrassing blunder in his 1,714th game.

It came at a most inopportune time. In the top of the eighth inning at Yankee Stadium, Detroit Tigers star George Kell was on second base with one out and his team ahead 3–2. The next batter, Bud Souchock, flied to deep center where DiMaggio made the catch. Unbelievably, DiMaggio leisurely started to trot in with the ball, erroneously thinking that there were three outs. But Kell knew differently. He tagged up at second and headed toward third, where coach Dick Bartell waved him around. By the time DiMaggio woke up from his mental fog, Kell was racing for home. DiMaggio's blunder allowed Kell—who could run only slightly faster than First Lady Bess Truman—to score from second base on the outfield fly.

The thinking man's player forgot to think

The 39,684 fans gasped in disbelief. Joe DiMaggio, the closest base-ball had to a perfect player, had pulled a boner—one that put the home team down by two runs, 4–2—with only two innings left to play.

Joltin' Joe was so ashamed that he figured there was only one way to atone for his mistake. In the bottom of the ninth inning, after the Yankees had tied the score, he drove in the winning run with a two-out single.

PEE WEE REESE
Shortstop · Brooklyn, NL · July 12, 1947

Pee Wee Reese found to his everlasting chagrin that courtesy has no business on the baseball diamond.

In the bottom of the third inning in a 6–5 victory over the Chicago Cubs, the Brooklyn Dodgers shortstop walked. He was taking a lead off first base when batter Carl Furillo swung mightily and missed. The bat slipped out of Furillo's hands and sailed toward first base.

Being the nice guy that he was, Reese carelessly ambled off the bag to retrieve the bat. Unfortunately, he had failed to call time. As the Little Colonel stooped down to pick up the bat, Cubs catcher Clyde McCullough fired the ball to first baseman Eddie Waitkus, who slapped the tag on Reese for the out.

Reese should have known better. After all, he played for four years under manager Leo Durocher, who famously said, "Nice guys finish last."

LOU WHITAKER
Second Baseman · Detroit, AL · July 16, 1985

Fans selected Detroit Tigers second baseman Lou Whitaker to start in the 1985 All-Star Game because of his glove and stick. He certainly wasn't chosen for his memory.

Whitaker arrived in Minneapolis ready to play, but with nothing to wear. That's because the American League All-Star forgot to bring his uniform and gear. He left everything in the back seat of his Mercedes at home in Bloomfield Hills, Michigan.

An emergency effort to get a uniform flown in from Detroit failed when the replacement was lost in transit. So Whitaker was forced to dress up like a Little Leaguer. He bought a Tigers jersey and cap from a Metrodome concession stand for $15 and had a number 1 written in blue felt-tip pen on the back. He borrowed a pair of pants, and the Twins loaned him a pair of the team's blue socks.

Fortunately, Mizuno, the company that paid Whitaker $5,000 a year to wear its baseball cleats, was on hand to present him with a pair of white spikes for the occasion. He then borrowed a glove from Baltimore Orioles shortstop Cal Ripken. But Whitaker had to tape over the brand name because a rival company paid him $9,000 a year to play with *its* glove. Wearing something old, something new, something borrowed, and something blue didn't help Whitaker. He went 0-for-2 in a 6–1 loss.

There was one item that no player was willing to share. Before the game, Whitaker lamented, "I don't even have a protective cup."

BABE HERMAN
Right Fielder · Cincinnati, NL · April 27, 1932

After beating the visiting St. Louis Cardinals 6–4, Babe Herman's Cincinnati Reds teammates headed home, leaving the day's triumphs and trials behind them at the ballpark. But not Herman. He left behind his little boy.

Herman didn't mean to do it. He just plum forgot his 7-year-old son Bobby.

About six weeks after Herman had been traded by the Brooklyn Dodgers to the Reds, the outfielder was caring for Bobby in Cincinnati while his wife remained in Brooklyn to tend to their ill 2-year-old son, Danny.

Herman with his forgotten son, Bobby NATIONAL BASEBALL HALL OF FAME LIBRARY

For the game against the Cardinals, Herman took his son to Crosley Field, got him a box seat and some food, and told the boy to wait for him by the back of the grandstands after the contest.

With his son cheering him on, Herman had a great game. He whacked two singles and a double, drove in a run, scored a run, and stole a base. Afterward, he showered, shaved, and dressed while mentally replaying his hits. Still on cloud nine, Herman hitched a ride home with Reds manager Dan Howley.

Meanwhile, Bobby dutifully did what he was told and stood outside the ballpark, waiting for his no-show father.

When Herman was almost home, Howley turned to him and said, "Geez, we left the kid!" Upon phoning the ballpark, Herman was relieved to learn that the team secretary had found Bobby and was bringing him home.

Recalled Herman with a chuckle, "I guess I had too much on my mind that day."

RICKY PETERS
Pinch Runner · Oakland, AL · June 25, 1986

Ricky Peters deserved an F in remedial arithmetic when he incorrectly added up the number of runners on base. Because two plus one doesn't equal four, his figures totaled up to a mortifying loss.

In a game against the Kansas City Royals, the visiting Oakland Athletics, who were tied for last place in the AL West, entered the top of the ninth inning tied 4–4. After Jerry Willard opened the frame with a single, Peters went in as a pinch runner and was sacrificed to second. Following a strikeout by Mike Davis for the second out, Carney Lansford was walked intentionally. With Jose Canseco at the plate, Royals hurler Steve Farr threw a wild pitch, and both runners advanced. Peters was now only 90 feet away with the potential winning run.

Farr then walked Canseco, triggering a mental blunder that seemed impossible in the Major Leagues. The Canseco walk should have loaded the bases. But, incredibly, Peters thought that the bases were *already* loaded and began to trot happily toward home plate. Third base coach Bob Didier was incredulous and shouted, "Back! Back! Back!"

When Peters realized his mistake, he wheeled around and sprinted back toward third, but it was too late. He was tagged out. The rally was killed and the inning was over. In the bottom of the ninth, the Royals won 5–4 with the help of an A's fielding error.

After the game, Farr, who was the winning pitcher, told reporters, "Gee, that's the first time I've ever gotten out of an inning on a walk."

A's manager Jackie Moore was so livid he could hardly talk. "Ricky thought the bases were loaded," Moore told reporters. "How could he? He had just run to third on a wild pitch. This is the big leagues—and this is embarrassing. The bottom line is we looked like a bunch of idiots. Every night something bad happens. I don't know what the answer is."

Apparently the front office did. Moore was fired as manager the next day. Presumably, he should have known better than to count on a pinch runner who couldn't count.

BOB SKINNER
Left Fielder
BILL VIRDON
Center Fielder
Pittsburgh, NL · June 17, 1959

Pittsburgh Pirates outfielders Bob Skinner and Bill Virdon helped lose a game when they both simply forgot what inning it was.

Because these two normally dependable players suffered a bad case of befuddlement, Chicago Cubs batter Cal Neeman huffed and puffed his way to a wacky game-winning "inside-the-beer-cup" home run.

It was the bottom of the eighth inning at Wrigley Field. With the score tied 2–2, the Cubs had runners Ernie Banks on second and Bobby Thomson on first and two out. Up to the plate stepped Neeman, Chicago's 200-pound catcher, known for neither his speed nor for his power.

Neeman drilled a sinking liner to left-center field, where Skinner tried for a shoestring catch but failed to snare the ball. As Banks scooted around third and headed for home, Skinner resignedly began jogging toward the Pittsburgh dugout. He mistakenly thought it was the ninth inning and that the game was over when Banks scored.

That an otherwise heads-up veteran like Skinner could make such a blunder was hard to imagine. Even more unimaginable was that his usually alert teammate, center fielder Bill Virdon, was just as unmindful. Instead of chasing after the ball, which was now bouncing toward the ivy-covered wall, Virdon began trotting in alongside Skinner.

Meanwhile, Thomson and Neeman were scampering around the bases. Pittsburgh shortstop Dick Groat was the only Pirate involved in the play who knew the game wasn't over. As he dashed into left field, he screamed at his two oblivious outfielders, "Get the ball! Get the damn ball!"

On the basepaths, Neeman couldn't understand why he was still running. When he last looked, he had hit what he thought was just an RBI single. "When I got to second base, I was amazed to see the third base coach waving me on," Neeman recalled. "And when I got near third, he was waving me on home. I had to look around to see if he was waving at somebody else. Nobody ever waved me home before."

Skinner and Virdon, now fully aware of what was happening, had turned and chased after the ball. But it was Groat who finally tracked it down. Given Neeman's speed—or rather lack thereof—the Pirates still had a chance to throw him out at the plate. But then fate decided to play a cruel joke on the three fielders.

"The bleacher fans had thrown all their beer cups and trash down onto the warning track," Skinner recalled. "When we got there, we couldn't find the ball. We finally found it—stuck in a cup! So Dick picked it up and threw it with the ball still inside. But it was too late. Neeman made it all the way around, even though he was the slowest runner in the league."

Because of Skinner and Virdon's snooze play, Neeman's single turned into a three-run inside-the-park home run to win the game 5–2.

MANNY RAMIREZ
Left Fielder · Los Angeles, NL · August 11, 2008

At the start of the ninth inning of his 10th game with the Los Angeles Dodgers, Manny Ramirez was supposed to be in left field. Instead he *left* the field.

Manny being Manny, he was missing in action because he went to the bathroom in the clubhouse without telling anyone. The game was held up for several minutes until he was found and ordered to return to his position.

The Dodgers were well aware of the hijinks they could expect from Ramirez when they acquired the 12-time All-Star from the Boston Red Sox at the July 31 non-waiver trade deadline. But the Dodgers were willing to put up with his antics because he was an awesome hitter.

It looked like the team had made a great acquisition; in his first 10 games, the dreadlocked slugger batted .475 (19-for-40) with four home runs and 13 RBIs.

It took less than two weeks, however, before Ramirez had one of his many Manny Moments.

In the bottom of the eighth inning of an 8–6 Dodgers win over the visiting Philadelphia Phillies, Ramirez got his second hit of the night, a single that set up an insurance run. Later in the inning, Ramirez was forced out at the plate, so he jogged into the dugout. And that's when the fun began.

"I was sitting there when Manny was forced at the plate, and then I realized that I didn't shake Manny's hand for getting the hit," manager Joe Torre told reporters after the game. "So he went by me and I put my fist out. He was probably 8 feet away, and he put his fist out and was starting to come back. I said, 'No, don't worry about it.'"

Manny being Manny, Ramirez took it to mean that he was done for the night. And because he needed to pee anyway, he headed up the tunnel to the clubhouse.

So when the ninth inning started, the Dodgers had only eight players on the diamond. Left field was empty and Ramirez was AWOL.

"I didn't know anything about it until [pinch hitter] Juan Pierre said, 'He took all his bats and went on in,'" Torre recalled. "So I said, 'Well, we'd better get him out here.'" Which they did.

While the umpires held up play, Ramirez finally reappeared and, with his dreadlocks flying, he hustled out to his position. Sporting a sheepish grin, he finished buttoning up his uniform.

After the game, he explained his absence to reporters. "I went to the bathroom in the bottom of the eighth. All the guys said, 'Hey, we play nine here.'"

Observed teammate Jeff Kent, "When he came out, his jersey was half undone. So if he was going to the bathroom, he takes his jersey off to do it?"

Manny being Manny, this was not the first, second, or third time he had spontaneously left his post during a game. He made several unscheduled trips inside the Green Monster at Fenway Park when he played left field for the Red Sox.

During a break in the action in a home game against the Tampa Bay Devil Rays on July 18, 2005, Ramirez thought a reliever was coming in because pitching coach Dave Wallace had gone to the mound to talk to starter Wade Miller. Relief was definitely on Ramirez's mind because he had to pee badly. So he used this opportunity to sneak into the Green Monster to take a leak. No one would have been the wiser except that there was no pitching change. The game was held up until he emptied his bladder and returned to the field. Afterward, when reminded that the scoreboard has no bathroom, Ramirez claimed that he peed in a cup.

In his final weeks with the Red Sox, Ramirez had several more Manny Moments. During a sixth-inning pitching change in a game against the Minnesota Twins on July 9, 2008, Ramirez stepped inside the scoreboard and could be seen through an opening between the balls and strikes counter talking on a cell phone (see photo).

Four days later, in the seventh inning of a game against the Baltimore Orioles, Ramirez waited out a pitching change by climbing into the wall and sipping on a sports drink. When he finished, he tipped his cap to the Fenway faithful and returned to his position.

Manny being Manny BOSTON GLOBE/GETTY IMAGES

Two weeks later, he told a reporter for ESPN Deportes, "The Red Sox don't deserve a player like me." He was traded to the Dodgers the very next day.

It was just Manny being Manny.

STEVE "PSYCHO" LYONS
First Baseman · Chicago, AL · July 16, 1990

Steve Lyons aired his dirty laundry during the middle of a game when he absentmindedly dropped his drawers at first base.

Lyons, a utility infielder for the Chicago White Sox, led off the top of the fifth inning in a 5–4 loss to the host Detroit Tigers. He laid down a perfect bunt toward first and then dived headlong into the bag, beating the throw from first baseman Cecil Fielder to pitcher Dan Petry for an infield single.

Feeling dirt trickling down inside his pant legs, Lyons unbuckled his belt and casually pulled down his pants to brush away the grime. His sliding shorts over his jock strap were clearly visible to the 14,770 fans at Tiger Stadium and to a TV audience.

Suddenly realizing where he was—and it wasn't in the privacy of the clubhouse—Lyons quickly yanked his pants back up, but he already had exposed himself to ridicule. While the fans roared with laughter, Lyons, his pants still unbuckled, put his hands on his hips, rolled his eyes skyward, and walked in a small circle while flashing an "I-can't-believe-I-pulled-my-pants-down" grin.

When the embarrassed player eventually returned to the dugout after the scoreless inning was over, giggling women in the stands waved dollar bills at him. One fan offered Lyons his belt.

In a postgame interview, Lyons explained, "I'm still not sure why I did it. I just kind of forgot where I was."

He said he was thankful he wasn't bare-assed naked or wearing dirty undies under his pants. He credited his mother Lillian for that. "She's the one who always told me to wear clean underwear in case something happened and I had to show them to strangers," Lyons said.

To the bemusement of players who actually had accomplished some amazing feats on the field, Lyons got more than his 15 minutes of fame. Within 24 hours of the incident, he did 20 radio interviews and seven live TV spots and was considered for a photo spread in *Playgirl* magazine (which he turned down).

"We've got a pitcher, Melido Perez, who earlier this month pitched a no-hitter, and I'll guarantee you he didn't do two live shots afterwards," Lyons told *Sports Illustrated* at the time. "I pull my pants down, and I do seven. Something's pretty skewed toward the zany in this game."

ORLANDO HUDSON
Second Baseman · San Diego, NL · July 26, 2011

MILTON BRADLEY
Right Fielder · Chicago, NL · June 12, 2009

LARRY WALKER
Right Fielder · Montreal, NL · April 24, 1994

You would think that it's virtually impossible for a Major Leaguer to lose track of the outs during a game, especially since all he has to do is look at the scoreboard or ask a teammate or simply count. You would think.

And that's the problem. Sometimes they don't think—like second baseman Orlando Hudson, of the San Diego Padres, or right fielders Milton Bradley, of the Chicago Cubs, and Larry Walker, of the Montreal Expos.

Hudson screwed up in a 2011 home game against the Arizona Diamondbacks in the top of the sixth inning with the Padres trailing 3–0. Arizona had runners Chris Young on second and Miguel Montero on first with one out when Brian Roberts hit a little flare to short right field. Hudson raced out and made a nice running catch for what everyone but Hudson knew was the second out.

Believing the inning was over, Hudson tossed the ball to the ball girl, who lobbed it to a fan in the box seats. Hudson started to jog toward the dugout when he saw first baseman Jesus Guzman race over to the stands and scream for the ball. The fan obediently threw it back, but by then it didn't matter. The umpires waved Young home and sent Montero to third. Hudson returned to his position at second and cracked a sheepish grin.

After the game, which the Padres lost 6–1, Hudson told reporters that he tried to laugh off his gaffe right after it happened. "I said [to his teammates on the field] 'Well, there's only two outs. I threw the ball away. Let's get the third out. My bad, boys. It happens. That's all I can say.' And then I started laughing. Life goes on. Nobody's perfect."

Milton Bradley can attest to that. During a 2009 game at Wrigley Field against the Minnesota Twins, Bradley was having just an awful day in the field. He lost an easy fly ball in the sun and later, by taking the wrong angle, he turned a single into a double. Adding to his woes, Bradley also was tagged out on a grounder to third when he could have remained safely perched on second.

In the top of the eighth inning, the Twins, who were winning 6–4, put runners Nick Punto on third and Brendan Harris on first with one out. The next batter, Joe Mauer, hit a shot to right. Bradley raced over and made a nice running catch for the second out. But for some reason, he thought it was the third out. He froze at the spot where he caught the ball and posed for a few seconds. Then he turned to the right field bleachers and tossed the ball into the crowd. As soon as he let go of the ball, it suddenly dawned on him that the inning was not really over.

Punto had already tagged up at third and scored. Meanwhile, Harris ran all the way to third from first. As more than 40,000 Cubs fans booed, Bradley rested both hands on top of his head and stared at the ground.

Hoping to win back the crowd, Bradley flipped a warm-up ball into the bleachers before the top of the ninth inning. Whoever caught it fired it right back at him in disgust.

After the game, which the Cubs lost 7–4, Chicago manager Lou Piniella said, "Do we have to go over the math? One, two, three. I don't know what else to say."

Bradley said he wasn't embarrassed, but acknowledged that the fans had every reason to be mad at him. "The fans have high expectations of me and I have high expectations for myself," he said. "I've never made a mistake like that in my life. Sue me. I guess I'll be in the bloopers with Larry Walker now. There are worse people I could be with."

Bradley was referring to Montreal Expos right fielder Larry Walker, who, in a 1994 game at Dodger Stadium, set the standard when it comes to counting—or rather miscounting—outs.

With one out and a man on first in the bottom of the third, Los Angeles catcher Mike Piazza sent a fly ball to right. Walker made the routine catch in foul territory for what he mistakenly thought was the

Bradley reacting to his brain sprain

last out of the inning. In a thoughtful gesture, Walker trotted over to the box seats on his way to the dugout and handed the ball to a boy sitting in the first row.

Hearing shouts of alarm from his teammates, Walker turned around and saw Dodgers runner Jose Offerman, who had tagged up from first, rounding second and hustling to third. Walker dashed over to the boy, snatched the ball from him, and fired it to third to keep Offerman from scoring. The next batter, Tim Wallach, walloped a home run.

As he took the field in the bottom of the fourth, Walker presented the boy with a new baseball. Walker's act of kindness triggered a standing ovation from the fans and a warm reception every time he came to bat.

It would have been an otherwise forgettable 7–1 Expos loss had it not been for Larry Walker's memorable memory lapse.

JIM HENRY
Pitcher · Boston, AL · September 25, 1936

Finding himself in a tight situation, rookie pitcher Jim Henry got so flustered that he couldn't tell the difference between a baseball and a resin bag.

Henry had won his first five decisions for the Boston Red Sox when he faced the host Washington Senators at Griffith Stadium. He breezed through the first two innings, but got in trouble in the bottom of the third. With two runs in and no outs, the Senators had runners Joe Kuhel on third and John Stone on first.

Trying to collect himself before facing Cecil Travis, who was a .320 hitter, Henry walked behind the mound, picked up the resin bag, and kept squeezing it with his pitching hand. He was working out in his mind how to pitch to Travis, and paying no attention to the runners.

With Henry's back to the plate, Kuhel broke for home while Stone sprinted for second in an attempted double steal. Taken by surprise, Henry threw to second, hoping to nail Stone. It was a good throw. It would have been better, though, had he flung the baseball instead of the resin bag.

Kuhel scored the third run of the inning and Stone was safe at second. As the crowd burst into laughter, Red Sox second baseman Ski Melillo picked up the resin bag and handed it back to the red-faced pitcher. Henry failed to recover from his gaffe. He was so unsettled that on the next pitch, he carelessly went into a full windup, allowing Stone to waltz into third with another steal.

Boston manager Joe Cronin had seen enough and yanked his rattled rookie. As Henry headed for the showers, a fan yelled, "Maybe you'll have better luck throwing a bar of soap!"

DAN FORD
Center Fielder · Minnesota, AL · September 5, 1978

Minnesota Twins manager Gene Mauch furiously paced around his office and declared, "All I've got to say is that the man will not get paid for tonight's game."

His ire was directed at Twins center fielder Dan Ford, who was cheering when he should have been running.

Trailing the visiting Chicago White Sox 4–0 in the bottom of the seventh inning, Minnesota loaded the bases with Ford on third, Jose Morales on second and Larry Wolfe on first. When Bombo Rivera lined a one-out single to center, Ford backpedaled down the third base line, waving his arms and yelling, "C'mon, Jose! C'mon, Jose!" to Morales, who was trying to score from second.

The problem with such cheerleading was that Ford had stopped short of home plate and continued to urge on his teammate, who then flew past him and touched home. Suddenly, Ford realized that *he* hadn't crossed the plate and immediately touched it with his toe. But White Sox catcher Bill Nahorodny noticed the mix-up and shouted at umpire Joe Brinkman, who called Morales out for passing Ford.

Mauch ran out of the dugout and, with a resigned look on his face, asked Brinkman, "Did what I think happened, happen?" The ump nodded. Mauch turned away without protest. As he headed back to the dugout with the downcast and chagrined Ford, Mauch growled, "Just keep right on going." Ford went straight into the clubhouse and left the stadium before the end of the game.

Instead of two runs and one out, the Twins had one run and two outs. The play took on added importance because Minnesota lost 4–3.

GARY GEIGER
Center Fielder · Boston, AL · June 8, 1961

Gary Geiger hit what he thought was a game-winning triple. Unfortunately, it wasn't.

In a lengthy night game against the visiting Los Angeles Angels, the Boston Red Sox entered the bottom of the 11th inning trailing 4–3. But leadoff hitter Chuck Schilling walked and Geiger smashed a pitch off the center field wall that drove Schilling home.

As Geiger pulled into third, the Boston players cheered. Now they were tied 4–4 with a runner on third and no one out. But to their stunned amazement, they watched Geiger trot jubilantly past third as if he were waiting for their congratulations.

It suddenly became clear that he had forgotten the score and failed to realize that his hit only tied the game; it didn't win it. Geiger was tagged out on a baserunning blunder that ultimately cost his team a victory.

"I thought the score was tied when I hit the ball," confessed the ashamed outfielder after the game. "When I ran to third, I saw Schilling score. I thought the winning run was in. Then I heard [third base coach] Billy Herman yelling at me and I turned back. I thought I was going to be congratulated for having knocked in the run. But then I got caught in a rundown and that was it."

The game ended in a tie because of a downpour in the 12th inning, forcing the entire game to be replayed the next day as part of a double-header. The Red Sox lost the makeup game 5–1.

EVERY TRICK
IN THE BOOK

For the Sneakiest Cheating of All Time,
The Baseball Hall of Shame™ Inducts:

LENNY RANDLE
Third Baseman · Seattle, AL · May 27, 1981

No third baseman ever blew a play more outrageously than Lenny Randle.

It happened in the top of the sixth inning at Seattle's Kingdome when Amos Otis of the visiting Kansas City Royals topped a ball down the third base line. Three Mariners converged on it, but they knew the roller was too slow for them to throw out Otis. All they could hope for was that the ball would turn foul.

The ball kept rolling straight, hugging the line in fair territory. Suddenly, Randle was struck with a brainstorm. He dropped down on all fours. Then he huffed and he puffed and he blew the ball foul.

Initially, plate umpire Larry McCoy signaled a foul ball. But after Royals manager Jim Frey protested, the call was changed to an infield single. The umpires ruled that a fielder cannot deliberately alter the course of a fair ball to make it go foul. Randle had done just that with his head's-down play.

Randle re-living his blown play   OWEN BLAUMAN

"I didn't blow on it," he told reporters after the game, won by the Royals, 8–5. "I used the power of suggestion. I was just telling the ball, 'Go foul, go foul.' The Bird [Detroit pitcher Mark Fidrych] used to talk to the ball and he didn't get into any trouble. How could they call it a hit? It was a foul ball."

Mariners manager Rene Lachemann backed up his infielder. "Lenny's breath from yelling must have moved it," he said with an impish smile.

The blown play, which didn't factor in any scoring, was "one of the big moments in the history of the Kingdome," declared Seattle's public relations director Bob Porter years later. "We didn't have any wind in our indoor stadium, but that night we had a breeze—and it was created by Lenny Randle."

HAL NEWHOUSER
Pitcher · Cleveland, AL · September 5, 1955

Hal Newhouser called on the US Army to help him steal the catcher's signs.

Between games of a doubleheader pitting the visiting Kansas City Athletics against the Indians at Cleveland Municipal Stadium, the US Army put on a show. Recalled Indians left fielder Ralph Kiner, "They rolled out tanks and all sorts of equipment, and drove them around the edge of the field. Then, before the second game started, they parked their equipment in an area behind the outfield fence."

A few yards away, in the bullpen, Indians pitcher Hal Newhouser noticed a telescopic rangefinder on one of the tanks. He furtively climbed into the tank and began focusing the rangefinder on home plate.

"He keyed in on the Kansas City catcher [Joe Astroth] big as life," said Kiner. "There were the signs staring Hal in the face. He called them out and somebody else got on the bullpen phone and alerted our dugout and they were passed on to our batters."

By getting tipped of the pitches, the Indians scored in the first five innings en route to a 9–2 drubbing of the A's.

"We were bombing the hell out of the Kansas City pitchers right from the start of the game," Kiner recalled. "[A's manager] Lou Boudreau knew we were getting the pitches from some place. He went nuts trying to find out, but never did."

MILLER HUGGINS
Manager · St. Louis, NL · August 7, 1915

Crafty St. Louis Cardinals skipper Miller Huggins tricked an opposing rookie pitcher into literally throwing the game away.

The Cardinals were playing host to the Brooklyn Dodgers (then known as the Robins) in a game that was deadlocked 4–all. In the bottom of the seventh inning, St. Louis loaded the bases with two outs against rookie hurler Ed "Whitey" Appleton.

With the pressure building, Huggins thought it was the perfect time to con Appleton. Coaching at third base, Huggins yelled to the mound, "Hey, Appleton! Let's see that old ball!"

Appleton had been raised to be polite and respectful toward his elders. Apparently he wasn't raised to be wary. Willing to accommodate so distinguished a baseball man as Miller Huggins, Appleton turned toward the coaching box and, without calling time-out, tossed him the ball. It happened so fast that the incredulous Brooklyn players didn't have time to stop him.

As the ball floated through the air, a grinning Huggins nimbly stepped aside and watched it bound toward the wall in front of the third base box seats. By the time the ball was retrieved, Jack "Dots" Miller and Tommy Long, the runners on third and second respectively, had scampered home with the winning runs in a 6–4 St. Louis victory.

"[Miller's] face was wreathed in a smile of sophistry," said an account in the *St. Louis Republic*. "Huggins, the arch perpetrator of the trick, scratched his chin and looked away from Umpire [Bill] Klem . . . Uncle Wilbert Robinson, who manages the Brooklyn outfit, seemed suddenly to have swallowed a catcher's mitt, if the fluidity of his face and his general incoherence could be taken to mean anything."

Because of Huggins's ploy, the rules were eventually amended to prohibit a coach from acting in any manner to draw a throw by a fielder. But the rule change came much too late for the humiliated Appleton, who lasted only two years in the bigs.

"It seemed hardly less than criminal to thus forever wreck this guileless youth's confidence in diamond nature," said the *Republic*. "But professional baseball is professional baseball with about as much sportsmanship to it as could be squeezed through the eye of a needle."

BOB MOOSE
Pitcher · Pittsburgh, NL · August 29, 1968

When Pittsburgh Pirates pitcher Bob Moose was a 20-year-old rookie, he felt the need to doctor the ball. He didn't bother throwing the tried-and-true spitter or Vaseline ball. No, he was an innovator. He threw a pine-tar ball.

In a home game against the league-leading St. Louis Cardinals, Moose coughed up two runs on three hits and two walks in the first inning. In the bottom of the frame, Moose was watching a teammate in the on-deck circle rub pine tar on his bat. Suddenly it dawned on Moose that the black goo might do wonders on a ball. So he rubbed his pitching hand with pine tar and went out to the mound for the second inning.

With his ball now dipping and diving, Moose looked like Cy Young. He struck out the side in the top of the second. When Moose fanned slugger Orlando Cepeda in the top of the third, St. Louis manager Red Schoendienst became suspicious. He called time and demanded that plate umpire Chris Pelekoudas inspect the hurler's hand. Sure enough, the ump found enough pine tar to make George Brett proud.

Following the umpire's orders, Moose went into the clubhouse and washed off the pine tar. Then he returned to the mound where he promptly gave up a double, walk, and two run-scoring singles in the inning before he was yanked for a reliever.

After the game, won by St. Louis 5–0, Cardinals outfielder Curt Flood, an African American, said of Moose's pine-tarred black hand, "Why it looked just like mine."

PETE ROSE
Third Baseman · Cincinnati, NL · July 11, 1978

Cincinnati Reds third baseman Pete Rose masterminded a clever plot that deliberately psyched out the American League team before the start of the 1978 All-Star Game.

Even though the National League had won six straight and 14 out of the previous 15 games, Rose was still looking for that extra edge against the junior circuit's All-Stars. So he concocted a scheme to make the National League hitters seem more powerful than they really were. He arranged for Mizuno, a Japanese sporting goods company, to ship him dozens of Japanese baseballs. Because they were made smaller and sewn tighter, they carried much farther than Major League baseballs.

"I brought the balls in for the National League's batting practice," Rose admitted to reporters later. "It was all for psychological warfare. There was all this talk going on about how the American League couldn't do anything against the National League. Well, I was always looking for ways to take advantage of that, kind of get under their skin and remind them in subtle ways that they really weren't as good as us."

When Rose had the Japanese balls smuggled into San Diego Stadium, the rest of the National Leaguers went along with the conspiracy and agreed to use the balls in batting practice. Then Rose went over to the American League's clubhouse and talked many of the players into watching the National League's BP.

"Everyone was hitting them out of the park," recalled Larry Bowa, an All-Star second baseman for the Philadelphia Phillies at the time. "I even hit a couple out in BP—something I never did before. It made me feel like Babe Ruth blasting those babies out of there. I remember some of the American League players were watching our guys wallop those balls, and they were just in awe with their mouths wide open.

"We thought it was funnier than hell. As soon as our BP was over, we made sure we gathered up all those balls and got them out of there. Then we sat around and watched the American League take their BP. They were just barely hitting them to the outfield wall. It was normal stuff, but after the way our balls were flying way up high into the stands, the American Leaguers looked like Little Leaguers."

The plot worked. The National League won for the seventh straight time, clubbing the American League 7–3.

"We were having a great time beating the American League all the time and using those Japanese balls was just one more way to psych them out and rub their noses in it," said Bowa. "Leave it to Pete Rose to come up with a new angle."

RENNIE STENNETT
Second Baseman · Pittsburgh, NL · August 10, 1976

Pittsburgh Pirates second baseman Rennie Stennett pulled a sleight-of-hand trick that gave teammate Willie Stargell credit for a catch he never made.

In a game against the visiting Los Angeles Dodgers at Three Rivers Stadium, Stennett hoodwinked everybody—including Stargell—with his cunning deception.

In the top of the ninth inning of a 5–1 Dodgers victory, Los Angeles batter Bill Russell lofted a pop fly into shallow right field. Stargell, who was playing first base, and Stennett charged after the ball while right fielder Dave Parker raced in.

"I was probably in the best position to make the catch," Stennett recalled, "but I could feel the ground shaking with those two guys closing in. I wasn't going to get caught between them, so I pulled up."

While Stennett, who weighed only 160 pounds, moved out of the way, the 230-pound Parker kept coming in and the 210-pound Stargell kept going out. They both reached for the ball at the same time and crashed into each other in a collision that triggered tremors of Richter scale proportions. Unnoticed by everyone in the stadium, the ball dropped between Parker and Stargell, whose bodies shielded the ball.

"They were pretty shaken up," Stennett said. "Dave was stretched out cold and Willie was groaning and trying to sit up. The ball was on the ground between them, but nobody else could see it. At first, I was going to throw it in, but I knew I'd never get the runner in time. So I reached down like I was checking to see if they were okay and then I stuck the ball in Willie's glove.

"Willie was so dazed he didn't know what was going on. I told him, 'Come on, Willie, get up! Show them the ball!'"

Stennett's ruse worked. As the umpire reached the crash site, Stargell staggered to his feet and held up his glove with the ball in it. Russell was called out, and Stennett calmly strolled back to his position sporting the grin of a cat that ate the canary.

BALTIMORE ORIOLES, NL
1892–1899

The Baltimore Orioles didn't invent cheating, but they developed it into a precise science, earning a reputation as the dirtiest team in baseball.

There was no trick in the book unknown to this rapscallion crew. Led by manager Ned Hanlon, crafty stars John McGraw, Willie Keeler, Wilbert Robinson, Hughie Jennings, and the rest of the conniving Orioles could fleece a con man out of his last dime.

The Orioles—no relation to the current team with that name—lasted only eight years in the National League, but they left an indelible mark in skullduggery, especially during home games where the fans were accomplices.

Rival infielders would boot easy grounders after being blinded by Orioles conspirators who used hand mirrors to reflect the sun into the players' eyes.

Back then, foul balls hit into the stands or out of the park were returned. But in Baltimore, furtive fans threw back substitute balls that had been soaked in water and deadened by the Orioles. Whenever a dead ball was hit by an opponent, it usually didn't make it out of the infield.

The players ordered head groundskeeper Tom Murphy to slope the third base foul line toward the infield so their bunts would curl fair. Murphy also kept the outfield grass so tall that it resembled a rye field, which allowed the Orioles to hide a baseball or two for one of their patented tricks. Often when an opposing slugger hit a long drive that appeared to fly past a Baltimore outfielder, the batter was held to only a single because the clever Oriole would pick up one of the strategically hidden balls and throw it back to the infield.

One time, however, the scheme backfired. Left fielder Joe Kelley made a perfect throw with a planted ball to shoot down a runner at third base only to see center fielder Steve Brodie chase down the real batted ball and fire it back to the infield too.

Baltimore took advantage of the fact that games were officiated by only one umpire who stood in the middle of the field. The Orioles mastered the fine art of taking shortcuts across the diamond behind the back of the arbiter when sprinting from first to third, or second to home.

Enemy runners took their lives in their hands. As they tried to dash around the bases, they were bumped, blocked, tripped, pushed, and spiked by the win-at-all-costs Orioles.

If an opposing player made it to third, Baltimore third baseman John McGraw liked to slip his fingers through the runner's belt and hold him just long enough to give an Orioles fielder a better chance of throwing him out at the plate.

Once in a game at Louisville in 1893, McGraw hooked his fingers inside the belt of Pete Browning, who was a runner on third. Tricking the trickster, Browning loosened his belt buckle. Then, when the batter put the ball in play, Browning raced home, leaving a startled McGraw holding nothing but the belt.

BYRON BROWNE
Center Fielder

GEORGE ALTMAN
Left Fielder

GLENN BECKERT
Second Baseman

JOE PROSKI
Trainer

Chicago, NL · March 28, 1966

The Chicago Cubs tried to steal a spring training game by resorting to some cloak-and-dagger trickery.

Then, when they were accused of cheating, the sneaky Cubs perpetrated an underhanded cover-up that even involved the team trainer.

In the second inning of a game against the San Francisco Giants in Phoenix, Giants batter Jim Ray Hart clubbed a deep drive that sent rookie center fielder Byron Browne racing back toward the wall. As he leaped, Browne crashed into the fence, and the ball bounced about 20 feet away. It looked like it would be a sure triple, if not an inside-the-park home run.

Browne collapsed with the wind knocked out of him. But before he fell, he made an incredible play. Somehow, without moving more than a couple of feet, he had fired the ball to shortstop Don Kessinger, whose perfect relay to Ron Santo at third nipped Hart.

To the Giants, it was unbelievable—too unbelievable. They had seen the ball bounce 20 feet away from Browne and couldn't figure out how he managed to retrieve it so quickly. Solving the mystery, the San Francisco bullpen crew pointed to the prone Browne and shouted to the umpires, "He threw the wrong ball!"

Their cries brought Giants manager Herman Franks out of the dugout to complain. Meanwhile, Browne's concerned teammates rushed to his side—as much to join in the fraud as to aid their fallen comrade. They discovered that an extra ball, left over from batting practice, had remained unnoticed near the base of the wall. The injured Browne, unable to reach the game ball, had grabbed the worn practice ball instead and thrown it in.

So left fielder George Altman started a cover-up. As he ran to Browne's side, Altman nonchalantly bent down, scooped up the game ball and stuffed it in his uniform. But this bit of chicanery did not go unnoticed. From the Giants dugout, eagle-eyed Willie Mays spotted Altman's attempt at hiding the evidence, so Mays added his voice to the protesting chorus.

Altman then secretly slipped the ball into the glove of second baseman Glenn Beckert, who was kneeling by Browne's side. Beckert surreptitiously handed the ball to trainer Joe Proski, who had rushed out to tend to Browne.

By now the entire Giants team was in an uproar, demanding the umpires take action against the Chicago con men. Finally, umpire Stan Landes waved his arms. "Everybody shut up!" he shouted. Turning to Cubs skipper Leo Durocher, the ump pointed to the four suspects and said, "Get all your guys over here and tell them to line up."

Once that was done, Landes went down the line, frisking the Cubs one by one. Last in line was Proski, who had no one left to take the hand-off of the evidence. The red-faced trainer sheepishly forked over the game ball to Landes. Comparing it with the dirty, grass-stained ball that had been used to tag Hart out at third, the umpire sent Hart to second base with a ground-rule double. And he sent the Cubs back to their positions, but with an admonishment not to try that scam again.

MARTY O'TOOLE
Pitcher · Pittsburgh, NL

FRED LUDERUS
First Baseman · Philadelphia, NL · 1912

Pittsburgh Pirates spitballer Marty O'Toole got a taste of his own medicine when a player on the opposing team loaded up the ball with burning-hot liniment that set the hurler's tongue on fire.

In 1912—eight years before the spitball was declared illegal—O'Toole faced the Philadelphia Phillies, who were fed up with his spitters. The Phils were especially vexed by his disgusting practice of holding the ball up to his face, hiding it with his glove, and licking it with his tongue. At least the Phillies spitballers didn't use their tongues.

Philadelphia first baseman Fred Luderus figured that if the pitcher could use a foreign substance on the ball, so could he. So Luderus took a small tube of a strong liniment onto the field with him, and every time he handled the ball, he rubbed the fiery hot salve on it.

Within a few innings, O'Toole's tongue was so inflamed, raw, and painful that he had to leave the game.

After the game, Pittsburgh manager Fred Clarke discovered what Luderus had done. The skipper was livid and issued a formal statement denouncing the player. "This liniment is the most powerful known," said Clarke. "Suppose a man should get a little of it on his hands and rub his eye. He could be blind for hours."

But Philadelphia manager Red Dooin issued his own statement claiming the liniment was used merely to protect the health of his players. "That ball may be carrying the germs of any one of many contagious diseases," argued Dooin. "So we put disinfectant on it whenever we face a spitball pitcher like O'Toole. I do not see how we can be refused the privilege of protecting ourselves."

O'Toole knew he was licked and no longer used his tongue to load up the ball.

GEORGE WILSON
Right Fielder · New York, NL · April 5, 1953

New York Giants right fielder George Wilson robbed a batter of an extra base hit by pretending a snowball was a baseball.

It happened in a 1953 spring training exhibition game in Denver between the Giants and the Cleveland Indians. Both teams had stopped in the Mile High City on their way east after breaking camp in Arizona.

Unexpectedly, a heavy winter storm had hit Denver the day before the contest. Snow plows had cleared most of the field, but they left a giant snow bank that followed the contour of the outfield wall.

"We agreed that any ball hit between the snow bank and the fence would be a ground-rule double," Indians manager Al Lopez recalled.

The game was played without incident until Cleveland batter Ray Boone hit a deep fly to right. Wilson went back for the ball and then tumbled over the snow bank and fell out of sight.

Just as Boone was rounding first, Wilson arose with his glove held high over his head with what seemed like the ball nestled in his mitt. The first base umpire signaled that Boone was out. But the ball wasn't a baseball. It was a snowball. Wilson had packed the snow into a ball, put it in his glove, and fooled the umpire.

"Wilson never caught the ball," Lopez recalled. "He didn't even come close. I yelled and yelled about it, but the umpire still called Boone out."

Meanwhile, Wilson sneakily retrieved the real ball a few seconds later and trotted in. Ray Boone wound up with the dubious honor of being the only Major Leaguer called out because of a snowball.

MORGAN MURPHY
Catcher · Philadelphia, NL · September 17, 1900

The Philadelphia Phillies resorted to an age-old scheme to steal signs from the opposing catcher. They used a spy.

Their undercover man was Morgan Murphy, a seldom-used second-string catcher who nevertheless became one of the club's most valuable players. His teammates relied on him to steal signals in their home ballpark to improve their weak hitting. It worked. The Phillies were 45-23 at home and 30-40 on the road.

Opponents did not know Philadelphia cheated until the Cincinnati Reds came to town and accidentally uncovered the secret.

In the third inning of a 4–2 Phillies win at Philadelphia Park, Reds shortstop Tommy Corcoran was coaching at third base when his spikes got caught on what looked like a vine underneath the surface. He kept scratching with his shoe until he uncovered a small metal box an inch or two below the ground. Opening the lid, he discovered a device that could emit electrical vibrations like a buzzer. When he pulled up the box, several yards of wire popped out of the ground. Corcoran called time and began yanking up the wire in a path that led across the field to the Phillies center field clubhouse.

And that's when the Phillies' ploy was exposed. Murphy would sit in the clubhouse behind a little peephole with a telegraph set and a spyglass and steal the signs from the opposing catcher. Murphy would tip off the Phillies third base coach—usually utility man Pearce "What's the Use" Chiles—by means of a buzzer system under the coach's box. One buzz meant fastball, two meant a curve, and three was a change-up. Forewarned, the coach signaled the batter what pitch was coming.

Phillies owner John I. Rogers thought this was perfectly fair and legitimate. The National League, however, declared that the ruse was definitely unfair and illegitimate.

THE FALL FOLLIES

*For the Most Atrocious World Series Screw-ups of
All Time, The Baseball Hall of Shame™ Inducts:*

BABE RUTH
Right Fielder · New York, AL · October 10, 1926

When the Babe pulled the biggest boneheaded play of his stellar career, it cost the New York Yankees their last shot at the 1926 world championship.

In the top of the ninth inning of the seventh and final game of the World Series, the St. Louis Cardinals were ahead 3–2. It is at historic moments like this that great heroes emerge. Or great goats are born. This happened to be the day of the goat. And his name was Ruth.

Cardinals relief pitcher Grover Cleveland "Old Pete" Alexander got the first two Yankees out. Then Ruth drew a walk, bringing up cleanup hitter Bob Meusel with Lou Gehrig on deck. Meusel was a .315 hitter that year and had batted in 81 runs in 108 regular season games. He also had doubled and tripled off Alexander in the Yankees' 10–2 loss the day before.

At this crucial moment in the game, with strong hitters coming up, even a rookie would have known not to risk the third out by trying to steal. But Ruth was no rookie. For his size and weight, he was always a rather aggressive—but not necessarily

What was Babe thinking?　　　NATIONAL BASEBALL HALL OF FAME LIBRARY

successful—baserunner. For the season, he had stolen only 11 bases in 20 attempts.

Without receiving any signal to steal, Ruth, one of the slowest runners on the team, took off for second. Catcher Bob O'Farrell had plenty of time to make the throw to second baseman Rogers Hornsby, who easily tagged Ruth out by a good 5 feet for the third out. End of inning. End of game. End of Series.

"He didn't say a word," Hornsby recalled. "He didn't even look at me. He just picked himself up off the ground and walked away."

Ruth explained later that he attempted to steal second base because he thought no one would expect it, and he had hoped to catch the Cardinals by surprise. Through the 2011 season, no other World Series had ever ended on a player caught stealing.

Said Yankees executive Ed Barrow, "It was Ruth's only dumb play of his life."

ST. LOUIS, AA VS. CHICAGO, NL
1885 World Series

It was the fielding—or more aptly the lack of it—that vaulted this World Series into the annals of fall foolishness. Never in baseball history have two teams displayed such amazing incompetence as the St. Louis Browns and the Chicago Cubs (known back then as the White Stockings). Incredibly, the teams made more errors than hits.

The blundering players muffed easy grounders, dropped routine pop flies, and threw wildly in every single Series game to rack up an astonishing 102 errors—six more than the number of hits they collected. But who needed hits with such phenomenally inept fielding?

Both teams worked hard at beating themselves. Of the 74 runs scored, only 19 were earned. The relentless error production began right from the start. There were 15 errors in the first game, which ended in a 5–5 tie, called at the end of the eighth inning because of darkness. Total errors over the next five games: 9, 16, 10, 8, and 17.

But the Boys of Bummer saved the worst for last. Floundering on the field in Game 7, St. Louis booted the ball 10 times only to be topped by 17 Chicago miscues. The fourth inning was a classic for Chicago's clod squad. With a flair for botchery seldom seen in baseball, Cap Anson let two feeble grounders trickle through his legs, left fielder Abner Dalrymple unleashed a wild throw two stories over the catcher's head, shortstop Ned Williamson pegged the ball into the seats, and catcher Frank "Silver" Flint let two strikes slip through his hands for passed balls. As a testament to the caliber of fielding, the record book shows that 13 of the 17 total runs scored in the game (won by the Browns, 13–4) were unearned.

So where did all this on-the-field ineptitude lead? Nowhere. The Series ended in a tie. And in controversy.

In the top of the sixth inning of the second game, which was played in St. Louis, the score was tied at 4–4 when Williamson beat out a dribbler down the first base line that scored the go-ahead run. At first, umpire Dan Sullivan called the ball foul and then changed his mind and called it fair. St. Louis player-manager Charlie Comiskey was so enraged he yanked his team off the field in protest. Sullivan countered by declaring the game a 9–0 forfeit. But St. Louis won a moral victory when Sullivan was relieved of his umpiring duties for the rest of the Series due to his poor officiating.

Because each team had won three games and tied one, Cap Anson declared he and his players were co-champions with St. Louis. But the Browns claimed the championship for themselves, insisting that the forfeited second game shouldn't count.

At least both teams could share one thing—their rightful place in The Baseball Hall of Shame™.

CINCINNATI, NL
1919 World Series

Everybody knows that the 1919 World Series was tainted by the infamous Black Sox Scandal when eight Chicago players were accused of taking payoffs to throw the Series.

But the Cincinnati Reds' performance was shameful as well. They almost lost to a team that was doing everything in its power to hand them victory.

Even though the White Sox fix was on, it looked like the Reds were the ones taking the dive in the best of nine series. After all, they committed just as many errors as the White Sox, 12.

For instance, in the second inning of the third game, Cincinnati pitcher Ray Fisher fielded a sacrifice bunt and flung the ball over second base and into center field. That put runners at second and third. A single brought them home, and Chicago reluctantly won, 3–0.

With the Reds ahead four games to one, the White Sox tried to toss them the sixth game, which would have given them the world championship, but Cincy refused to take it. Doing everything but pick up the Reds and carry them around the bases, the White Sox committed three errors on the way to a 4–0 Cincinnati lead. But the Reds successfully fought off victory with an abominable display of baseball.

In the top of the sixth inning, Chicago batter Buck Weaver looped a pop fly to short left field that should have been an easy catch for either left fielder Pat Duncan or shortstop Larry Kopf. Instead, they stood around and watched to see how high the ball would bounce when it hit the ground. Weaver ran at less than full speed, but the Reds still couldn't throw him out. The goof paved the way for a 5–4 Chicago victory.

The Reds' bats went silent in Game 7 while their fielding racked up three errors, so the White Sox won again, 4–1.

With back-to-back victories that closed the Series' gap to four games to three, there was real desperation in the Chicago clubhouse that they might actually win the crown after all. But Cincy finally came through in Game 8, winning 10–5 to capture the title after White Sox hurler Claude "Lefty" Williams (who lost all three games he started) grooved enough pitches to get bombed in the first inning.

The better team probably didn't win the Series. The better loser lost it.

FRED SNODGRASS
Center Fielder

CHIEF MEYERS
Catcher

CHRISTY MATHEWSON
Pitcher

FRED MERKLE
First Baseman

New York, NL · October 16, 1912

No team ever handed a Series championship to its opponents the way the New York Giants did.

The Giants and Boston Red Sox had each won three games. Because Game 2 had ended in a 6–6 tie due to darkness, the teams played an unusual eighth and decisive game at Fenway Park.

After nine innings, they were deadlocked 1–1. In the top of the 10th, New York took a 2–1 lead after Red Murray doubled and was driven home on a single by Fred Merkle. The Giants could taste victory, only three outs away.

Leading off in the Boston half of the inning, pinch hitter Clyde Engle hit an ordinary fly ball to center, the territory of sure-handed Fred Snodgrass. But the unbelievable happened. The ball hit his glove and plopped to the ground. His teammates stood in disbelief as the tying run for Boston was now perched on second base. The visibly shaken Snodgrass tried to atone for his grave mistake on the next play by making a spectacular grab of a low liner hit by Harry Hooper. After the catch, Engle tagged up and advanced to third with one out.

Still shaken by Snodgrass's muff, the Giants began to fall apart at the seams. The famous control of pitcher Christy Mathewson unexpectedly vanished and he walked weak-hitting Steve Yerkes. That brought up the always dangerous Tris Speaker.

On the first pitch, Speaker hit a lazy foul pop-up between first and home. Any one of three players could have caught it with his eyes closed. Mathewson moved over from the mound, catcher Chief Meyers broke from the plate, and first baseman Fred Merkle trotted down the baseline. What followed was a scene straight out of a Marx Brothers flick. Mathewson called for Meyers to take it. But Meyers thought Merkle would take it. Merkle assumed Mathewson or Meyers would take it. The result: Nobody took it. All three stood there and watched the ball fall at their feet. And with that blunder, the outcome was inevitable—and everyone in Fenway Park knew it.

Given a new lease on life, Speaker singled to right to drive in Engle with the tying run. With Yerkes at third and Speaker on first, Duffy Lewis was walked intentionally. Larry Gardner then belted a fly ball to Josh Devore in right field that was deep enough for Yerkes to tag up and score the Series-winning run.

For the stunned Giants, it was an unbelievable finish to what had otherwise been a great season—and they had nobody to blame but themselves.

HACK WILSON
Center Fielder · Chicago, NL · October 12, 1929

When the 1929 World Series had faded into painful memory, Chicagoans were mournfully singing "The Wrigley Field Blues." It was sung slowly and with great feeling to the tune of "My Old Kentucky Home."

The first stanza went: "Oh! The sun shone bright in our great Hack Wilson's eyes . . ." And it concluded: "Weep no more, dear Cub fan/Oh, weep no more today/For we'll sing one song for the game and fighting Cubs/For the record-whiffing Cubs far away."

The Chicago fans had a right to vent their bitterness not only over the Cubs' loss to the Philadelphia Athletics in five games, but also over Hack Wilson's absentmindedness. He had opened the way for an astonishing come-from-behind victory by the A's in Game 4.

Going into the bottom of the seventh inning at Shibe Park, Cubs ace Charlie Root was throwing a three-hitter, smugly anticipating victory with what looked like an insurmountable 8–0 lead. A win by the Cubs would even the Series at two games apiece.

The A's Al Simmons opened the inning with a home run and Jimmie Foxx singled, but there was little cause for alarm. Next, Bing Miller

If only Hack had worn these shades . . .

lofted a short fly to center. Wilson ran in and reached to flip down his sunglasses. Everybody wore sunglasses in the outfield at Shibe because of the glare. Everybody, that is, except Wilson. He had left his pair back in the dugout. Not that they would have done much good. Two innings earlier, in the fifth, Wilson, with his shades on, had lost Jimmy Dykes's fly ball in the sun and muffed it for an error.

Now, in the seventh without the sunglasses, he was blinded even worse by the sun and let the ball drop for a single.

Incredibly, before the next batter stepped up, Wilson did not call time to fetch his sunglasses.

The A's kept the rally going and quickly cut the lead to 8–4. With one out and runners on the corners, Cubs reliever Art Nehf came on to pitch. Mule Haas then smashed a long fly ball toward Wilson. The center fielder had room to make the catch. But for the third time in the game, he was blinded by the sun. With his bare hand, Wilson made a desperate but futile stab at the ball as it sailed over his head and rolled all the way to the wall for a three-run inside-the-park home run. The A's went on to tally 10 runs in the inning to set a Series record. The stunned Cubs couldn't recover and fell 10–8.

Devastated by the loss, Chicago blew a 2–0 ninth-inning lead in Game 5, losing 3–2 to close out the Series on the short end.

Although Wilson led all batters in hitting during the Series with a lofty .471 batting average, he took the blame for the balls he lost in the sun.

"Looks like I'm the big chump of the Series," he told reporters. "I play good ball all season, and in the most important game I've ever been in, I blow up. They'll be calling me a long lost brother of Snodgrass and Merkle. And to think the weatherman promised we'd have a cloudy day. If he'd only been right."

JOHNNY BENCH
Catcher · Cincinnati, NL · October 18, 1972

Johnny Bench, who played in 23 World Series games, was often an October hero. But in the third game of the 1972 Fall Classic, he looked more like an April fool.

The Cincinnati Reds star was at bat with runners on second and third, one out, and his team ahead 1–0 in the top of the eighth inning. After Bench ran the count to 3-and-2, Oakland Athletics manager Dick

Williams went out to the mound to talk to relief pitcher Rollie Fingers and catcher Gene Tenace.

It was a crucial moment in a tight game. Bench, who was batting cleanup, figured the A's were discussing whether to pitch to him or walk him intentionally and face the next batter, Tony Perez. While on the mound, Williams pointed toward first and held up four fingers and then trotted back to the dugout. When play resumed, Bench figured that he was about to get an intentional walk.

Standing behind and to the right of the plate, Tenace extended his hand, the traditional gesture for an intentional base on balls. Bench relaxed and waited for the expected wide pitch.

As Fingers threw, Tenace suddenly crouched behind the plate. The ball caught the outside corner for strike three. To his utter distress, Johnny Bench, the thinking man's ballplayer, realized he had been suckered into a called third strike. Casting his eyes to the ground, he shuffled back to the dugout, a victim of a baseball con job.

Fingers then gave Perez a free pass to load the bases and got Denis Menke to foul out to end the threat. The Reds won 1–0, but much of the talk after the game was over duping Bench.

Recalled Fingers, "Dick Williams came to the mound and told me, 'We're going to fake an intentional pass to Bench, but throw a strike. Don't throw a fastball because he's a fastball hitter.' I said, 'What are you talking about? Is this Little League or what?' I threw probably the best slider I'd ever thrown in my life.

"When I see Johnny Bench, I never mention it. But he usually brings it up and says, 'That was the most embarrassing moment of my life.'"

RED FABER
Pitcher · Chicago, AL · October 7, 1917

In the 1917 World Series, Hall of Fame pitcher Red Faber scored his biggest triumph—and committed one of the Fall Classic's biggest base-running blunders.

As a pitcher for the Chicago White Sox, Faber dominated the New York Giants, beating them three times as the Sox drubbed the Giants, four games to two.

However, as a baserunner, Faber would have been better off sitting on the bench. That, apparently, was where he left his brains during the fifth inning of Game 2.

With teammate Buck Weaver on second base, Faber drilled a base hit to right field, but a strong throw home from Dave Robertson kept Weaver at third. Meanwhile, Faber, running with his head down, took second on the throw. Faber, who collected only four hits during the entire season for an abysmal .058 batting average, was thrilled with his World Series single. Assuming that Weaver had scored, Faber was so pumped that he failed to realize that Weaver was standing on third.

As the next batter, Nemo Leibold, dug in at the plate, Giants pitcher Pol Perritt didn't even bother glancing back to second base. There was little reason for him to do so. Faber was a slow runner, and besides, Weaver was already on third. With two out and two on and the White Sox ahead 7–2, Perritt went into his windup.

Faber figured that even though he was no speed merchant on the basepaths, he could surely steal third because Perritt wasn't pitching from the stretch. Faber just couldn't resist the temptation and blindly scampered to third base, arriving in a nifty slide—and bewilderment.

Much to his astonishment, Faber looked up and saw Weaver peering down on him. After Faber was tagged out by third baseman Heinie Zimmerman on a peg from catcher Bill Rariden, Weaver asked his embarrassed teammate, "What the hell are you doing here?"

As Faber dusted himself off, he replied, "Why, I'm just going out to pitch, of course."

ROGER PECKINPAUGH
Shortstop · Washington, AL · 1925 World Series

On the eve of the 1925 World Series, Washington Senators shortstop Roger Peckinpaugh was named the American League's Most Valuable Player. Unfortunately, he was anything but that in the Fall Classic.

Peckinpaugh set a futility record that no one has come close to matching—he pecked and pawed his way to eight errors in one World Series.

Playing as if his glove was made of Portland cement, the fumbling shortstop contributed to three of his team's losses. As a result, the Pittsburgh Pirates overcame a three-games-to-one deficit to win the world championship right out from under the shell-shocked Senators.

Peckinpaugh ranged to his right and to his left and deep in the hole to bungle balls throughout the Series.

He helped blow the second game in the eighth inning. With the score knotted at 1–1, Peckinpaugh bobbled Eddie Moore's easy grounder. Moments later, Kiki Cuyler belted a homer, scoring Moore ahead of him, giving the Pirates a 3–2 victory.

After five games, Peckinpaugh had five errors, but the Senators were still ahead three games to two. In the sixth game, he made his sixth error, but fortunately for him it proved harmless. However, in the third inning, he failed to field a double-play ball cleanly, resulting in a fielder's choice that left runners at first and second. A sacrifice, an infield out, and a single drove home two runs as Pittsburgh won 3–2 to even the Series.

It seemed impossible that Peckinpaugh could play any worse, but he did in the seventh and deciding game. Washington held a 6–4 lead in the seventh inning when the hapless Senator was afflicted with the dropsies. Moore hit a high pop-up to Peckinpaugh, but the snake-bit shortstop muffed it. His seventh error of the Series was followed by a double and a triple that tied the score at 6–6.

In the top of the eighth, however, Peckinpaugh smashed a home run to give the Senators a 7–6 lead. It looked like he had redeemed himself. But that was short-lived.

With two out in the bottom of the eighth, Pittsburgh tied the game with back-to-back doubles. Then, after Moore walked, Max Carey rapped an easy grounder to Peckinpaugh for what should have been the third out. The shortstop scooped it up, but he botched the force-out on Moore at second by making a bad throw. Peckinpaugh's record-setting eighth error filled the bases and set the stage for Cuyler, who promptly doubled home the two winning runs as the Pirates captured the Series with a 9–7 victory.

Needless to say there was no fancy dinner in Washington to celebrate Peckinpaugh's MVP award.

JOHNNY MILJUS
Pitcher · Pittsburgh, NL · October 8, 1927

Johnny "The Big Serb" Miljus caused the wildest ending ever to a World Series.

Going up against the New York Yankees' "Murderers' Row" powered by Babe Ruth (60 homers) and Lou Gehrig (175 RBIs), the Pittsburgh Pirates were decidedly the underdogs in the 1927 postseason classic.

The Yankees took the first three games and were leading 3–1 in Game 4 on a two-run blast by Ruth, but the Pirates fought back to tie it in the top of the seventh inning, compliments of two New York errors.

Pittsburgh then brought in Miljus to face the Yankees in the bottom of the seventh. Miljus, a Pittsburgh native, had posted an 8-3 record and a stellar 1.90 ERA during the regular season. In Game 1, he had hand-cuffed New York, twirling four scoreless innings in relief.

He continued his mastery over the Yankees by holding them score-less through the eighth inning. The Pirates couldn't push across a run either, so going into the bottom of the ninth, the game remained dead-locked 3–3.

Miljus then committed the cardinal sin of pitchers—walking the leadoff batter, in this case Earle Combs. Mark Koenig then beat out a bunt down the third base line, putting runners on first and second with Ruth coming to the plate. In the Babe's previous at-bat, Miljus had coaxed him to hit into a double play.

Knowing the Series-winning run was in scoring position, Miljus hurled a pitch he hoped would lead to another twin killing. But the ball bounded by catcher Johnny Gooch for a wild pitch, which moved the runners to second and third. Now the winning run was only 90 feet away.

Pirates manager Donie Bush then ordered an intentional walk to Ruth. As Miljus tossed the first of four wide pitches for the walk, the Bambino shouted to the pitcher, "Give me a chance!" No such luck. Babe got three more balls for the free pass. In frustration, Ruth pointed to on-deck hitter Lou Gehrig and yelled, "The Buster will do it if I don't."

With the bases loaded and nobody out, the Pittsburgh infielders and outfielders moved in. Miljus bore down and struck out Gehrig and then Bob Meusel, who had batted .325 during the season. To the dismay of Yankees fans who were yelling at Miljus in an attempt to rattle him, it looked as though the hurler might actually wriggle out of this incredibly tight jam.

After the fielders returned to normal playing depth, Tony Lazzeri, a .302 regular season hitter, stepped to the plate. He hit a long foul ball for strike one. Gooch then called for a curve and dropped down on one knee to give Miljus a low target. The hurler nodded, figuring this would be the pitch that would end the inning. And so it did, but not in the way he hoped.

Miljus let fly with a curve that didn't break. To his horror, it sailed high and wide. Gooch leaped up and lunged for the ball, but it glanced off his glove and rolled about 12 feet away—far enough for Combs to scamper across the plate with the Series-winning run.

Recalled Pirates star outfielder Lloyd Waner, "For a couple seconds I didn't budge. I just stood there in center field. I couldn't believe it, really. It's no way to end a ballgame much less a World Series on a dog-gone wild pitch."

It was the only time a Series ended in such a shameful way.

ALL FOULED UP

For the Foulest Foul Balls of All Time,
The Baseball Hall of Shame™ Inducts:

RICHIE ASHBURN
Center Fielder · Philadelphia, NL · August 17, 1957

It wasn't enough that Richie Ashburn hit a foul into the stands that smacked a grandmother in the face. No, as the injured fan was being carried out on a stretcher, Ashburn whacked another foul that struck poor Granny again!

"I didn't mean to do it," Ashburn recalled. "When I saw what happened, I felt terrible."

Not as terrible as Alice Roth, who had taken her two grandsons to see the New York Giants play the home Philadelphia Phillies at Connie Mack Stadium. Mrs. Roth, the wife of Earl Roth, sports editor of the *Philadelphia Bulletin*, and her grandsons were sitting behind third base when Ashburn, the Phillies center fielder, came to the plate. "Richie was fouling off a lot of balls," recalled Mrs. Roth's grandson Preston, who was 8 years old at the time. "My grandmother was fixing my cap and never saw the ball coming. It hit her square in the face."

The blow broke Mrs. Roth's nose and left her dazed and bleeding. Medical personnel immediately rushed to her aid and placed her on a stretcher. Preston suffered a blow of sorts too. Although he and his brother Tom were upset, Preston had the presence of mind to notice that a man sitting in front of them had ended up with the ball. Preston recalled, "I asked him if I could have the ball. He just looked at me and said, 'Go to hell, kid.'"

Mrs. Roth's ordeal wasn't over yet. Play on the field had halted momentarily while the teams focused their attention on the injured woman. When Mrs. Roth was placed on a stretcher, the game resumed, and Ashburn stepped back into the batter's box. Too bad the medical personnel didn't take her out just a little bit quicker. While Mrs. Roth was being carried off on the stretcher, Ashburn swatted another wicked foul. Unbelievably, the same helpless woman was struck again.

Ashburn felt so bad about the incident that he visited Mrs. Roth regularly in the hospital and brought her bouquets. The team gave her grandsons free tickets and a tour of the clubhouse, where they met players and received an autographed baseball. Apparently, the boys forgot the painful reason for the red carpet treatment. Recalled their mother, Mrs. Dorothy Roth, "For my two sons, this was quite exciting. When poor Grandma was still suffering in the hospital, the boys went to visit her. One of them asked, 'Grandma, do you think you could go to an Eagles game and get hit in the face with a football?'"

GEORGE BURNS
First Baseman · Detroit, AL · 1915

Detroit Tigers first baseman George Burns hit the most scorching foul ball ever to land in the grandstands. It reportedly started a fire in a fan's coat pocket.

The crazy incident occurred during a scoreless game with the visiting Boston Red Sox at Briggs Stadium. In the bottom of the seventh inning, Burns—no relation to the comedian with the same name—came to bat and worked the count full. On the next pitch, he fouled the ball into the crowd. There was the usual flurry in the stands as some fans scattered to avoid the ball while others lunged for it.

Burns walked on the next pitch. But before he reached first base, the commotion in the stands where his foul ball had landed flared up even more—especially when a fan yelled, "There's a man on fire here!"

Players and fans saw a middle-aged man hopping up and down, with smoke coming out of the pocket of his sportcoat. A quick-thinking soft drink vendor raced to the rescue. He ran up to the smoking fan, opened a bottle of soda pop, poured it into the man's pocket, and squelched the fire.

Incredible as it sounds, the foul ball had hit the fan's coat and touched off a box of matches inside. After the fan took off his singed sportcoat, he muttered to those around him, "It figures this would happen on a ball hit by a player named Burns."

BOB FELLER
Pitcher · Cleveland, AL · May 14, 1939

Cleveland Indians star pitcher Bob Feller threw a pitch that was fouled off into the worst possible place imaginable—the face of his mother, Lena.

On Mother's Day 1939, Feller's family had journeyed from their home in Van Meter, Iowa, to Chicago to watch Rapid Robert pitch against the White Sox at Comiskey Park. Feller had arranged for his folks to sit in box seats on the first base side close to the field so he could see them from the mound.

He set the White Sox down in the first two innings and was cruising along with a comfy 6–0 lead when near disaster struck. With two on and two out, batter Marv Owen lashed a nasty foul ball into the stands. Out of 28,000 people, the ball hit Mrs. Feller in the face just above her right eye. The impact broke the poor lady's glasses and opened up a deep cut.

Feller rushed to the stands to check on his mother, who was hurt and bleeding but still conscious. "I felt sick," Feller later recalled. "I saw the police and ushers leading her out of the stands so they could take her to the hospital. There wasn't anything I could do, so I went on pitching."

Feller and mom, Lena, before her Mother's Day surprise

But he was so shaken up that he lost his control, walked several batters, and gave up three runs in the inning. However, he settled down and finished the game, winning it 9–4. Then he rushed to the hospital, where his mom had received six stitches and was kept under observation for two days.

"Mother looked up from the hospital bed, her face bruised and both eyes blackened, and she was still able to smile reassuringly," Feller recalled. "She told me, 'My head aches, Robert, but I'm all right. Now don't go blaming yourself. It wasn't your fault.'

"It was a one-in-a-million shot that my mother, while sitting in a crowd, would be struck by a foul ball resulting from a pitch I had made."

And on Mother's Day, no less.

DENARD SPAN
Outfielder · Minnesota, AL · March 31, 2010

As unfathomable as it seems for a mom to get nailed by a foul ball off a pitch thrown by her son, it's even more unbelievable that a mother would get struck by a foul ball hit by her son. Yet Minnesota Twins outfielder Denard Span did just that.

He swatted the odds-defying foul ball during a spring training game with the home team New York Yankees at George M. Steinbrenner Field in Tampa. Span, a Tampa native, had left 20 tickets for relatives and friends in prime seats three rows from the field directly to the left of the Twins' third base dugout. He was thrilled to be playing in front of his family, especially his mother, Wanda Wilson, who was proudly wearing a Twins jersey with Span's name on the back. The game was his last homecoming before the start of the 2010 season.

His family and friends were just settling into their seats when Span led off the game. With the count 3-and-2, he fouled off the pitch. The low liner zipped past the Twins' dugout and slammed right into the chest of his mother below her shoulder.

"When it first happened, I kind of froze a little bit," Span told reporters. "I couldn't believe it actually hit her. When I realized what happened, that's when I took off running."

Span dropped his bat and sprinted into the grandstand to console his mother while paramedics stationed at the ballpark went to her aid. "It just seemed like everything was in slow motion when I hit the ball," Span recalled. "I didn't see her before I got up to the plate. But as soon as the ball was in the air, I realized it was going after my mom. When I saw her go down, I couldn't do anything but just run after her and make sure she was okay."

Fortunately, she was not seriously hurt, although she was sore. Paramedics suggested Wilson get checked out at the hospital, but she declined to go. After all, she had come to see her son play. Although Wilson remained in the stadium, she moved to a different seat farther away from the field and under the grandstand roof.

The game had been held up for a few minutes while Span stayed with his mother. When play resumed, he was still so rattled that he took a called third strike. Assured that his mom was okay, he played in the outfield for the next two innings.

Before the bottom of the third, Yankees shortstop Derek Jeter pulled Span aside and suggested that Span should be with his mother. "He was just like, 'You go see about your mom,'" Span recalled. "I was already feeling that way, but to have him say it to me, I was like, 'You know what? He's right.' Mentally, my mind wasn't into the game. It was on her well-being."

Span said that his mother scolded him when he took himself out of the game. "She got mad at me because everyone came to see me play," he recalled. "She was madder at me for coming out of the game than for me hitting her."

BO WYBLE

Fan · Houston, NL · August 9, 2010

Houston Astros fan Bo Wyble proved that chivalry is dead, at least at the ballpark, after Houston's Chris Johnson hit a foul into the stands.

Wyble had taken his 19-year-old girlfriend of five months, Sara Saco-Vertiz, to a game against the visiting Atlanta Braves at Minute Maid Park. Early in the contest, the couple moved down to better seats that hugged the left field foul line. Minutes later, in the bottom of the fourth inning, Johnson stroked a foul line drive that headed straight for them.

Wyble stood up as if he was ready to catch the ball for his girlfriend, or at the very least, protect her from getting hit. But, as the video that went viral painfully shows, at the last second, he dodged out of the way, leaving Sara directly in the path of the ball, which smacked her right on the elbow.

And where was Wyble? He was bent over snatching the ball. Only after he had secured the ball did he check on his girlfriend's condition. Luckily, she wasn't hurt, other than having a sore elbow.

An inning later, during the game telecast, FOX Sports Houston reporter Patti Smith interviewed the couple live. Sara told her, "As soon as we got here and saw where we were sitting I said, 'Baby, I'm going to get hit.' And he said, 'No, no you're not. I'll catch it if you do' . . . And sure enough the ball comes at me and I shout, 'Baby!' and he just bails." Sara then held up her arm to show the seam marks from the impact of the baseball on her elbow.

When Smith asked Wyble what happened, he explained, "The ball was coming. I was going to catch it. But then it was in the lights and I lost track of it."

Smith pulled out some sunglasses, handed them to him, and scolded him.

"If you lose it [the ball] next time, you should go towards your girl-friend, protect her. Don't go the other way like a little chicken."

Wyble nodded meekly.

Then Smith turned to Sara and asked, "You think this maybe is a foreshadowing for the future that he might not be by your side?"

Sara hesitated and said, "Maybe I do need to reconsider . . ."

Three days later, after video of the foul play was seen repeatedly on ESPN's *SportsCenter* and got tens of thousands of hits on YouTube, the Foul Ball Couple appeared on CBS's *The Early Show.*

"I just lost sight of it, so I moved, and I figured she wasn't sitting still," said Wyble, who in the blogoshere was called Bo the Bailer. "I figured she'd move."

Sara said she wasn't too upset by Wyble jumping out of the way, adding that the pain in her elbow was "a six" on a scale to 10. "Honestly, it wasn't that bad," she said. "I have a high pain tolerance."

Sara added that she was surprised by all the attention. "The fact that so many people watched it, I didn't think that was going to happen."

At the end of the interview, the couple awkwardly announced they were no longer a couple. Wyble got the ball, but he lost the girl.

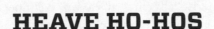

HEAVE HO-HOS

For the Most Inglorious Ejections of All Time,
The Baseball Hall of Shame™ Inducts:

BOB "FATS" FOTHERGILL
Pinch Hitter · Detroit, AL · May 24, 1926

Bob "Fats" Fothergill got ejected for losing his temper with the home plate umpire, but at least he left a lasting impression—literally.

The roly-poly Detroit Tigers outfielder had two passions in life: playing baseball and eating. His official weight was listed at 230 pounds, but the 5-foot-10 player often tipped the scales at well over 250 pounds. Columnist Joe Williams wrote that Fothergill's "barrier to greatness is a Graf Zeppelin belt line." Teammate Charlie Gehringer once said Fothergill "was about as round as he was tall."

One day, Fothergill was seen carrying a big bundle under his arm in the clubhouse and was asked if that was his laundry. Fothergill replied, "Laundry, nothing. It's my lunch."

Most every year, Fothergill reported to spring training well over his playing weight. It was too bad because the leaner he was, the better he hit—and he ended up with a lifetime batting average of .325.

In 1926, Fothergill was so overweight at the start of the season that he went on a crash weight-reduction program. He exercised for hours in a rubber suit, took Turkish baths, and followed a strict diet. It was too much for him. He grew increasingly testy until he cracked during a pinch-hitting appearance in a game against the Cleveland Indians.

Called out on strikes by home plate umpire Bill Dinneen, Fothergill became uncharacteristically enraged. He seized Dinneen and bit him on the arm. For his shocking display of cannibalism, Fothergill was tossed out of the game.

"It's okay by me," Fothergill muttered to the ump. "That's the first bite of meat I've had in a month."

EDD ROUSH
Center Fielder · Cincinnati, NL · June 8, 1920

Edd Roush never said a word. He never made a gesture. Yet he was ejected from a game for conduct unbecoming a Major Leaguer.

Roush was given the boot for taking a nap in center field!

In the eighth inning of a 4–4 game between the Cincinnati Reds and the host New York Giants at the Polo Grounds, Giants batter George Burns slapped a grounder over third base smack dab down the left field line. Home plate umpire Barry McCormick called the ball fair, whereupon Reds catcher Ivey Wingo tossed his glove in the air in protest. McCormick did him one better. The ump tossed his mask *and* his thumb in the air, signaling Wingo to the showers. Meanwhile, Burns, who was credited with a double, ended up at third on the play because of an error by left fielder Pat Duncan.

After time was called, the entire Reds infield swooped in on McCormick and angrily complained that the ball was foul. While the battle raged at home plate, Roush became bored in center field. So he placed his glove and cap on the ground and used them as a pillow while he stretched out for a short snooze. He quickly fell into a deep sleep.

Roush slumbered through the stormy dispute and all its fury: the rantings of third baseman Heinie Groh; the Spanish obscenities uttered

A rude awakening for Roush   NATIONAL BASEBALL HALL OF FAME LIBRARY

by pitcher Dolf Luque; the pleadings of Reds manager Pat Moran; and the wild departure of Wingo, who threw his catching gear all over the field as he stomped to the dugout.

Once the squabble ended, McCormick sent the Reds back to their positions and was just about to shout "Play ball!" when he noticed that Roush was using center field as a sofa. Teammates yelled at Roush to get up, but their calls failed to rouse him. Finally, Groh raced out to center and managed to awaken the team's Rip Van Winkle. But by then, it was too late.

When Roush opened his eyes, the first sight he saw was McCormick's thumb. The ejection immediately woke up Roush's temper and the heretofore dozing player launched into a tirade against the umpire. Roush, who wanted to duke it out with McCormick, was restrained by his teammates, who eventually ushered him to the dugout.

Moran couldn't understand why a player should be thrown out of a game simply for taking a nap in the outfield. "A lot of players have been caught sleeping on plays and they don't get the boot," he complained.

BILL SHARMAN
Outfielder · Brooklyn, NL · September 27, 1951

MIKE KEKICH
Pitcher · Los Angeles, NL · 1965

Basketball Hall of Famer Bill Sharman not only left his mark on the court but also on the baseball diamond. He was kicked out of a game without ever having played in one.

Before becoming an NBA legend for the Boston Celtics, Sharman was a minor league outfielder, and was once called up by the Brooklyn Dodgers toward the end of the 1951 season. In the bottom of the eighth inning of a 3–3 tie, the Boston Braves put runners on the corners. On the next play, a grounder to short, Braves runner Bob Addis raced home from third. It was a bang-bang play at the plate, and umpire Frank Dascoli called Addis safe.

Brooklyn catcher Roy Campanella and coach Cookie Lavagetto exploded in rage and were immediately ejected. The Dodgers bench then bombarded Dascoli with a volley of verbal abuse. In retaliation, Dascoli kicked out everyone in the entire Brooklyn dugout. That included rookie Sharman, who was sitting at the end of the bench, mouthing off like his teammates. Officially, they weren't ejected. They were ordered to stay in the clubhouse and could have been summoned to play if needed. The Dodgers lost 4–3.

Sharman never did play in the Majors and finished his baseball career a year later in the minors. Then he went on to basketball fame with the Celtics . . . but not before leaving a baseball legacy of his own for being kicked out of a game without ever having played in one.

Los Angeles Dodgers pitcher Mike Kekich identified with Sharman. He got ejected before he played in his first Major League game. In fact, it was the only time he was tossed in his entire nine-year career.

In 1965, when he was a rookie, Kekich was sitting in the dugout when an umpire made a close call that went against the Dodgers. Wanting to do his part for the team, Kekich joined other bench jockeys in riding the ump.

Suddenly all the other Dodgers quit yapping at once, except Kekich. Now only his voice was heard. His lone cutting remarks infuriated the arbiter, who then kicked him out of the game.

"That won't happen again," veteran Wally Moon told the press afterward. "All the kid needs is to get his timing down pat."

DICK DROTT
Pitcher · Chicago, NL · April 24, 1957

When Dick Drott tried to play nurse, he was thumbed out of the game by a rather humorless umpire.

Drott, a rookie pitching sensation with the Chicago Cubs, was in the dugout watching his roommate, hurler Moe Drabowsky, bat against Joe Nuxhall of the home Cincinnati Reds at Crosley Field. On a 2-2 count, Drabowsky fouled a pitch that struck his foot. The batter looked for sympathy but found none on the stoic face of home plate umpire Stan Landes. So Drabowsky launched into a performance worthy of an Oscar by crumpling to the ground and writhing in pain.

Drott decided that he couldn't just sit there and watch his roommate roll in the dirt in agony. As luck would have it, a disabled singer who had sung the national anthem before the start of the game was sitting in a front-row seat next to the Cubs dugout. Her wheelchair was by her side.

"Okay, if I borrow it?" Drott asked her. Then, before hearing her answer, he grabbed the wheelchair and rolled it up to home plate. "Roomie," he said to his injured comrade, "get in the wheelchair."

That seemed like a terrific idea to Drabowsky, but not to Landes. "What the hell are you doing?" the ump shouted at Drott.

"I'm only trying to help my roommate," Drott replied with a straight face. "He's hurt and he could use a hand."

Drabowsky did not get a hand. However, Drott did get the thumb. "You're out of the game!" thundered the unamused Landes. "And take that damn wheelchair with you!"

A few days later, Drott received a letter from Warren Giles, then president of the National League. "Warren indicated that he didn't know if Dick was trying to make a travesty of the game or if he really had my welfare at heart," recalled Drabowsky. "Not knowing what Dick's motives were, Warren was reluctant to fine him. However, he did tell Dick that such behavior would not be condoned in the future."

Drabowsky, who was one of baseball's greatest pranksters, added, "I've seen a lot of crazy things in my 17 years in the Majors, but that was really one of the funniest things I ever saw—and I didn't even pull it."

EDDIE KASKO
Manager · Boston, AL · July 7, 1972

Boston Red Sox manager Eddie Kasko was booted out of a game for lying down on the job—he faked a faint while protesting an umpire's call.

Kasko's swoon came in the top of the ninth inning of a game against the host California Angels. With Boston leading 3–2 and Ben Oglivie on third base with one out, Luis Tiant hit a grounder to shortstop Leo Cardenas, who fired the ball to catcher Jeff Torborg, trying to nail Oglivie at the plate. As Torborg was about to make the tag, the runner sidestepped him and then slid across the plate for what seemed like an insurance run.

Torborg and Angels manager Del Rice claimed that Oglivie had run out of the baseline. Plate umpire Hank Morgenweck disagreed, but then huddled with crew chief John Rice, who was working second base. Eventually, the umps reversed the decision and called Oglivie out.

Kasko stormed out of the dugout. Turning his wrath on Rice, Kasko shouted, "I don't believe this, John. Are you standing there telling me that even though you were on the outside part of the infield by second base, you saw the play at home better than Morgenweck?"

The ump replied, "Yeah, that's exactly what I'm telling you."

Kasko was so upset he didn't know what to say. But he felt obligated to make a statement of some sort—so he keeled over backward on the grass as if he had fainted from disbelief over the call. At first, the umps were irritated over Kasko's showboating. But when he lay there spread-eagled, flat on his back for nearly a minute, they became alarmed.

"My God, he's had a heart attack!" declared Rice. "Get a doctor out here!" But as the ump bent over, he saw Kasko open his eyes and grin. "Never mind the doctor," Rice told his colleagues. Then, staring down at the prone manager, the ump bellowed, "You're out of the game!"

"For what?" asked Kasko.

"For fainting."

Kasko left the field, but the umpires hadn't seen the last of him. In true Hall of Shame style, Kasko managed to get ejected twice in the same game.

After the Angels had tied the score in the bottom of the ninth, Bosox utility man Phil Gagliano started mouthing off to Morgenweck from the dugout in the top of the 10th. Kasko, who was now watching the game from the tunnel leading to the clubhouse, charged out onto the field to protect his player from getting booted.

Rice immediately ran in from his position near second, confronted Kasko, and said, "I don't know if you remember it or not, but while you were passed out in the last inning, I threw you out. So get out of here!"

GRANNY HAMNER
Shortstop · Philadelphia, NL · June 21, 1957

Philadelphia Phillies shortstop Granny Hamner was kicked out of a game after arguing over a play in which he was called *safe!*

In the top of the sixth inning of a 6–1 win over the host Milwaukee Braves, Hamner hit a bouncer to deep short where Johnny Logan made a hurried throw that pulled Frank Torre off first base. Torre made a desperate swipe at Hamner but missed him.

As he crossed the bag, Hamner yelled, "No! No!" It was his way of saying that he had not been tagged.

But first base umpire Ken Burkhart took exception to Hamner's words. "I'm doing the umpiring here," said the arbiter caustically. Alluding to Hamner's previous run-ins with umps, Burkhart added, "In fact, you've been umpiring long enough."

Hamner shouted back, "Hey, it's a free country. I can say what I want, especially when it's true."

Because he had beaten the throw to first anyway, Hamner was called safe and credited with an infield single. That should have ended things, but it didn't. The next batter, Solly Hemus, hit a single to right that sent Hamner to third.

Like a fire that was never doused and flares up again, Hamner began jawing with Burkhart from across the diamond as players from both sides—unaware of the beef's origin—wondered why a runner would argue over being called safe. Finally, Burkhart warned, "One more word out of you and you're gone!"

Responded Hamner, "One more word."

So Burkhart gave him the heave-ho.

BOB ELLIOTT

Third Baseman

BOBBY HOFMAN

Pinch Hitter

New York, NL · August 23, 1952

In one of the most bizarre double-barreled ejections in baseball history, a hitter was tossed out of the game before finishing his turn at bat—and moments later so was his pinch hitter.

The visiting New York Giants were trailing the St. Louis Cardinals 3–0 in the top of the seventh inning when Bob Elliott came up to bat. Plate umpire Augie Donatelli called the first pitch a strike and Elliott squawked in protest. When the next pitch was called a strike, he blew a gasket, launching into a tirade that he capped off by kicking dirt on the arbiter.

Donatelli wasted no time in banishing Elliott from the game. But the hotheaded player refused to leave. Instead he tried to get at Donatelli's throat and had to be held back by the other umpires. His coaches finally hustled him to the showers to cool off.

Meanwhile, Bobby Hofman was sent up to finish Elliott's turn at bat with the count 0-and-2. Hofman mumbled something unfriendly to Donatelli and then settled into the batter's box. He took the next pitch and then heard Donatelli bellow, "Steeerrriiiike threeeee!"

That was Hofman's cue to reprise Elliott's hopping-mad performance. After venting his spleen, he too kicked dirt on the ump and was promptly thumbed out of the game.

For Elliott and Hofman, it was one, two, three strikes you're (both thrown) out of the old ball game.

GENE MAUCH

Manager · Montreal, NL · May 7, 1969

Gene Mauch was kicked out of a game because he kicked too much.

The Montreal Expos skipper turned into a punter in a game against the host Atlanta Braves. In the bottom of the fifth inning, Montreal was

Mauch displaying his punting skills

clinging to a 3–2 lead with Atlanta runner Felipe Alou on third and two outs. As starting pitcher Mike Wegener got ready to pitch, third base umpire Stan Landes called a balk, allowing Alou to trot home with the tying run.

Infuriated by the call, Mauch leaped out of the dugout and confronted Landes. Yelling at the top of his lungs, the soon-hoarse manager appealed to the other umpires to override Landes's ruling.

When they refused, he stomped to the pitcher's mound and punted the resin bag 10 feet in the air. Not satisfied with his kick, Mauch ran after it and then punted it another 20 feet. Still not done, Mauch snatched the ball out of his startled hurler's hand and punted it high into the air.

The next boot was of Mauch himself—right out of the game.

AL LOPEZ
Catcher · Brooklyn, NL · September 20, 1934

Brooklyn Dodger Al Lopez used a photo to prove umpire Bill Klem had blown a call. But when the ump got the picture, the catcher got the thumb.

As a result, Lopez was in the showers 10 minutes before the game even started in one of the earliest ejections ever.

The disputed call came during the first game of a doubleheader with the visiting Pittsburgh Pirates. Umpiring the contest were Klem calling balls and strikes and George Barr handling the bases.

Brooklyn hurler Van Mungo was pitching a shutout into the ninth inning with a 4–0 cushion. But on a close play at the plate, Klem called Pittsburgh runner Paul Waner safe. "I knew I had the plate blocked," recalled Lopez, "but Klem called the guy safe. I came off the ground yelling my head off. Klem wouldn't listen. He just indicated that the runner had slid in under the tag."

But after the second game and a troubled night's rest, much to Lopez's delight, a morning newspaper published a picture of that very play. It clearly showed the catcher had indeed made the tag.

That afternoon, Klem strode to home plate before the start of the game and noticed the plate was covered with dirt. He took out his whisk broom and brushed it off—and found a newspaper photo taped to the plate. Upon closer inspection, he saw it was a picture of the disputed play.

Klem furiously ripped the picture off the plate, thrust it under Lopez's nose and bellowed, "You're outta here!"

For Lopez, there was no Klemency.

DON ZIMMER
Manager · Boston, AL · August 2, 1980

In a heated argument over an umpire's call, Boston Red Sox manager Don Zimmer lost his cool—and his teeth.

At the time, the 49-year-old skipper had been chewing tobacco for more than 30 years. Zimmer, who earned the nickname Popeye because he looked like the cartoon character, walked around with a bulge of chaw in his cheek that was as big as a baseball. He had to chew the sticky stuff carefully because he had false teeth.

His love for chewing tobacco proved to be his undoing when he was ejected during a verbal clash with umpire John Shulock, who was also a hard-core tobacco chewer.

The quarrel started in the top of the fourth inning in a 1–0 win over the host Texas Rangers. After Boston's Jim Rice drew a walk, Texas center fielder Mickey Rivers robbed Carlton Fisk of extra bases on a sensational catch. Rice, who was near second, made a U-turn and headed back toward first. Trying to double up the runner, Rivers fired the ball to the relay man, who threw to first. Shulock called Rice out on a close play.

"I came running across the field," Zimmer told the *New York Times* 10 years later. "During the argument, I took out my chaw and slammed it down into the dirt, then Shulock slammed his chaw down. I took my pouch of tobacco out of my back pocket and slammed it down, so Shulock took out his pouch and slammed it down. But when I slammed my chaw down, my teeth had gone with it. I had to go down and get my teeth out of the chaw."

TOM GORMAN
Umpire, NL · July 1, 1963

Umpire Tom Gorman deserved the thumb for knowingly throwing out the wrong player.

Gorman was calling balls and strikes in a game between the visiting Pittsburgh Pirates and the Philadelphia Phillies when one of the Phillies started blasting the ump from the dugout with digs such as "Where's your seeing-eye dog?" and "Why don't you punch a hole in your mask so you can see?" The tormentor wouldn't let up, and by the seventh inning, Gorman had taken enough guff.

The ump decided to take a shot at somebody, so he figured he'd toss out third baseman Don Hoak, who had had a run-in with him the previous week. Besides, it wouldn't hurt the team much, reasoned Gorman, because Hoak had a leg injury and wasn't even playing.

Pointing toward the corner of the dugout where he thought he had spotted Hoak, Gorman shouted, "Okay, Hoak, you're out of here!"

Philly manager Gene Mauch rushed to the plate to protest. "Why are you picking on my ballplayers?" Mauch complained. "So far you've been working a pretty good game, not bad for you. You've only missed six or seven pitches."

"Don't play around with me," Gorman warned. "Get that donkey Hoak out of the dugout."

Mauch put his hands on his hips and pushed his face to within inches of the umpire's. "Let me tell you something," snapped the manager. "Hoak isn't in the dugout." Pointing to a spot 380 feet away, Mauch said, "He's in the bullpen. What are you going to do now?"

Trying hard not to turn red from embarrassment, Gorman replied, "Get him over here."

Mauch waved to the bullpen and Hoak jogged in, thinking he was going to pinch-hit. Mauch told him, "Gorman just put you out."

"What?" stammered Hoak. He started ranting and raving and jumping up and down. But Gorman would not be swayed. He ordered Hoak to leave the premises.

The next day Hoak bumped into Gorman in the clubhouse runway leading to the field. "Answer me one thing, Tom," said Hoak. "How the hell did you know I was hollering at you from down in the bullpen?"

HEINIE MANUSH
Left Fielder · Washington, AL · October 6, 1933

Heinie Manush was fit to be tied with an umpire's call—and it cost him an inglorious World Series ejection.

After batting .336 for the season, Manush was anticipating a great performance in the 1933 World Series between his Washington Senators and the New York Giants. But it didn't turn out the way he had hoped. Entering Game 4, his team was down two games to one, and he had collected one measly hit in 13 at-bats. Disappointed by his poor batting performance, the slumping left fielder took out his frustration on an umpire.

In the bottom of the sixth inning of Game 4, the Senators trailed 1–0, but had the tying run on second with one out. Manush slapped a hard grounder past a diving Bill Terry at first for what looked like a sure hit. But second baseman Howie Critz tracked it down and fired to pitcher Carl Hubbell, who raced over to cover the bag. Umpire Charlie Moran called Manush out on the whisker-close play.

Manush was furious over the call and so was Washington player-manager Joe Cronin. They sandwiched Moran and blasted him for his poor eyesight and bad judgment and every other fault they could conjure up. Plate umpire Red Ormsby finally entered the fray and ordered Cronin and Manush back to the dugout.

Cronin reluctantly returned to the bench, but Manush didn't. He lashed out at Moran one more time as irate Washington fans heaved hundreds of soda pop bottles at the umpire. Moran didn't back down.

"I was too smart to lay a hand on Moran when I was arguing the call," Manush recalled years later. "But when he bellied up to me and asked me what I wanted to make of it, there was a temptation that was too great."

Moran, like the other umpires in those days, wore a black bow tie held on by an elastic band under the shirt collar. "What I did was grab the tie," Manush recalled. He pulled it out as far as he could and then "I let it snap back into Moran's neck."

The impact left the umpire speechless. When he finally got his voice back, his first words were, "You're out of the game!"

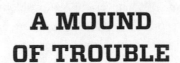

A MOUND
OF TROUBLE

*For the Most Pitiful Pitching Performances of All
Time, The Baseball Hall of Shame™ Inducts:*

TOM GORMAN   MARK FREEMAN
GEORGE BRUNET
Pitchers · Kansas City, AL · April 22, 1959

It was the sorriest exhibition of pitching control ever seen in one inning.

Kansas City Athletics hurlers Tom Gorman, Mark Freeman, and George Brunet were so wild they couldn't find home plate with a compass.

In one deplorable inning, the struggling pitchers walked 10 batters and hit another while allowing the visiting Chicago White Sox to score 11 runs *on only one single.* What's worse, eight of those runs were forced in by bases-loaded walks. (For this reason, the A's performance is even more shameful than the Washington Senators' record-setting 11 free passes in one inning on September 11, 1949.)

The White Sox were winning 8–6 in the seventh inning when Gorman came in to pitch. A hit and three errors brought in two runs and put a runner on third base with no outs. Gorman could have escaped further damage if the strike zone had been high and outside. But it wasn't, and he started the pitiful base-on-balls procession.

He walked two batters in a row to load the bases, and then threw two straight balls to the next hitter before manager Harry Craft yanked him and brought in Freeman. Whatever control problems afflicted Gorman were passed on to Freeman, who tossed two more balls, which finished the walk and forced in the third run. Then he issued two more free passes sandwiched around a force-out at home for another two tallies.

Brunet came in to relieve. In keeping with the tradition already established by his colleagues, Brunet forced in the final six runs with a walk, walk, hit batsman (to break up the monotony), walk, strikeout (no big deal because it was the opposing pitcher), walk, walk, and, mercifully, an inning-ending groundout.

Seventeen White Sox came to the plate in the walkathon half-inning that took 45 minutes to complete. The final score: Chicago 20, Kansas City 6.

ROGER MASON
Pitcher · San Francisco, NL · April 13, 1987

JEFF AUSTIN
Pitcher · Cincinnati, NL · May 28, 2003

PHIL DUMATRAIT
Pitcher · Cincinnati, NL · September 9, 2007

Giving up back-to-back-to-back home runs is a shameful way for a pitcher to start the game. No one knows that better than Roger Mason, Jeff Austin, and Phil Dumatrait—the only three hurlers in baseball history to have achieved such a dubious deed.

Mason set the standard for pitching ignobility when he started a 1987 game for the visiting San Francisco Giants against the San Diego

Padres. He needed his whole repertoire of pitches to make it into the record books.

On an 0-2 pitch, he tried to slip a slider past leadoff hitter Marvell Wynne, who hammered it for a homer. Next, with the count 1-and-2, Mason hurled a fastball to Tony Gwynn, who also went yard. Finally, Mason threw a split-fingered fastball on a 2-2 pitch to John Kruk, who smashed it for a four-bagger. It was the first time in the Majors that a pitcher gave up three consecutive home runs to the first three batters in a game. It could have been worse. The next batter, Steve Garvey, walloped a full-count pitch to the warning track.

After the contest, which the Giants lost 13-6, Mason told reporters, "I'm glad I didn't have a fourth pitch."

Sixteen years later, Cincinnati Reds hurler Jeff Austin matched Mason's futile feat—but with an added flourish. At the start of a 2003 game against the host Atlanta Braves, Austin served a leadoff homer to Rafael Furcal, whose drive landed in the right field seats. On the very next pitch, Mark DeRosa homered to center. Gary Sheffield then launched a shot into the stands in left, causing Austin to stomp around the mound in disgust. The three record-tying homers came in the span of only six pitches.

But then Austin bettered (or worsened) Mason's performance. After retiring the next two hitters—including a flyout by Andruw Jones that was caught at the edge of the warning track—the pitcher gave up a walk and then *another* homer, this one to Javy Lopez.

After kneeling on the mound in disbelief, Austin turned his back to the Reds dugout because he didn't want to see manager Bob Boone come out and yank him, which is what Boone did. Austin then jogged off the mound to sarcastic cheers from the Turner Field crowd.

Austin became the first pitcher in 11 years to get knocked out of two straight starts without making it through the first inning. In his previous start against the Florida Marlins, the right-hander had failed to get an out, giving up five runs on three hits and four walks in an 8–4 loss.

After the Braves' 15–3 shellacking of the Reds, Boone said, "It was awful. Austin feels horrible."

Not surprisingly, Austin, who had a 2-3 record, was demoted to Class AAA Louisville right after the game. "My goodness, this team is definitely better without me on it," he told reporters. "I'm surprised I've stayed here this long."

He never pitched in the Majors again.

It took only four years before another Reds pitcher, Phil Dumatrait, duplicated the triple-homer start. His game-opening gopher ball achievement came at home against the Milwaukee Brewers. Leadoff batter Rickie Weeks sent a 2-1 pitch into the Reds' bullpen in left-center field. J. J. Hardy followed two pitches later with a drive into the Brewers' bullpen down the right field line. Ryan Braun then hit Dumatrait's ninth pitch over the fence in center.

Dumatrait, who was 0-4, faced five batters in the inning, allowing five hits and four runs before being pulled by manager Pete Mackanin. "Phil just didn't have any command of his pitches, and the Brewers let him know about it," Mackanin said. "That might be my quickest hook ever."

JACK CHESBRO
Pitcher · New York, AL · October 10, 1904

BOB MOOSE
Pitcher · Pittsburgh, NL · October 11, 1972

Twice pitchers have thrown ninth-inning wild pitches that lost a pennant. "Happy Jack" Chesbro turned into a Sad Sack after throwing a historically disastrous wild pitch.

In 1904, Chesbro had pitched phenomenally, winning 41 games to set a record that has never been threatened. On the strength of his arm, the New York Yankees (then known as the Highlanders) fought the Boston Red Sox (then known as the Americans) down to the wire for the pennant that year.

On the last day of the season, New York trailed Boston by a single game, but the Highlanders could capture the pennant with a doubleheader sweep over the visiting Americans. With Chesbro getting the call in that critical first game, the New York fans had good reason to expect a pennant. About 30,000 rooters were on hand, an astonishing number for those days.

The game was a nail-biter, and the two teams entered the top of the ninth inning tied at 2–2. Chesbro got the first two outs, but in the process had seen Boston runner Lou Criger make it to third. The pitcher desperately wanted that final out of the inning, so he did what he always did in a jam. He went to his spitter.

But the pitch that had brought Chesbro so many victories that season betrayed him in the end. He threw the wettest and wildest pitch of his career. Catcher Red Kleinow leaped for the ball, but it sailed past him and headed for infamy. Criger scampered home with the winning run as a collective moan of despair swept through the stunned crowd. New York failed to score in the last of the ninth and lost the pennant to Boston.

At least Chesbro's calamitous wild pitch had occurred in the top of the ninth, giving his team a chance to recover. Sixty-eight years later, Pittsburgh Pirates pitcher Bob Moose didn't give his team any such opportunity. He hurled a pennant-losing *walk-off* wild pitch.

In 1972, the world champion Pirates were just three outs away from winning their second straight pennant. In the fifth and deciding game of the National League Championship Series at Riverfront Stadium in Cincinnati, the Pirates held a 3–2 lead over the Reds entering the bottom of the ninth inning. With ace reliever Dave Giusti on the mound, Pittsburgh could already taste the champagne.

But on this day, of all days, Giusti didn't have his stuff. He gave up a game-tying home run to Johnny Bench and back-to-back singles before right-hander Bob Moose, normally a starting pitcher, relieved him. Moose retired the next batter, Cesar Geronimo, on a long fly that advanced runner George Foster to third base. Moose bore down and coaxed Darrel Chaney to pop up. Now there were two outs. To send the game into extra innings, Moose needed to retire hitter Hal McRae.

The count went to 1-and-1. Then Moose threw a hard slider down and away—but a little too down and a little too far away. The

The wild pitch that sank the Pirates

ball skipped into the dirt to the right of home plate and bounced over catcher Manny Sanguillen's head. The catcher frantically retrieved the ball, but it was much too late. Foster had already raced across the plate with the pennant-winning run. There was nothing Sanguillen could do but fire the ball into center field in a final gesture of frustration over the inglorious end to the Pirates' reign as world champs—all because of that pennant-losing, walk-off wild pitch.

PAUL LAPALME
Pitcher · Chicago, AL · May 18, 1957

Chicago White Sox pitcher Paul LaPalme had the easiest pitching assignment ever given a hurler. Just hold the ball. That's all. Just hold the ball.

But, incredibly, he didn't. And he cost his team the game.

With the Chicago White Sox leading 4–3 over the host Baltimore Orioles, LaPalme went out to the mound to pitch in the bottom of the ninth inning. Sox manager Al Lopez gave him one strict and simple instruction: Stall. Under a prearranged agreement, the umpires were to halt the game at exactly 10:20 p.m. to give Chicago time to catch a train for Boston. It was 10:18 p.m. when Oriole Dick Williams led off the frame. Unable to think of any creative way to dawdle, LaPalme threw a strike and a ball.

By now, time was almost up. Just a few seconds remained before the White Sox could leave town a winner. All LaPalme had to do was simply stand there. Or tie his shoelaces. Or pick his nose. Or scratch his butt. He could do anything except throw the ball.

But he threw the ball anyway—and not way outside or into the ground or any other spot that would have been impossible to hit. No, Paul LaPalme threw the ball right down the pipe, and Williams walloped it. As the minute hand struck 10:20 p.m., the ball landed high in the left field bleachers for a dramatic game-tying home run. The umps then called the game with the score knotted 4–4.

Under American League rules, the tie meant the game had to be replayed in its entirety at a later date. The Orioles won the rematch.

As for LaPalme, his time ran out. After that year, he never pitched in the Majors again.

PHIL MARCHILDON
Pitcher · Philadelphia, AL · August 1, 1948

Phil Marchildon threw the wildest wild pitch in baseball history. His wayward ball sailed into the 10th row of the grandstand and conked a fan smack on the noggin.

The Philadelphia Athletics' Canadian-born hurler was never known for his control. In fact, in his nine-year career, he chalked up 203 more walks than strikeouts and twice led the American League in issuing free passes. So it wasn't unusual for the right-hander to uncork a wild pitch now and then. Even so, the one he flung in a 1948 game against the host Detroit Tigers was a doozy that astonished even veteran players.

In the bottom of the fourth inning, Detroit's Vic Wertz stepped to the plate. Meanwhile, sitting in a 10th-row box seat between third and home, fan Sam Wexler, of Toledo, Ohio, leaned over to light a cigar. Just then Marchildon went into his windup and cut loose with a pitch so wild that it flew into the grandstand and nailed Wexler right on the head.

Wexler didn't know what hit him. At first the Briggs Stadium crowd was hushed. But once they saw that the slightly dazed Wexler was not seriously hurt, they burst into raucous laughter.

"It was just a fastball that got away from me," Marchildon recalled. "I couldn't believe it went that far. It just sailed right into the stands and hit that poor fan. Everybody was laughing—even my own teammates. I turned to [catcher] Buddy Rosar and said, 'I guess that was a little high.' Then I shouted to [plate umpire] Ed Rommel, 'You don't call 'em that high and outside, do you?'"

Marchildon's teammates were amazed. "The first thing I thought was, 'Holy hell, what did I just see?'" recalled A's left fielder Barney McCosky. "I've never seen a wild pitch that wild before. I turned to [center fielder] Sam Chapman and he broke into a smile and shook his head."

As for the beaning victim, Wexler was escorted by stadium ushers to the first aid room, but he didn't need any treatment. After thanking everyone for their concern, Wexler returned to his seat amid a big ovation from the crowd. Then he lit a fresh cigar—while keeping a wary eye on Phil Marchildon.

LEE GRISSOM
Pitcher · Cincinnati, NL · 1938

Suffering from a chronically sore arm in 1938, Cincinnati Reds southpaw Lefty Grissom adopted a painfully bad solution in the hopes of pitching better.

He eagerly listened up when someone told him that hurler Lefty Grove, by then destined for the Hall of Fame, once had two teeth pulled to restore his throwing arm. As ridiculous as it sounded, Grissom thought it was worth a try. So he rushed to a dentist and had two teeth extracted—and then had two more taken out for good measure. He never stopped to wonder how yanking four good teeth had any bearing on his pitching arm. Until later.

"I think somebody was filling me full of it," Grissom ruefully recalled years later. "But it seemed like a good idea when I heard about it. I figured if I could win some games, it was worth it.

"The teeth-pulling didn't hurt me. I was back to pitching in a couple of days. But it damn sure didn't help my arm none."

Grissom's record that ruthless, toothless season: two wins, three losses, and one bill for false choppers.

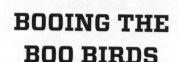

BOOING THE
BOO BIRDS

*For the Most Obnoxious Fan Behavior of All
Time, The Baseball Hall of Shame™ Inducts:*

KESSLER BROTHERS
Philadelphia, AL · 1932

One was born with a bullhorn for a throat and the other with a loudspeaker for a mouth.

They were the Kessler Brothers, Bull and Eddie. They sat on opposite sides of the diamond at old Shibe Park, and together they drove Philadelphia Athletics manager Connie Mack out of his mind and A's third baseman Jimmy Dykes out of town.

The Kesslers were the first to turn a Philadelphia tradition—verbally abusing the home team—into an art form. Whenever the A's were home, the Kesslers, who worked on the docks in the morning, turned up their astonishingly loud voices and aimed their vitriolic raps at both home and visiting players.

For some strange reason, they unmercifully harassed Dykes, who was a Philadelphia native. It wasn't like Dykes was a bad fielder or hitter. He made only 11 errors in 152 games and batted .265 for the 1932 season.

But from their seats, Bull and Eddie loudly debated Dykes's ability on the field and questioned the circumstances of his birth for all to hear. Their nonstop slams made Dykes dread homestands.

Whenever he couldn't reach a grounder, the Kesslers hooted and hollered. "The little round man missed another one!" they announced to most of Philadelphia and part of New Jersey. Whenever Dykes fanned, Bull bellowed from his first base seat, "Who always strikes out with men on base?" And Eddie replied from his third base seat, "Stand up, Jimmy Dykes!"

At times the torrent of abuse got to the normally unflappable infielder, and he booted an easy ball or failed to drive in runners in scoring position. With games at stake, Connie Mack tried everything to shut up the booming tongue-lashers. He pleaded. He cajoled. He threatened. He even bribed them with season passes.

For a while that worked. But after a few games, the Kesslers couldn't stand the sounds of silence any longer. They turned in their passes and turned on their mouths.

In desperation, Mack hauled the Kesslers into court and sought an injunction to muzzle them. But the judge threw the request out quicker than a Walter Johnson fastball.

Finally when Dykes no longer could take any more of the Bull and Eddie Show, Mack was left with two choices—cut off Dykes's ears or get rid of him. At the end of the season, Mack sold Dykes to the Chicago White Sox.

Without their favorite target of abuse, baseball was no longer fun for the Kesslers and they faded away . . . somewhat quietly.

FOOD-FLINGERS
Cleveland, AL · September 27, 1940

The fans in the cheap seats at Municipal Stadium made sure they were fortified with fruits and vegetables when the Detroit Tigers came to town for a crucial three-game series with the second-place Cleveland

Indians. The Tigers needed only one more victory to clinch the pennant.

It was Ladies Day, but the 45,000-plus fans in the stands made it look more like a convention of produce peddlers. They brought with them eggplant, cauliflower, tomatoes, and overly ripe fruits and veggies . . . and none of them were for eating. The food was ammo because it was payback time after the Tigers had called the Indians such names as the Crybabies, Boohoo Indians, and Papeese (plural for papoose). The Detroit players had aimed their slurs at the Cleveland players for trying to get Indians manager Oscar Vitt fired.

As soon as the Tigers took the field, they were pelted by produce hurled from the stands. In the first inning, Hank Greenberg circled under a fly ball in left field and was nearly buried in a deluge of fruits and vegetables.

Umpire Bill Summers stopped the game twice and threatened to declare a forfeit, which would have handed the pennant to Detroit. He and Vitt got on the public address system and pleaded with fans to curb their enthusiasm, or at least the food-flinging. The shower slowed but didn't stop. By the time Detroit's Rudy York smacked one of Bob Feller's pitches for a two-run homer—the only runs of the game—the diamond looked like a giant vegetable plate.

Meanwhile, stadium police were roving through the crowd, grabbing the worst offenders and hustling them out. As the cops approached a particularly rowdy group in the upper deck, one of the troublemakers gathered all his ammunition—tomatoes, eggs, bottles, and other assorted trash—into one basket and dropped it over the side into the Tigers bullpen. The basket landed right on the head of Detroit catcher Birdie Tebbetts, knocking him out cold.

When he was revived, Tebbetts was taken to the clubhouse for treatment. The cops, waiting there with his assailant, asked Tebbetts if he wanted to press assault charges against him. Tebbetts declined and said he would settle the matter personally in his own way.

Exactly how the fan left the stadium with a busted nose is not quite clear.

STEVE BARTMAN
Chicago, NL · October 14, 2003

Die-hard Cubs fan Steve Bartman will go down in baseball history as an unwitting Cubs traitor.

By reaching for a potentially catchable foul ball, he singlehandedly changed the course of a game, ruined the Cubs' chances to reach the World Series, and proved that they are indeed the most cursed team of all time.

At least that's what millions of his fellow fans believed.

Whether or not Bartman should be blamed—and you can build a strong argument that he shouldn't—he was responsible for triggering the most outrageous reaction ever by fans over a loss. Fueled by the smoldering remains of decades of dashed hopes and dreams, Cubs fans took out their frustration, anger, and heartbreak on him.

It was Game 6 of the National League Championship Series at Wrigley Field between the visiting Florida Marlins and the Chicago Cubs, who were up three games to two in the best of seven series. With Mark Prior hurling a three-hit masterpiece, the Cubs were ahead 3–0 in the top of the eighth—only five outs away from going to their first World Series since 1945.

Florida had a runner on second and one out when second baseman Luis Castillo sent a high foul ball down the left field line toward Bartman, a 26-year-old global human resources worker, who was sitting in Aisle 4, Row 8, Seat 113, an arm's length away from the foul line. Cubs outfielder Moisés Alou leaped to make the play. But the bespectacled Bartman, wearing an old Walkman headset over his Cubs cap, reached up for the ball, and inadvertently deflected it away from Alou. The outfielder slammed his glove to the ground and yelled at Bartman.

Given new life, Castillo walked . . . and then the Cubs collapsed. After a single, an error on a double-play ball, a double, a walk, a sacrifice fly, a walk, and a bases-clearing double, the Marlins had scored eight runs—six unearned—and won 8–3.

Upset fans turned their wrath on Bartman, pelting him with drinks and other debris. It was so bad that he was rushed out of the park with his jacket over his head and given a police escort home.

Then things got really bad. Bartman was outed on a Major League Baseball online message board that gave his address and phone number. Six police cars were on call outside his house. Rod Blagojevich, the since disgraced governor of Illinois, announced that Bartman should join the witness protection program. Florida governor Jeb Bush graciously offered Bartman political asylum, adding, "I promise we will expedite his safe passage."

Bartman was crushed and issued a heartfelt apology: "There are few words to describe how awful I feel and what I have experienced within these last 24 hours . . . I am so truly sorry from the bottom of this Cubs fan's broken heart. I ask that Cubs fans everywhere redirect the negative energy that has been vented towards my family, my friends, and myself into the usual positive support for our beloved team on their way to being National League champs."

The Cubs had a chance to do their part the next day to save Bartman from eternal damnation in Cubdom. A win would make him a mere footnote in baseball history, a fan forgiven for doing what every other fan would have done in the same situation. The delirium of finally making it to the World Series and a chance for a championship that had eluded the team for nearly 100 years would have automatically pardoned him.

As manager Dusty Baker said at the time, "We've got to win for that kid. For us, it's just a ballgame. For him, it's the rest of his life."

But this was Chicago. And they were the Cubs.

In the seventh and deciding game, Chicago charged out to a 5–3 lead. Everything looked great . . . until it didn't. The Cubs lost 9–6. And the Marlins went on to win the World Series.

At the suggestion of police, Bartman disconnected his phone and went into hiding. He was vilified on the Internet in "Death to Steve Bartman" message boards. Blogs encouraged Cubs fans to "not let him do this to us" and to "seek revenge." He was Photoshopped hiding in

Bartman about to catch hell

Saddam Hussein's bunker, pushing a button that caused the collapse of the Twin Towers, and holding a match to the burning *Hindenburg*. An FBI "Ten Most Wanted" poster on the Internet showed Bartman's photo over the caption, "Considered ignorant and extremely stupid. Wanted for interfering with crucial play . . . [and] breaking the heart of an entire city."

Furious Cubs fans wore their feelings on their T-shirts: SIT DOWN, STEVE; THE CURSE LIVES—THANKS, STEVE; and CUB FAN RULE NO. 1: KEEP BOTH HANDS ON YOUR OLD STYLE.

And then there was this MasterCard parody:

Tickets to Cubs game: $200
Chicago Cubs hat: $20
1987 Walkman: $10
[Screwing] up your team's chances of winning the
World Series: Priceless

Eventually, the dastardly ball that Bartman deflected from Alou was bought at auction for $113,824.16 on behalf of Harry Caray's Restaurant Group. On February 26, 2004, it was blown up at a special ceremony. The remains were cooked, and the steam from the process was captured, distilled, and added to the restaurant's pasta sauce in a good-bye bad ball dinner. But the memory of that fateful day at Wrigley Field was still awfully hard to swallow.

FIRE-STARTERS
Boston, NL · May 15, 1894

When the rowdies in the right field bleachers at Boston's South End Grounds tried to light a fire under the home team, they ended up burning down most of the neighborhood instead.

The 3,500 fans were getting hot under the collar during a bitter game against the visiting Baltimore Orioles (no connection to the current O's), who had boiled the Beaneaters (ancestors of the Atlanta Braves) badly the day before, 16–5.

In the third inning, Orioles third baseman John McGraw sent the hostile crowd into a frenzy when he started a fistfight with local hero and first baseman Tommy "Foghorn" Tucker. While the two traded punches, a gang of hoodlums decided to inflame the passions of fans and their team by setting a small fire in the 25-cent seats in right field. Almost everyone laughed at the prank . . . until it was no longer funny.

The flames began to spread in the bleachers, so the umpire halted the game. Rather than leave, the fans in the grandstands became infuriated that such a small fire should stop play. Impatiently, they shouted, "Play ball! Play ball!"

The players ran out to right field to help fight the fire, but once they felt the heat of the blaze, which was now raging, they high-tailed it for the clubhouse, cleaned out their lockers, and got the hell out of the neighborhood.

With the speed of a forest fire, the inferno engulfed the grandstand and jumped across the street, devouring block after block. Three hours after the right field idiots had torched the ballpark, the fire had wiped out 12 acres of the South End, including more than 170 homes, schools, churches, stores, stables, and warehouses. Fortunately, no one was killed. Unfortunately, the fire-starters got away.

The Beaneaters played their home games at the Congress Street Grounds until the ballpark was rebuilt in an astonishingly fast 10 weeks.

GUNSLINGERS
Chicago, NL · July 4, 1900

Thousands of gunslinging fans turned a Fourth of July doubleheader into a shootout at the OK Corral, spreading fear among unarmed players and spectators.

Bullets sang, darted, and whizzed over the players' heads as the rambunctious fans fired round after round whenever the Cubs (then known as the Orphans) scored against the gun-shy Philadelphia Phillies. The visiting team was so intimidated it lost both games of the twin-bill at Chicago's West Side Grounds, 10–6 and 5–4.

In the sixth inning of the opener, the Cubs triggered an explosive six-run rally as guns and firecrackers blasted away from all corners of the ballpark. When the inning finally ended, the shell-shocked Philly outfielders emerged from a haze of gunpowder smoke that hung over the field like a battleground pall.

In the second game, Chicago tied the score in the bottom of the ninth as the fans cheered them on with gunfire. First, the left field bleachers let loose with a salvo. Then the right field bleachers responded. Hundreds of spectators in the grandstand were so happy they began shooting holes in the roof, causing flying splinters to fall on their heads.

In the bottom of the 12th inning, ammo was running short for many fans, so they pounded their seats with the butts of their guns. But others, who were still well supplied with bullets, fired a fusillade to rattle Phils hurler Al Orth and his teammates.

The barrage worked. Philadelphia misplayed two balls for an error and an infield hit, and the strain began to show on Orth. Chicago's Barry McCormick laid down a sacrifice bunt that was fielded by Orth, but the nettled pitcher threw wildly past first, allowing the winning run to score.

When Chicago won, one armed-to-the-teeth fan stood up and shouted to his cohorts, "Load! Load at will! Fire!" And they did. The last remaining ammo was spent in one booming volley.

Said the *Daily Inter Ocean,* one of Chicago's major newspapers: "The actions of the spectators and the noise of the revolver shots reminded one of a pleasant little afternoon—at a lynching bee."

FRANK GERMANO
Brooklyn, NL · September 16, 1940

The cry of "Kill the umpire!" is as old as baseball itself. Fans don't really mean it, although some wouldn't mind if an ump got roughed up a little. And that's what fan Frank Germano was counting on.

After the last out in a 4–3 Brooklyn Dodgers loss to the visiting Cincinnati Reds, Germano rushed down on the field and blindsided burly, 6-foot, 3-inch, 230-pound umpire George Magerkurth, knocking him to the ground. Magerkurth had made a disputed call in the top of the 10th inning that ultimately led to Cincy's winning run.

Everyone at Ebbets Field was shocked when the snarling fan, who was half the size of the mighty Mage, landed several good punches before he was pulled off by the other umpires. In the confusion, fellow

Germano getting in his licks © BETTMANN/CORBIS

ump Bill Stewart caught a kick in the head that opened up a gash. The only bruises Magerkurth suffered were to his ego.

Germano was arrested for assault and battery. At the arraignment later, Magerkurth learned the 21-year-old punk was on parole for a petty larceny conviction. The big-hearted ump asked authorities to drop the charges, explaining, "I'm the father of a boy myself." But the charges weren't dropped, so Germano was sent back to the clink. As for the umpire, he shouldn't have been so forgiving.

A few years later, Germano appeared before Brooklyn judge Samuel Leibowitz on a pickpocketing charge. Remembering him from the

Magerkurth assault, the judge asked Germano, "How did you come to lose your head that day? Were you really all that stirred up because the Dodgers lost the game?"

"I was pretty stirred up," Germano admitted. "I was mad enough to slug Magerkurth, all right. The Dodgers shoulda won easy." Then he lowered his voice and confessed, "But just between you and me, Judge, I had a partner in the stands that day. We wuz doin' a little business."

What Germano was doing was creating a disturbance so his partner could pick a few pockets.

PETE ADELIS
Philadelphia, AL, NL · 1940–1955

Pete Adelis—better known as "The Iron Lung of Shibe Park"—was one of baseball's most outrageous hecklers.

The 6-foot, 280-pound department store employee wore a size-52 coat and owned a booming voice that could shatter glass. He was such a tenacious tormentor that his favorite team, the hometown Philadelphia Athletics, once took him on the road to harangue their opponents. The New York Yankees, among his most abused targets, tried to get on his good side by giving him free tickets to Yankee Stadium. It worked. More than once they imported him to New York to intimidate their foes—but never the A's.

Also known as "Leather Lungs," "Foghorn," and "Loud Mouth," Adelis would yell and howl and bang on pans and a helmet he wore. But he was most known for his incessant, biting tongue-lashings of players, managers, and umpires. Although he was partial to the A's, he also taunted on behalf of the Phillies.

He was such a famous heckler that the *Sporting News* published his seven "Rules of Scientific Heckling" in its September 8, 1948, issue. They were:

1. No profanity.
2. Nothing purely personal.
3. Keep pouring it on.
4. Know your players.
5. Don't be shouted down.
6. Take it as well as give it.
7. Give the old timer a chance—he was a rookie once.

Adelis did not follow his own Rule No. 2, however. Like a gumshoe who enjoys digging up dirt, he diligently collected juicy tidbits on the private lives of the players and then bellowed the malicious gossip for all the players and fans to hear. "When Pete boomed out something personal, you could see the player just start shaking," recalled his brother Walter.

"Pete used little known facts like if a player was out the night before with some woman and got drunk. These were things a player just wouldn't expect to hear on the field. The player would say to himself, 'Who is this guy and how did he know about that?' The things Pete yelled at them really surprised and shamed them. They just couldn't escape his voice because it carried all over the park."

Once in 1948, umpire Larry Goetz stopped a game for 15 minutes in a futile effort to get someone with authority to throw Adelis out of the park because of his heckling.

Dozens of players wished The Iron Lung of Shibe Park would have been barred from entering the stadium. "One of the players Pete got on the most was Pat Seerey, an outfielder for the Chicago White Sox in 1948," recalled Walter. "It so happened that Pete and I were in New York to see the Yankees on the day Seerey hit four home runs against the A's at Shibe Park [on June 18]. After the game, Seerey wanted to know where Pete was. Seerey figured the only reason he had such a good day was because Pete wasn't there."

MARY "THE HORSE LADY" OTT
St. Louis, NL, AL · 1926–1955

With a raucous, scornful hee-hawing laugh, Mary "The Horse Lady" Ott tormented umpires and opposing players at Sportsman's Park in St. Louis for nearly 30 years.

Nicknamed for her shrill, sarcastic whinny, Mary sat behind the home-team dugout at both Cardinals and Browns games. From her box seat, the squat 180-pound Horse Lady had the lung power to make afternoons miserable for players by jangling their nerves and rattling their concentration. With subtle nuances, her loud neighing would convey derision, disdain, or disrespect toward her target. Her loud voice was kept well lubricated by a constant supply of beer.

"I like scientific rooting—something that helps the home boys win and makes the other guys sore," she once told a reporter. "I figure if I really work on them, I can knock a lot of them pitchers out of the box in three innings."

Mary first attracted attention in 1926 when she harassed plate umpire Bill Klem with her insulting braying. The veteran arbiter threatened to have her bodily removed from the park, but she just laughed at him.

"There was never anybody like Mary," recalled Bob Burns, retired reporter for the *St. Louis Globe-Democrat,* who saw—and, more accurately, heard—her at hundreds of games. "She had a voice that you can't describe. Everybody in the stadium could hear her hee-hawing.

"She didn't have specific cheers, or words or yells. She just had this awful screeching laugh. She had a whole repertoire of them. If an opposing player struck out or made an error, she gave a sarcastic, insulting, braying laugh that carried like nothing I've ever heard before."

The Horse Lady drove Philadelphia Athletics Hall of Famer Al Simmons crazy. One time when he struck out, Mary cut loose with one of her special whinnies. Simmons just smiled. When he struck out a second time, Mary really unloaded on him. This time, he stomped back to the dugout. The third time up, Mary bellowed her horse laugh while he was in the batter's box. "You could see Al shaking from all the way up in the press box," Burns recalled. "He struck out again and this time he blew up. He thought about going into the stands after her, but some teammates pulled him back. [Manager] Connie Mack had to take him out of the game because he was so shook up."

In the late 1930s, Mary loved to harass Philadelphia Phillies outfielder Morrie Arnovich. During a doubleheader she hounded him with her ridiculing laugh. Late in the nightcap, she blasted Arnovich just as he was getting ready to swing. "He must have jumped 5 feet out of the box," Burns recalled. "Then he got into a big argument with the umpire. Morrie waved his bat and pointed over at Mary's box, wanting the umpire to shut her up. The umpire refused. Morrie was so frustrated that he started pounding the ground with his bat."

Mary disliked catchers, especially Shanty Hogan, who played mostly for the Braves and Giants in a career that spanned from 1925 to 1937. "He tried to get back at her by imitating her laugh," said Burns. "But he couldn't come close to equaling it."

The Horse Lady wasn't content to annoy opposing players on the field. She liked to ambush them after the game at the clubhouse door, offering up her sarcastic laugh as they left the stadium.

"Nobody ever knew exactly who she was or where she came from," said Burns. "There was one story that she was really the madame of one of the city's better houses of ill repute. Another story said that she was the widow of a wealthy plumber. She always loved baseball, but when her husband was alive, he wouldn't let her go to the games. So when he died, she used his money to buy season tickets every year."

And she brayed and neighed at game after game while players prayed and prayed she'd just shut up.

JEFFREY MAIER
New York, AL · October 9, 1996

All 12-year-old Jeffrey Maier wanted was a baseball. But in his effort to get one, he turned a potential flyout into a crucial home run that helped the New York Yankees to a controversial come-from-behind playoff victory.

In the first game of the 1996 American League Championship Series, the Baltimore Orioles were leading New York 4–3 in the bottom of the eighth inning at Yankee Stadium. With one out and nobody on base, Derek Jeter hit a deep fly ball that sent O's right fielder Tony Tarasco to the wall. Jeffrey, a Yankees fan who was at the game as a birthday present, reached over the fence separating the stands from the field 9 feet below and tried to glove the ball, but instead deflected it into the crowd.

"I didn't mean to do anything bad," said Jeffrey at the time. "I'm just a 12-year-old kid trying to catch a ball."

Right field umpire Rich Garcia immediately signaled a home run, which tied the game at 4–4. Tarasco and Baltimore manager Davey Johnson protested vehemently, claiming the kid in the black T-shirt, pointing to Jeffrey, had interfered with a catchable ball and, thus, Jeter should have been called out for spectator interference. Garcia stuck to his ruling and tossed Johnson for arguing too fiercely. The Yankees won in the 11th inning on a Bernie Williams walk-off homer.

The Orioles had played the game under protest, but their appeal was denied by American League president Gene Budig, who said judgment calls, which this one was, can't be protested.

For a kid from Old Tappan, New Jersey, who was just trying to catch a ball, Jeffrey gave a boost to his team.

Propelled by the tainted victory, the Yankees won the ALCS in five games and went on to beat the Atlanta Braves in six games in the World Series to claim their first championship since 1978.

The Orioles, convinced they lost because of Jeffrey's interference, were furious. Tarasco claimed he would have made the catch if it hadn't been for Jeffrey. Replays clearly showed that the boy had indeed interfered.

Even Garcia admitted that it was fan interference after seeing the replay. But by then it was too late.

"I've seen it a hundred times on replay," the umpire told *Referee* magazine in 2001. "I've seen it a hundred times in my dreams. I'm

Maier, the Yankees' 10th man

waiting for the ball to hit his glove or go over the wall or do whatever and, all of a sudden, [Tarasco] jumped up and there's no ball anywhere. I never saw the kid reach out and [deflect] the ball. My first instinct was that the ball had to be above his glove and it had to be above the fence, so it had to be a home run. There was no doubt in my mind."

As a result of the play, Yankees owner George Steinbrenner had a railing installed on the top of the right field wall to prevent fans from reaching over it.

That did little to mollify Orioles fans who began wearing T-shirts that read, "Beat the Yanks, Beat the Umps, Spank the Kids."

Meanwhile, in New York, Jeffrey had his 15 minutes of fame. The *New York Daily News* arranged for Jeffrey and his family to sit behind the Yankees dugout for Game 2 in exchange for photos and a story about his experience. He appeared on national talk shows, including *Good Morning America, Regis & Kathie Lee,* and *The Late Show with David Letterman.* He was even awarded the key to New York City by Mayor Rudy Giuliani.

Ever since, Jeffrey has been asked to tell how he helped the Yankees win the pennant.

"Being 12, I had never seen a ball hit that high before," he told the *Washington Post* in 2006. "But I was able to get to the spot. I had a pretty good idea of where it was going. It's what every kid wants to do at a ball-game—catch a ball. It was my ballplayer instincts. I saw a ball in the air, and I was going to go get it."

Hard-core Baltimore fans have never forgotten Jeffrey, said Tony Pente, who operates the fan website, orioleshangout.com. "I hate to say it," he said in the *Post* article, "but for some people, there's almost a hatred of him—to this day."

BAT GRABBER
New York, AL · September 22, 1927

Babe Ruth had an easier time hitting his 56th home run of the 1927 season than he did circling the bases because of an over-eager fan.

In a thrilling game against the Detroit Tigers at Yankee Stadium, Ruth stepped to the plate in the bottom of the ninth inning. New York was trailing 7–6 but had the tying run on first and no outs.

In the seats behind first, a freckle-faced youngster in knickers pleaded at the top of his lungs for the Babe to get a hit. Ruth, who had gone hitless in four previous plate appearances, couldn't help but hear the kid, who had been imploring him to do something all afternoon.

With the stage set, the tension high, and the youngster on tenterhooks, Ruth belted a booming drive that chipped a piece out of a seat six rows from the top of the right field bleachers for a dramatic game-winning two-run homer.

Ruth, who decided to carry his bat with him, went into his famous home run trot. Meanwhile, the ecstatic young fan leaped out of his seat, cut across the diamond, and caught up with the slugger near third.

Flailing away with both hands, the deliriously happy boy, who was about 10 years old, pounded the Babe on the back—and then tried to swipe his bat. But Ruth wasn't about to let go of his cherished piece of lumber. Instead, he gripped the bat handle tighter and continued toward home plate. However, the kid wouldn't give up his hold on the bat either, creating one of the most bizarre scenes ever witnessed on a home run trot. Ruth had to lug the little boy across home plate.

As the *New York Times* reported the next day, "The youngster was like the tail of a flying comet, holding onto the bat for dear life and being dragged into the dugout by the Babe."

STADIUM RAIDERS
Washington, AL · September 30, 1971

The Washington Senators were just one out away from winning their final game in the nation's capital. The franchise was packing up and moving to Texas to begin play the following year as the Rangers.

There was a collective lump in the throats of the Senators as they were about to give their fans a going-away gift to remember—a victory. Instead, the fans gave the Senators something to remember—a forfeit.

For Washington's farewell home game, the 14,460 fans on hand came out to Robert F. Kennedy Stadium not so much to cheer their team against the New York Yankees as to express their contempt for owner Bob Short. Chants of "We want Short! We want Short!" throughout the game kept the crowd in a frenzy. Adding to the electric atmosphere, the Senators stormed back from a 5–1 deficit to vault into a 7–5 lead entering the ninth inning.

Washington pitcher Joe Grzenda got the first two Yankees out. With victory all but secured, the fans weren't ready to say good-bye to baseball without making a statement. As Grzenda prepared to pitch to Horace Clarke, thousands of boisterous fans spontaneously swarmed onto the field. Police were powerless to stop the crowd from swiping the bases and home plate and ripping up the turf. Fans began dancing on the bullpen roofs, which nearly collapsed under their weight. People attacked the scoreboard, pulling down letters and even the lightbulbs for souvenirs.

Within minutes, the game, the ballpark, and the Senators' franchise were in shambles. The umpires then ordered the contest forfeited to the Yankees. Instead of a triumphant 7–5 finale, the Washington Senators lost 9–0 in their final game ever, all thanks to their fans.

PILOT ERROR

*For the Most Outlandish Managerial Actions of
All Time, The Baseball Hall of Shame™ Inducts:*

BILLY MARTIN
Manager · New York, AL · September 20, 1985

New York Yankees skipper Billy Martin scratched his nose at the worst possible moment and helped trigger an opponent's rally that cost his team the game during a tight pennant race.

Martin put his nose out of joint in a rare mental lapse when he forgot that when your sign for a pitchout is rubbing your schnozz, you need to resist the urge to scratch it.

In the bottom of the seventh inning of a 2–2 game against the host Baltimore Orioles, the O's had two outs with runner Alan Wiggins on first and Lee Lacy at the plate. Before the first pitch to Lacy, Yankees catcher Butch Wynegar glanced over at the New York dugout. At that exact moment, Martin had an itch on his nose and rubbed it. Naturally, Wynegar assumed the manager had ordered a pitchout. So the catcher called for one, and pitcher Rich Bordi complied, much to Martin's surprise. Wiggins wasn't running and Lacy drew ball one.

After the count went to 2-and-0, Wynegar saw Martin scratch his nose again. Assuming that his skipper had stolen the Orioles' signs, Wynegar ordered another pitchout, which Bordi threw for ball three. Wiggins wasn't running. Now way behind in the count, Bordi eventually walked Lacy. The next two batters drove in run-scoring singles, and the Yankees went on to lose 4–2. It was New York's eighth straight loss and halted their last-ditch drive to catch the eventual division winners, the Toronto Blue Jays.

After the game, Martin, who had seen just about everything else go wrong in the previous week, admitted he should have known better. "At first, I couldn't believe it when I saw the pitchouts," he said. "I couldn't understand why Butch called for them. Then I realized what *I* had done."

DICK WILLIAMS
Manager

OZZIE VIRGIL
Acting Manager

JACK KROL
Acting-Acting Manager
San Diego, NL · August 12, 1984

During a beanball war that masqueraded as a baseball game, the San Diego Padres needed four managers. That's because the manager, the acting manager, and the acting-acting manager were all ejected. Fortunately, the acting-acting-acting manager kept his cool.

The game got off on a bad note when, on the very first pitch, Atlanta Braves hurler Pascual Perez drilled San Diego's leadoff hitter Alan Wiggins with a fastball. The ticked-off batter jawed with Perez all the way to first base.

After that, Perez was a marked man every time he came to bat. He ducked out of the way of a high fastball behind his head in the second inning. Two frames later, Padres starting pitcher Ed Whitson came close to knocking off Perez's noggin with a steamer. Home plate umpire Steve Rippley had seen enough and ejected Padres manager Dick Williams for ordering the beanball and Whitson for throwing it.

Coach Ozzie Virgil replaced Williams, and Greg Booker relieved Whitson. But Virgil and Booker were sent to the showers in the sixth inning after Booker threw at Perez's head, triggering a bench-clearing brawl.

Coach Jack Krol took Virgil's place in the dugout while reliever Greg Harris went to the mound. Meanwhile, Perez was still pitching and doing a damn good job of dodging beanballs.

But in the eighth inning, San Diego hurler Craig Lefferts finally nailed Perez on the elbow with a pitch—prompting another free-for-all between the teams and getting Krol and Lefferts booted out of the game.

The Padres were now piloted by Coach Harry Dunlop, their fourth manager of the game. But the beanball war went on.

Braves manager Joe Torre wisely brought in reliever Donnie Moore to pitch the ninth, but unwisely ordered him to plunk leadoff batter Graig Nettles, which Moore did. That ignited the third brawl of the game. When the dust was settling, Rippley tossed Torre and Moore. Torre's ejection meant a record total of six managers were used by both teams in the shameful game won by the Braves 5–3.

Said umpire crew chief John McSherry, "I would think it was one of the stranger days I've ever seen, if not the strangest."

WILBERT ROBINSON
Manager · Brooklyn, NL · 1925

Wilbert Robinson was a charter member of the Bonehead Club of Ebbets Field, which he founded at the beginning of the 1925 season.

As manager of the Brooklyn Dodgers (then known as the Robins), Robinson came up with the idea as a way to cut down on the mental and physical blunders that were trademarks of the team back then. The rules were simple. Every time a player pulled a boner, he put $10 in the pot and gained automatic membership in the Bonehead Club. The manager figured that given a typical Brooklyn season, by the end of the year they would have more money in the pot than they would get from

Robinson, charter member of the Bonehead Club

the winner's share of the World Series take—assuming they made it that far (which they didn't).

The club didn't last long—only one game. Robinson called the whole thing off after he handed the umpires the wrong lineup card at the start of the game and had to ante up the first 10 bucks.

LOU BOUDREAU
Manager · Cleveland, AL · 1942

Lou Boudreau had a cold. Lou Boudreau blew his nose—and the game along with it.

During his first year as the Cleveland Indians player-manager, Boudreau came down with a terrible cold, so he took himself out of the lineup. Although he didn't feel well enough to play his regular position at shortstop, he could still manage and flash signs from the dugout to his third base coach, Ski "Spinach" Melillo. One of Boudreau's signals, putting a towel to his face, meant a double steal.

But Boudreau promptly forgot it. Late in a tie game, the Indians had two of the team's slowest runners on first and second base with two outs.

After a sneezing jag, Boudreau unthinkingly reached for a towel to blow his runny nose. The next thing the young 25-year-old manager knew, both runners lumbered toward third and second respectively. The only people in the stadium more stunned than Boudreau were the opposing infielders, who never expected to be handed such a gift. The lead runner was easily thrown out at third, ending the Indians' scoring threat.

After the inning, Boudreau barked at Melillo for putting on such a stupid play "with those truck horses on base."

Melillo calmly explained that it was Boudreau who gave the signal—and it was Boudreau who blew it.

Years later Boudreau recalled, "After the game, which we lost, [team owner] Bill Veeck asked me to explain my strategy and I 'fessed up. Bill told me, 'Next time you have to blow your nose, go into the runway out of sight.'"

CHUCK DRESSEN
Manager · Brooklyn, NL · October 3, 1951

Brooklyn Dodgers hurler Ralph Branca took the fall for "The Shot Heard 'Round the World." But it was his manager, Chuck Dressen, who was just as responsible for the most famous home run in all of baseball.

Dressen made at least five critical decisions, which all proved to be dead wrong, that ripped the 1951 National League pennant right out of the Dodgers' fingers . . . and saddled Branca with the blame.

Brooklyn held a seemingly insurmountable 13½-game lead over the New York Giants on August 11. But the Giants went on a historic streak, winning 37 of their last 44 games to force a best-of-three playoff to determine who would challenge the New York Yankees for the world championship.

Even before the first pitch of the playoff, Dressen blundered. Because Brooklyn won the coin toss to decide home-field advantage, he was given the choice to play the first game at home and the next two on the road or play the first game on the road and the next two at home. Against conventional wisdom, he chose the former, reasoning that if the Dodgers won their only home game, they would have two chances to win one on the road. Apparently, he hadn't thought of the consequences if his team lost the opener and would be forced to win the next two on the road.

Brooklyn did lose their only home game, 3–1. But the team roared back to take the second contest at the Polo Grounds, 10–0. It seemed Dressen's decision wasn't going to matter because in the finale, the Dodgers carried a 4–1 lead into the bottom of the ninth inning and looked like they would be the National League champs.

Unfortunately for Brooklyn and its fans, Dressen still had to make several more decisions—ones that all backfired.

Starter Don Newcombe, pitching with only two days' rest, threw brilliantly throughout the game, but by the ninth he had run out of gas. Although Newcombe wanted to take himself out, Dressen left him in—a decision he would regret.

Alvin Dark led off the bottom of the frame with a single. With a three-run lead in the last inning, the manager could have positioned his infielders for a possible double play. That meant moving first baseman Gil Hodges a few steps toward second base. But Dressen had Hodges guarding the line, opening up a huge gap between first and second, which is exactly where the next batter, Don Mueller, placed a single.

The tying run was now at the plate, causing Dodgers fans to squirm. But Monte Irvin hit a pop foul to Hodges for the first out. However, Whitey Lockman followed with a double down the left field line, scoring Dark and moving Mueller to third. Mueller injured his ankle sliding into the bag and was replaced by Clint Hartung.

Finally realizing that Newcombe was spent, Dressen decided he needed a new pitcher to face slugger Bobby Thomson. The manager checked with bullpen coach Clyde Sukeforth on which reliever to bring in—Carl Erskine or Ralph Branca, who were both warming up. Erskine was a rested 16-game winner. Branca had pitched eight innings two days earlier in the opener and was the losing pitcher, having served up a two-run homer to Thomson that proved to be the winning margin. So what did Dressen do? He brought in Branca.

Dressen and Branca discussed whether or not to intentionally walk Thomson, who had 31 homers—including two earlier in the season off Branca—and 98 RBIs while batting .292. With first base open and a young, unproven rookie outfielder named Willie Mays on deck, an intentional walk made sense, but Dressen decided to pitch to Thomson. Of all the wrong decisions the manager made, this one proved the most disastrous.

On Branca's second pitch, Thomson blasted a line drive into the left field stands. As Giants broadcaster Russ Hodges put it, "The Giants win the pennant! The Giants win the pennant! The Giants win the pennant! The Giants win the pennant! The Giants win the pennant!"

That probably wouldn't have happened had Chuck Dressen made just one right decision in the last inning.

GENE MAUCH
Manager · Philadelphia, NL · August 16, 1961

The 1961 Philadelphia Phillies were so inept that they lost everything but their way to the ballpark. By late summer, baseball's biggest bumblers had piled up 19 losses in a row—and manager Gene Mauch was going crazy.

After trying everything to no avail, Mauch resorted to one of the zaniest managerial decisions ever. He imposed a reverse curfew during a stay in Milwaukee.

"Gene told us, 'It's a $100 fine if I catch any of you in your room *before* 4:30 in the morning,'" recalled pitcher Jack Baldschun. "So we all went out for nice long dinners or to the movies, and then to some bar. Only, the taverns closed around two. When I got back to the hotel, there was half the team in the lobby, trying to sleep."

Incredibly, Mauch's wacky plan almost worked. Later that day his team was leading the Braves in the eighth inning. But Milwaukee tied the game, forcing it into extra innings, and the pooped Phils ran out of steam, losing 7–6.

The Phillies didn't break their skein until they had dropped three more games for a total of 23 straight—the longest losing streak in modern baseball history.

JOHN MCNAMARA
Manager · Boston, AL · October 25, 1986

Boston Red Sox manager John McNamara let his heart rule his mind in a decision that left fans second-guessing, turned an All-Star into an undeserved scapegoat, and let the team's first World Series title in 68 years slip away.

The Red Sox had taken a 3-games-to-2 lead in the 1986 World Series entering Game 6 against the New York Mets at Shea Stadium. In a pitching duel between Boston's Roger Clemens and New York's Bob Ojeda, the contest went into extra innings. The Red Sox then scored two runs in the top of the 10th to go up 5–3.

Normally in the late innings, for defensive purposes, McNamara would use Dave Stapleton to replace 36-year-old first baseman Bill Buckner, who was hampered by sore and injured legs. But the skipper wanted Buckner to experience the joy of winning a championship while playing his regular position at first. As well-meaning as it was, McNamara's good intention turned into a very bad decision.

Reliever Calvin Schiraldi retired the first two batters in the bottom of the 10th. The Red Sox needed just one more out to claim their first World Series title since 1918. Just one more. But then Gary Carter and Kevin Mitchell hit singles. Schiraldi got two quick strikes on the next batter, Ray Knight. Boston was now one little strike away from that long-sought championship. Just one little strike. Alas, Knight singled to center field to score Carter and send Mitchell to third. It was now 5–4.

McNamara then brought in reliever Bob Stanley to face Mookie Wilson. However, Stanley uncorked a wild pitch, allowing Mitchell to score the tying run and moving Knight to second. Stanley settled down and coaxed Wilson to hit a slow roller down the first base line right to Buckner. But as the Red Sox Nation gasped in horror, the ball trickled through Buckner's battered legs. Knight raced around third and scored the winning run, forcing a Game 7, which the Mets won 8–5 to claim the World Series title.

Although there was plenty of blame to go around—McNamara pulled Clemens in the seventh even though the hurler was still throwing heat; Schiraldi couldn't get the last out; Stanley flung a disastrous wild pitch—Buckner was held responsible for the most crushing loss in the anguished history of the Red Sox. He was the recipient of hate mail, obscene calls, and sports show tirades. He was the brunt of cruel jokes like "Did you hear Bill Buckner tried to commit suicide after the World Series? He stepped in front of a bus, but it went between his legs."

Eventually the Red Sox Nation forgave Buckner and, four years later, gave him a resounding minute-long standing ovation on Opening Day in 1990. Yes, he had committed a crucial error. But it never would have happened had McNamara just stuck to his winning policy of replacing the aging first baseman in the late innings.

ROUND TRIP-UPS

For the Most Ridiculous Home Runs of All Time,
The Baseball Hall of Shame™ Inducts:

ED DELAHANTY
Center Fielder · Philadelphia, NL · June 1, 1891

If ever there was a four-bag travesty, this was it.

Ed Delahanty unwittingly took part in a round-tripper that was so outrageous even the fans who witnessed it didn't believe what they saw.

It happened at the Philadelphia Baseball Park (also known as the Huntingdon Street Grounds) where the Philadelphia Phillies were playing host to the Chicago Cubs (then known as the Colts). The stadium had one unique characteristic—a "doghouse." It was a tiny structure with an arched doorway that looked like it had been built for man's best friend. The doghouse, as it was called, rested at the base of the flagpole in left-center field and was used to store numbers for the scoreboard.

Even though it was in fair territory, no one had ever paid any attention to the doghouse until the top of the eighth inning in this particular game. Chicago first baseman Cap Anson stepped to the plate with two runners on base and the score deadlocked 3–3. On the first pitch, Anson drilled a high drive that hit the flagpole and dropped straight down into the narrow space between the doghouse and the outfield fence.

Delahanty, who was playing center field, quickly draped himself over the roof of the little house and tried to recover the ball but failed. In desperation, he dropped to his knees and crawled partway through the narrow door of the doghouse, hoping to get to the ball. But then he remembered why he was nicknamed "Big Ed." At 6-foot-1, he was the most muscular player on the team. He couldn't squeeze any more of his body through the opening and he couldn't back out. Big Ed was stuck in the doghouse.

"From the grandstand, all that was visible was the rear elevation of his county seat," wrote Dr. W. N. Pringle, a spectator whose account of the bizarre incident was published 16 years later. "His heels [were] kicking in the air in a lively manner in his frantic effort to extricate himself.

"In the meantime, Mr. Anson was clearing the bases at a lively clip amid the greatest excitement I ever saw on a ball field. I do not think there were a dozen people in that immense crowd who were not on their feet, laughing, cheering and yelling themselves hoarse, and throwing hats, canes and umbrellas in the air."

By the time left fielder Billy Hamilton rushed over and yanked Delahanty free, Anson had crossed home plate with a three-run, inside-the-doghouse home run—the decisive blow in Chicago's 6–3 victory.

JIMMY MCALEER
Center Fielder · Cleveland, NL · 1892

In one of the most bizarre plays in baseball history, Jimmy McAleer was credited with a home run even though he was tagged out at the plate with the ball stuck in a tomato can.

It reportedly happened in a National League game between the Boston Braves (then known as the Beaneaters) and the Cleveland Spiders at the Congress Street Park in Boston. The ballpark was unusual because it had no outfield fence. Instead, the outfield was bordered by a garbage dump filled with trash and old tin cans.

The score was tied late in the game when McAleer belted a line drive past Boston's center fielder Hugh Duffy and into a pile of cans in the dump. Duffy raced over to the spot where the ball had landed and, to his dismay, discovered it had wound up smack inside a rusty tomato can. Try as he might, he couldn't yank that ball out. It was stuck tight.

By now, McAleer was rounding second base. Duffy had to do something fast. In desperation, he picked up the can—with the ball still inside—and heaved it to teammate Billy Nash at third base. But it was too late. McAleer had already sped past third and was steaming for home with the lead run.

When Nash caught the tomato can, he looked at it in amazement for a split second, then relayed it with rifle-like velocity to catcher Charlie Bennett at the plate. Bennett snared the can and put the tag on McAleer as the Cleveland runner slid across the plate. Boston fans whooped because Bennett had clearly tagged McAleer before the runner had reached home. But even though the umpire saw the ball in the tomato can, he insisted that McAleer was safe.

When the Boston players began to argue, the ump lifted his hand to silence them and said, "Gentlemen, since when is a runner out just because he's been tagged with a rusty tomato can?"

LU CLINTON
Right Fielder · Boston, AL · August 9, 1960

Lu Clinton made a football and baseball play at the same time . . . in the same game. He drop-kicked a winner for the other team.

During his rookie year with the Boston Red Sox, Clinton was playing right field in a 1960 game against the home Cleveland Indians. In the bottom of the fifth inning, Cleveland's Vic Power stepped to the plate with the score knotted at 3–3 and a runner on first and two out. He slammed a high drive over Clinton's head. The ball hit the top of the wire fence and bounced back toward Clinton, who was running with his back to the infield.

Before the right fielder could react to the carom, the ball fell in front of him. But it never touched the ground. Instead, the ball hit the foot of the still-running Clinton—who then accidentally kicked it right over the fence. Because the ball never touched the ground, the hit was ruled a home run—one that proved to be the game-winner.

"Our pitcher that day was Bill Monbouquette," recalled Clinton. "He didn't say a whole lot after the game. He didn't have to. I knew he was really hacked off at me."

HANK AARON
Right Fielder · Milwaukee, NL · August 18, 1965

Milwaukee Braves slugger Hank Aaron blasted a monster homer onto the roof of the old Busch Stadium in St. Louis, only to be called out because he had stepped out of the batter's box.

The homer that wasn't occurred in the top of the eighth inning of a 3–3 tie on a pitch from Cardinals hurler Curt Simmons. "Simmons used to drive me crazy with his herky-jerky delivery and his floating change of pace," Aaron wrote in his biography, *I Had a Hammer*.

Aaron decided to wait for the change-up, and when it floated toward the plate, Hammerin' Hank just couldn't help himself. He walked up on the pitch and clubbed it about 450 feet onto the pavilion roof in right field for an apparent tie-breaking home run.

Aaron was halfway to first base when Cardinals catcher Bob Uecker began jumping up and down and shouting at plate umpire Chris Pelekoudas that Aaron had hit the pitch when his left foot was completely out of the batter's box. The umpire agreed and called the hitter out.

"Aaron was running up on the change-up," the umpire explained later. "His foot was at least 3 feet out when he hit the home run."

Fiery Milwaukee manager Bobby Bragan charged out of the dugout to protest the ruling and got a quick thumb. "I told Pelekoudas it was either a grudge call or he just wanted to get his name in the papers," said Bragan after the game, which the Braves won 5–3. "That's when he threw me out."

In his biography, Aaron wrote, "I'm sure Pelekoudas never doubted that he was right, and I won't swear to you that I didn't step over the line of the batter's box, but it was nothing that I or other hitters hadn't done before. Really, I blame the whole thing on that damn Uecker."

Without that infraction, Aaron would have finished his career with 756 home runs rather than 755—a record that stood for 33 years.

JOSE CANSECO
Right Fielder · Texas, AL · May 26, 1993

Jose Canseco became the first player to hit 40 homers and steal 40 bases in a season. But the on-the-field moment for which he will be remembered most is misplaying a fly ball off his head for a home run—a blunder that will live in infamy on every classic blooper reel on TV, DVD, and the Internet.

In a game against the Cleveland Indians, Canseco was playing right field for the visiting Texas Rangers, who were leading 3–1 in the bottom of the fourth inning, when Carlos Martinez came to the plate. Martinez was not considered much of a power hitter and Canseco was not considered much of a fielder, but together they combined for one of the most hilarious home runs ever hit in Major League history.

Martinez lofted a deep fly to right-center field. Canseco raced to the warning track, reached up with his glove, and then . . . boink! . . . the ball landed on top of his noggin and bounced over the fence for a home run.

As a befuddled Canseco looked around for the ball and adjusted his cap, center fielder David Hulse burst out laughing and then told him the bad news—his header went for a homer.

"I really didn't feel it," said Canseco after the game, which Texas lost 7–6. "I really don't know what happened other than I was looking for the wall, and the ball nicked off my glove and hit my head. I'll be on ESPN for a month. I guess I'm just an entertainer."

Canseco's header for a homer   RON KUNTZ

When reporters asked teammate Julio Franco if he had ever seen such a play, the Texas infielder replied, "Yeah, in a cartoon."

Playing along to hide his embarrassment, Canseco rubbed his head and asked, "Anybody got a bandage?"

The chagrined outfielder autographed his cap and wrote the date and city in which the mortifying event took place. Then he gave away the hat, which ended up in collector Seth Swirsky's baseball memorabilia collection alongside the ball that Bill Buckner booted in Game 6 of the 1986 World Series.

The day after the heady homer, the Harrisburg Heat of the National Professional Soccer League offered Canseco a contract. "I haven't had the opportunity to fully evaluate his foot skills," Heat coach Jim Pollihan told reporters at the time, "but he certainly possesses great potential for the head ball. In these days of the two-sport star, we think Jose could help us tremendously."

In 1998, *This Week in Baseball* ranked Canseco's misplay as the greatest blooper in the show's history.

ABNER POWELL
Right Fielder · Cincinnati, NL · August 22, 1886

William Van Winkle "Chicken" Wolf of the Louisville Colonels hit an inside-the-park home run that could only be described as a doggone shame.

He never would have made it around the bases had Cincinnati Red Stockings right fielder Abner Powell not tangled with a snarling canine.

At the time, Louisville was in the American Association, a major league that battled the National League for supremacy. In the game in Louisville, the score was knotted 3–3 when Wolf, the Colonels' right fielder, stepped to the plate. All eyes were on Wolf, who had smacked a game-tying homer in his last at-bat. No eyes were on the curled-up mangy mongrel dozing at the base of the center field fence.

That would soon change. Wolf slammed a drive toward Powell in deep right-center field. With the crack of the bat, Powell took off—and so did the suddenly awakened dog. The mutt reached Powell before the outfielder reached the ball.

Like a hound after a mailman, the dog clamped its iron jaws on Powell's pants just below the back of the knee and wouldn't let go. While Wolf galloped around the bases, Powell tried to shake himself free. Then in desperation he started hopping toward the ball, dragging the dog behind him.

By the time Powell broke free from the mutt's grip, Wolf had crossed home plate with the winning "inside-the-bark" home run.

Poor Powell. He's best remembered after more than a century and a quarter for dogging it in the outfield.

JASON MICHAELS
Center Fielder · Philadelphia, NL · September 9, 2004

Philadelphia Phillies center fielder Jason Michaels was oh so close to making a circus catch. But instead, he ended up accidentally swatting the ball with his hands into the seats for a ridiculously bizarre home run.

With the home team Atlanta Braves trailing 4–3 in the fourth inning, Braves batter Charles Thomas led off with a deep drive to center field. Michaels got a great jump on the ball and raced to the edge of the warning track and reached up. The ball deflected off his glove and headed toward the ground. Trying to snare the ball before it landed, Michaels slapped at it while still on the run. To his horror, he inadvertently knocked the ball into the first row of seats for a game-tying—and the year's weirdest—home run.

Michaels planted his face against the outfield wall, not believing what had just happened.

"I was at a loss for words," Michaels told reporters after the game, which, to his relief, the Phillies won 9–4. "I was like, 'You've got to be kidding me.' I almost didn't think it was real."

Phillies manager Larry Bowa had never seen anything like it during all his years in baseball. "It was like jai alai," he said. "He had it on his hand and flipped it out."

Michaels' combination of great effort and lousy luck was deserving of national recognition. Fans voted his uncanny trick of turning a would-be spectacular catch into a home run as Blooper of the Year in MLB.com's This Year in Baseball Awards. Michaels beat out an adventuresome squirrel that held up a Yankees-Indians game with an unsupervised tour of Jacobs Field.

CAP ANSON
First Baseman · Chicago, NL · June 24, 1892

Tom Brown of the Louisville Colonels raced around the bases for the only score of the game because of Cap Anson's horseplay—literally.

In a pitching duel at South Side Park, home of the Chicago Cubs (then known as the Colts), Brown slapped a grounder to shortstop Bill Dahlen. But Dahlen's throw to Anson at first was wide, and the ball ricocheted off the grandstand wall and bounded in foul territory down toward the right field corner.

Anson reportedly went chasing after the ball when he saw a huge white sway-backed horse galloping hell-bent for leather straight at him. It was Sam, a nag belonging to the team's groundskeeper, who used the horse to pull a lawnmower. Someone had forgotten to close the gate to Sam's corral. And the horse, who for some reason always hated Anson, went after the first baseman with a vengeance.

Anson forgot about the ball and concentrated on running for his life. While Sam was chasing Anson, Brown was galloping around the bases. By the time Sam was corralled, Brown had already scored the game-winning run on an error-triggered "home run" that left fans roaring until they were hoarse.

LASTINGS MILLEDGE
Left Fielder · Pittsburgh, NL · May 6, 2010

When Pittsburgh Pirates hitter Lastings Milledge drove the ball deep into left field at PNC Park, the fans cheered, fireworks exploded, music blared, and he went into a home run trot. There was just one problem. It wasn't a home run.

In a home game against the Chicago Cubs, the Pirates were enjoying an 8–0 cushion when Milledge came to bat with one out and the bases loaded. He then smashed a liner that Cubs left fielder Alfonso Soriano assumed would clear the wall. The crowd assumed the same thing. So did Pirates broadcaster Tim Neverett, who told his audience, "Milledge hammers one to left . . . this ball is back . . . It iiiiiis gone!" The pyrotechnics that explode every time a Pirate goes deep thundered.

Convinced he had gone yard for his first career grand slam, Milledge raised his fist rounding first base, humbly but proudly put his head down, and went into a triumphant trot. Only the thing was, the ball had not cleared the wall. It hit the top and bounced back in the field of play where Soriano gloved it and fired to shortstop Ryan Theriot.

As Neverett corrected himself, his announcing partner Bob Walk interjected, "Uh oh, uh oh, uh oh, uh oh, we've got a problem here."

Milledge had just rounded second base when he realized the Cubs had him boxed in. He didn't put up any fight. Theriot flipped the ball to second baseman Jeff Baker, who tagged him out. The supposed grand slam turned into a two-run double. Fortunately for Milledge, the Pirates didn't need the lost runs, winning 11–1.

After the game, Milledge told the press, "It was my fault. I didn't look at the ball. I was running hard, making sure that I had a double, and I looked up and all the fireworks were going off and I had a lapse for a second."

Turning a lemon into lemonade, he added, "I think that was the most exciting double in PNC Park history."

STEVE SAX
Second Baseman · Los Angeles, NL · July 30, 1985

Los Angeles Dodgers second baseman Steve Sax did more than hurt the opposing team with a walk-off home run. He also hurt his own coach.

Playing in Dodger Stadium against the rival San Francisco Giants, Sax stepped to the plate with a runner on base in the bottom of the ninth inning of a 2–2 game. No one really considered Sax a home run threat because he hadn't hit one out in more than a year. But somehow he got all of a Mark Davis pitch and lofted a drive that cleared the wall for a dramatic 4–2 Los Angeles victory.

Because of his inexperience in home run trots, Sax didn't give just an ordinary hand slap to Dodgers coach Joe Amalfitano after rounding third. No, the exuberant Sax delivered a hyperactive low five so hard that it broke the coach's thumb.

"I should have known better," said Amalfitano after his thumb was put in a splint. "I saw the crazed look in his eyes when he hit third base."

In a 2010 *Sports Illustrated* article, Sax recalled, "All I remember is, after I hit [Amalfitano], I turned around and saw him jumping up and down and I figured, 'Damn, he's really excited that I hit a home run. I was like, wham, and he was like, 'Yeeee-ahhh,' and I was like, 'Right on, Joey.' He came to the park the next day, and he had a cast on."

The following year, when Sax hit his first homer of the 1986 season, he trotted around the bases. But when Sax rounded third base, Amalfitano broke with baseball tradition and refused to hold out his hand. Instead, the coach just pointed and pulled an imaginary trigger.

PHIL RIZZUTO'S FIRST HOMER
Shortstop · New York, AL · April 23, 1941

In his second week of the season, New York Yankees rookie shortstop Phil Rizzuto hit the first homer of his illustrious career. And what a homer it was—a two-run, game-winning shot in the bottom of the 11th inning to beat the rival Boston Red Sox 4–2.

The round-tripper was also memorable for another reason. It led him to a bitter introduction into the penny-pinching side of Yankees president Ed Barrow.

After Rizzuto socked the game-winner—a hit that every young player dreams about—he hopped around the bases while a bunch of happy fans came out of the stands to celebrate. As Rizzuto rounded third base, one of the fans grabbed his hat and took off.

The next morning, Rizzuto was summoned to Barrow's office. The rookie was expecting praise from the owner over the heroic homer. Instead, Rizzuto's jaw fell to the carpet when he heard Barrow say, "You have to pay for your lost cap."

It might have been the only time a player was billed by his own team for winning a game.

PITIFUL PICKOFFS

For the Most Boneheaded Pickoffs of All Time,
The Baseball Hall of Shame™ Inducts:

FRENCHY BORDAGARAY
Center Fielder · Brooklyn, NL · 1935

Brooklyn Dodgers outfielder Frenchy Bordagaray had a penchant for getting picked off base, but for utter craziness none could compare with the time he was nailed while still standing on the bag.

It happened during a home game against the Chicago Cubs. After Bordagaray hit a double, Brooklyn manager Casey Stengel, who was coaching first base, held up the game and went out to talk to his baserunner.

"Now look here, Frenchy," Stengel said. "I want you to stand on second until Frey [the next batter Lonny Frey] actually hits the ball. I mean stand right on the bag. Don't take a lead. Don't even move away from it six inches. Do you understand?"

"Why, certainly, Boss," Bordagaray replied.

Moments later, Cubs hurler Larry French whirled and fired a bullet toward second base. Shortstop Billy Jurges caught the ball and slapped the tag on Bordagaray for the out.

Frenchy, tapping and napping NATIONAL BASEBALL HALL OF FAME LIBRARY

As Bordagaray passed Stengel on the way to the dugout, the disgusted manager hissed, "What were you doing out there? Weren't you standing on the bag?"

Bordagaray nodded and said, "I was on the bag."

"Well then, how could they pick you off?"

"I haven't the slightest idea, Boss," answered the beleaguered player. "I did just like you told me. I didn't move from the base even three inches. I was just standing there tapping my foot on the bag, waiting for Frey to bang one."

"I see," said Stengel, wiping the sweat from his fevered brow. "In that case, how did Jurges manage to put you out?"

Bordagaray sighed and threw his hands up in defeat. "It beats me, Boss. He must have put the tag on me between taps."

GEORGE BRETT
Designated Hitter · Kansas City, AL · September 30, 1992

Of all the players who've collected at least 3,000 hits, only George Brett had his moment of glory tarnished by an embarrassing gaffe. While the future Hall of Famer was still savoring his amazing feat, he got picked off first like an excited rookie.

In the last week of the 1992 season, the Kansas City Royals superstar needed four hits to gain admittance into the exclusive club, which as of 2011 has just 28 members. The only man ever to win a batting title in three different decades, Brett had remained a consistent hitter year in and year out. In 1980, he batted .390, the highest average for a full season since Ted Williams of the Boston Red Sox hit .406 in 1941.

Although Brett had hoped to have the chance to reach the 3,000-hit milestone in Kansas City, he felt fortunate that he was playing against the California Angels at Anaheim Stadium because it was near where he grew up. With friends and family in the stands, and his brother Ken, a former Major Leaguer, broadcasting the game, Brett doubled to left field and scored in the first inning, singled to right in the third, and singled to center in the fifth for his 2,999th career hit.

In the seventh inning, Brett had his first opportunity to make history. He wasted no time by rocketing a sharp one-hopper past Angels second baseman Ken Oberkfell into right field. At the time, Brett had become only the 18th player to reach the lofty 3,000-hit mark. The 17,000 fans at the ballpark rose to their feet to give the popular veteran a standing ovation while teammates mobbed him, and opposing players congratulated him. With fireworks bursting overhead, he doffed his helmet and waved to the crowd. The ball and the first base bag were taken to the Royals clubhouse where a bottle of Dom Perignon was being chilled.

Standing on first base, Brett thought about the three men who helped shape his life as a hitter—his father Jack, his hitting coach Charlie Lau, and his former manager Dick Howser, who were all deceased.

Getting misty-eyed, Brett was still lost in the moment even when play resumed. After Kansas City's Gregg Jefferies flied out, Brett carried on a brief conversation with Angels first baseman Gary Gaetti, who was asking about the star's family.

Although the Angels were happy for Brett, they weren't about to cut him any slack. After all, he was an opposing player, and they wanted to beat him and his team. While a thrilled Brett was still relishing his accomplishment, Anaheim pitcher Tim Fortugno, who gave up the 3,000th hit, snapped the ball over to first. Gaetti caught it and tagged out Brett for the most inglorious pickoff in baseball history.

"I was right in the middle of a sentence to Gaetti and they picked me off," Brett sheepishly said after the game. "He asked me if my wife was here and I said, yes, and I had friends here from Kansas City. He didn't even let me finish the sentence."

BARRY BONNELL
Left Fielder

DAVE COLLINS
Pinch Hitter

WILLIE UPSHAW
First Baseman
Toronto, AL · August 24, 1983

In the most stunning display of baserunning ineptness in one inning, three Toronto Blue Jays reached first base—and all three were picked off.

Toronto and the home team Baltimore Orioles were knotted up at 3–3 when designated hitter Cliff Johnson led off the top of the 10th inning by blasting a home run off Tim Stoddard. After the next batter, Barry Bonnell, slapped a single up the middle, Baltimore manager Joe Altobelli brought in relief pitcher Tippy Martinez. Because the Orioles had used up their two regular catchers and now had second baseman Lenn Sakata behind the plate, Blue Jays manager Bobby Cox flashed the steal sign to Bonnell. Cox figured it would be a cinch to steal against the inexperienced catcher.

Bonnell took a big lead off first, eager to test Sakata's arm. Unfortunately, Bonnell was a little too eager. Martinez went into his stretch and whipped the ball to first, catching Bonnell flat-footed. Knowing he was an easy out at first, he took off for second and was tagged out.

The next batter, pinch hitter Dave Collins, walked. He had the look of a man ready to take candy from a baby—but instead got his own pocket picked. He strayed too far off first to become the inning's second pickoff victim.

With two out and no one on, Willie Upshaw legged out an infield single. Now it was his turn to join the pickoff parade. He was all set to steal off Sakata when, leaning the wrong way, he was picked off first just like his two teammates.

Incredibly, Martinez had retired the side without getting a batter out. The Blue Jay runners did all the work for him.

If that wasn't embarrassing enough for Toronto, in the bottom of the 10th, the Orioles tied the score on a leadoff homer by Cal Ripken. Then, later in the inning, with two on and two out, Sakata—the very guy from whom the Blue Jays were going to steal the game—socked a three-run walk-off homer to win the game for Baltimore, 7–4.

HERB WASHINGTON
Designated Runner · Oakland, AL · October 13, 1974

Herb Washington proved that the idea of a designated runner—the brainchild of Oakland Athletics owner Charlie Finley—was way off base.

That was never more apparent than during the second game of the 1974 World Series when the Los Angeles Dodgers picked Washington off first, snuffing out a ninth-inning rally.

Before the 1974 season, Finley plucked Washington from the college track circuit, where the Michigan State University sprinter and four-time All-American had broken several world records. Even though his only baseball experience was in high school, Washington was signed by the eccentric owner to a contract solely as a "designated runner." His job was to steal bases, so he wouldn't need to wear a glove or hold a bat.

Throughout the season, Washington never really got off the blocks the way Finley had hoped. The runner stole only 29 bases and was caught 16

Designated runner Washington bites the dust   ASSOCIATED PRESS

times. In the American League Championship Series against the Baltimore Orioles, Washington attempted two steals and was thrown out both times.

Nevertheless, Finley waited for the World Series to prove that the designated runner was an innovation that would pay dividends. At last, Herb Washington could show the baseball world his dazzling speed, his daring baserunning, his ability to win once for the A's with his legs.

His golden opportunity came in the ninth inning of Game 2 with one out. He went in to pinch-run for Joe Rudi, who had just knocked in two runs with a single to cut the Dodgers' lead to 3–2.

Representing the tying run, Washington edged off first. Ever so carefully, he widened his lead, his feet itching to sprint toward second. He stared at pitcher Mike Marshall, who stared right back. Washington stared. Marshall stared. Suddenly, Marshall made his move. Washington didn't. The next sound the designated runner heard was the ball slapping into the glove of first baseman Steve Garvey. The next sensation he felt was getting tagged on the hand. The next thing he saw was umpire Doug Harvey's thumb in the air. The A's lost 3–2.

It was one of the last things Herb Washington experienced in the Majors. He was released early the next season.

BILLY ROGELL
Shortstop · Detroit, AL · April 30, 1934

To his everlasting chagrin, Detroit Tigers shortstop Billy Rogell learned a valuable lesson: Never tick off an infielder because, when you least expect it, he will get his revenge. In Rogell's case, it was a mortifying pickoff.

During the offseason, Rogell supplemented his modest Detroit Tigers salary by delivering milk in his hometown of Chicago for $41 a week. One of his customers was St. Louis Browns second baseman Ski "Spinach" Melillo.

Because they were friendly rivals on the diamond, Rogell decided to have some fun at Melillo's expense during the winter before the 1934 season. Rogell made sure that he delivered the milk to Melillo as early as possible, before 6:00 a.m. Rogell would put the milk on Melillo's back porch, rattle the bottles, and shout up to the bedroom window, "Here's your milk, Ski!"

This never failed to wake up—and irritate—Melillo. Being a patient man, Melillo waited for his revenge. It came the first time that the two teams met in the new season. With the hometown Tigers trailing 4–1 midway through the game, Rogell slid into second with a double. Feeling pleased about the hit, Rogell brushed the dirt off his uniform. Then, taking a few steps off the base, he turned his attention toward St. Louis hurler Ivy Andrews.

Melillo, who was playing second base, sauntered close to the bag and said to Rogell, "Billy, remember how you'd wake me up in the morning, shouting, 'Here's your milk'?"

Rogell grinned and nodded. "Boy, do I. That sure made my day."

"Well, this is going to make my day," retorted Melillo, who then tagged out Rogell with the old hidden ball trick. "Now you've got some explaining to do to [Tigers manager Mickey] Cochrane. Who knows, you might wind up delivering milk again sooner than you think."

The following winter, Rogell was somewhat quieter in his deliveries to the Melillo household. But he was determined to get the last laugh.

"Back then, the infielders used to leave their gloves on the field when they went to bat," Rogell recalled. "It just so happened I found a dead sparrow in the dugout, and I knew Ski was afraid of anything dead. So I secretly put the dead sparrow in his glove. When he took his position in the field the next inning and saw that dead sparrow in his glove, he threw his glove in the air and took off running."

RON LEFLORE
Left Fielder · Montreal, NL · July 28, 1980

Montreal Expos left fielder Ron LeFlore knew that stealing a base requires concentration. But he learned the hard way that *staying* on base also requires concentration.

In the bottom of the seventh inning of a 5–4 victory over the visiting Cincinnati Reds, LeFlore, the Expos' best baserunner, singled and easily swiped second for his 67th theft of the year. As he stood up and brushed himself off, he noticed that the electronic scoreboard at Olympic Stadium had flashed an interesting message: It was 115 years ago to the day that the first stolen base had been recorded by Ed Cuthbert.

For a player who would finish the season with a league-leading 97 stolen bases, LeFlore found this little piece of historical trivia fascinating. Maybe too much so. While he was standing there reading about baseball, he forgot about *playing* baseball—and was promptly picked off second by reliever Dick Tomlin.

SUPER-SILLY SUPERSTITIONS

For the Nuttiest Habits and Idiosyncrasies of All Time, The Baseball Hall of Shame™ Inducts:

LOU "THE MAD RUSSIAN" NOVIKOFF
Outfielder · Chicago, NL · 1941–1944

Chicago Cubs outfielder Lou Novikoff had the weirdest superstition of any batter in baseball—he insisted that his wife Esther taunt him from the stands.

He claimed that her shouts of derision inspired him.

The superstition began when Novikoff played for the Los Angeles Angels in the Pacific Coast League in 1940. Esther discovered that he seemed to do better the angrier he got, so she decided to test her theory. As he came to bat, she shouted from her box seat behind home plate, "You big bum! You can't hit!"

The words turned Novikoff's ears red. He swung on the first pitch and sent the ball sailing over the left field wall for a home run. Later, when fans asked Esther why she kept shouting nasty things to her husband, she explained, "I yell at him like that to make him mad. And when he gets mad, he gets hits."

After that game, Novikoff insisted that his wife continue to berate him every time he batted. On road trips or when she couldn't make a home game, he tried to picture what slander she'd hurl at him to fire him up. It worked. He batted .363 and clubbed 41 homers that season.

The following year, Novikoff was called up to the Cubs and left his family behind in Los Angeles. But without his wife insulting him from the stands, Novikoff batted only .241 in his first season. The promising rookie didn't look so promising.

The next year, the Cubs played the cross-town rival White Sox in a preseason exhibition game. When Novikoff came to bat, Sox manager Jimmy Dykes yelled to him from the dugout, "Mad Russian, eh? If I couldn't hit any better than you, I'd be mad too." Novikoff was so ticked off that he laced a base hit.

Realizing how much he missed his wife—and her insults—the peculiar outfielder summoned her to the Windy City. A few days later, when he stepped to the plate at Wrigley Field for the Cubs' home opener, a piercing female voice rose above the crowd, yelling, "Strike the big bum out! He can't hit!" It was his loving wife Esther. Novikoff then smacked a run-scoring base hit. With her in the stands at most home games, he went on to bat an even .300 in his first full year in the Majors.

When Esther's taunting didn't work, Novikoff turned to another superstition—singing. Blessed with a fine baritone voice, he believed that singing could change his, and the team's, luck. Unfortunately for those around him, he sometimes sang at the oddest times—like in the middle of the night on the train.

One night in 1943 in Philadelphia, Cubs manager Charlie Grimm turned on the radio and listened to a show that was broadcasting live from a Philly nightclub. "Ladies and gentlemen," said the master of ceremonies, "we will now hear several songs from one of our guests here tonight, Lou Novikoff, the great Cubs outfielder."

Grimm leaped into his clothes and into a taxi. He arrived at the nightclub in time to catch Novikoff's closing number, "My Wild Irish Rose." Grimm applauded politely and then informed Novikoff that he had just been fined for violating curfew. But the Mad Russian protested, saying, "I only sang tonight because I thought it would bring our team good luck."

He had a point. The Cubs won three out of four from the Phillies.

BABE RUTH
Pitcher, Outfielder, First Baseman · Boston, New York, AL; Boston, NL · 1914–1935

Babe Ruth was so superstitious that he used to wear women's silk hose because he believed they protected him from jinxes.

The Sultan of Swat heard that Hall of Famer Honus Wagner wore ladies silken stockings when not playing. For some crazy reason, Wagner felt that women's hose—not men's—guarded him from batting slumps.

It certainly seemed to work for Wagner. In his 21 years in the bigs (1897–1917), the Pittsburgh Pirates shortstop batted over .300 in each of 16 seasons and finished with a lifetime average of .328.

Toward the end of Wagner's career, the Babe, who was then a pitcher for the Boston Red Sox, learned about Wagner's strange superstition. Ruth wasn't about to argue with success, so when not in uniform, he chose to sport knee-length ladies' silken hose.

Whether it's coincidence or not, Ruth hit over .300 in 17 of his 22 years in the Majors and ended up with a lifetime batting average of .342.

Ruth had plenty of other quirks. When jogging in from the outfield, he always would step on second base. And on the rare occasions when he forgot to touch the bag, he would trot back out of the dugout and kick the base.

Although Ruth was a generous man, he would never loan one of his bats to a teammate. Ruth once explained, "Bats have so many hits in them, and each time I lend one to a guy and he whacks a couple of hits, all I'm doing is lopping a few points off Babe Ruth's batting average. That's why nobody uses Babe Ruth's bat but Babe Ruth."

The Babe dressing like a babe   NATIONAL BASEBALL HALL OF FAME LIBRARY

TURK WENDELL

Pitcher · Chicago, New York, Philadelphia, Colorado, NL
1993-2004

Turk Wendell was one of the most eccentric and superstitious relievers in baseball.

He posted some solid seasons in the Majors, including 18 saves for the Chicago Cubs in 1996. But he's most remembered for his wacky superstitions.

Whenever he headed to the mound to pitch, he stuffed exactly four pieces of black licorice in his mouth. At the end of each inning, he would spit them out, return to the dugout, whip out his toothbrush, and brush his teeth. While brushing, he often hid in the dugout, either by ducking behind objects or by facing the wall.

Getting ready to pitch for the first time in any game, he would draw three crosses in the dirt on the mound. If his catcher was standing, Wendell would squat and if the catcher was squatting then the hurler would stand. Before facing the first batter in each inning, Wendell would turn his back to home plate and wave to the center fielder. The reliever wouldn't pitch until the center fielder waved back.

On his way to and from the mound each inning that he pitched, he leaped—not stepped—over the baseline, a superstition known as Wendell's 3-foot kangaroo hop.

Because he was an avid hunter, Wendell believed that parts of animals were lucky charms. When he pitched, he wore a necklace adorned with trophies from animals he had harvested, including mountain lion claws and the teeth of wild pigs and buffalo.

Wendell had a thing about the number 9, which he was convinced was lucky. He wore uniform number 99 in honor of Rick "Wild Thing" Vaughn, one of the main characters in the movie *Major League*, portrayed by Charlie Sheen. In 2000, Wendell signed a contract with the New York Mets that would have been worth $10 million, but he insisted that the agreement be for $9,999,999.99.

CHARLES "VICTORY" FAUST
Human Good Luck Charm · New York, NL · 1911

The 1911 New York Giants were the most superstitious team in baseball history—and relied on a human good luck charm to carry them to the National League pennant.

The team believed that a player who found a stray hairpin would get a double, but looking at a cross-eyed girl would lead to a hitless day at the plate, and leaving more than a 25-cent tip was bad luck. The players rubbed their bats with ham bones in the belief that it would attract hits. They wore lucky medallions, lucky ties, lucky shoes, and lucky hankies.

Early in the season second baseman Laughing Larry Doyle fell into a batting slump. On his way to the ballpark one day, he spotted a wagonload of beer barrels. That day he got three hits. But the next day he didn't hit the ball out of the infield. "Maybe those barrels brought you luck," said Giants manager John McGraw—and a new baseball superstition was born. From then on, players believed it was good fortune to see a load of beer barrels before a game.

A few weeks later, the Giants were playing poorly, having lost five of seven. Trying to snap them out of the slump, McGraw paid a beer-cart driver $2 to travel past his players as they entered the clubhouse. Seeing those beer barrels, the players were jubilant and went on a tear, winning 10 of their next 12 games.

But the one belief that mattered most to the players was their faith in their lucky mascot—Charles "Victory" Faust. He was a tall, lanky 30-year-old Kansas farmer who got a tryout with the Giants in St. Louis in July after a fortune teller told him he would become a great pitcher. He failed miserably in his audition, but McGraw and the players liked him, and let him sit on the bench for the games against the Cardinals. The Giants won three straight.

When they headed for Pittsburgh, the Giants assumed they had seen the last of Faust. But by hopping freight trains, he caught up with them in Philadelphia. During that time, New York had lost five of seven. After letting Faust sit on the bench again, the Giants won six straight.

Faust, the Giants' good luck charm

There was no doubt that Faust had to remain on the team. McGraw, who was just as superstitious as his players, announced, "We're taking Charlie along to help us win the pennant."

Although Faust was never formally given a contract, the club issued him a uniform and paid his expenses. The players were convinced he had special powers. One day, he told catcher Chief Meyers that the backstop would get a single and double that afternoon. Meyers did. The next day, Faust predicted that Meyers would get three hits. And, incredibly, Meyers did.

If Faust wasn't sitting in the dugout, he was in the bullpen spreading his brand of good fortune. From the time Faust sat on the Giants bench in St. Louis to the day the team clinched the pennant, the Giants had a record of 39-9.

Faust was getting so much attention from the press and fans that he signed a $200 a week vaudeville contract. But in his first week away from the club, New York won only one of its next four games, so Faust broke his showbiz contract and returned to the team. The Giants won their next 10 games and went on to capture the pennant—their first in six years—by seven and a half games.

Out of gratitude, McGraw let Faust pitch briefly after clinching the pennant. In each of two appearances, he pitched the ninth inning, giving up a total of two hits and two runs.

But Faust's luck ran out in the postseason. Despite his prediction of a world championship for New York, the Giants lost the Series to the Philadelphia Athletics. The faith the team had in Charles "Victory" Faust was shaken . . . and he never donned a Giants uniform again.

GEORGE STALLINGS
Manager · Boston, NL · 1914

George Stallings feared jinxes more than any other manager in baseball.

He truly believed that part of his job as skipper of the Boston Braves was to spot jinxes and ward them off. So he went to extraordinarily wacky lengths to defuse their bad influence, especially in 1914.

Off the field, Stallings was a dignified, soft-spoken Southern gentleman, courtly of manner and meticulous in dress. But when he stepped onto the baseball diamond, he turned into a superstitious "jinx-dodger." To Stallings, even the most innocent of objects could cause his team harm.

The eccentric manager had an uncontrollable phobia over, of all things, pieces of paper. He hated them. He regarded any loose paper in front of the dugout as an omen of bad luck. The site of a piece of paper on the floor of the Braves dugout sent him into a frenzy.

Gabe Paul, who became one of baseball's most respected general managers, used to cater to this idiosyncrasy when he was Stallings's bat boy. Paul painstakingly kept the dugout area clean of any pieces of paper. "If one little scrap of paper escaped me," Paul recalled, "Mr. Stallings's roar scared the life out of me."

To thwart any ill fortune and to encourage a rally, Stallings stayed literally frozen in place whenever a Brave got a hit. Once, Stallings was bending over to pick up a peanut shell—another sign of bad luck—when a Brave socked a single. Stallings refused to move from his stooped position until the last Brave was out, which was a half hour later because the team went wild and scored seven runs in the inning. When the rally finally ended, Stallings couldn't straighten up. Two players had to carry him back to the clubhouse where the trainer applied hot towels to unbend him.

Stallings was constantly finding signs of bad luck and then creating ways to nullify their power. If the team's bats were crossed, he uncrossed them so his players wouldn't get hurt or go hitless that day. Sometimes he shook the bats to "wake up the lumber." He made sure his players left their gloves sitting right side up for fear they were risking an error. In close games, he slid up and down the length of the bench, hoping to pick up good luck and rub out the bad luck. Naturally, his players had to jump off the bench and make way for him when he went into his sliding mode.

Stallings seldom saw outfielder Josh Devore catch a ball. Devore, who was traded to Boston late in the year, had cement hands. One day, late in a tie game, a high fly was hit to him in right field. Devore circled under the ball with uncertainty. The tension over whether or not he would catch it was too much for Stallings to bear. The manager rushed to the clubhouse door with his back to the diamond. After several seconds ticked off, he asked, "Did he catch it?" Devore did. After that, whenever there was a high fly hit to Devore, Stallings turned his back on him.

The manager's obsession with jinxes had a bizarrely positive effect on the team. The Braves, who had only one .300 hitter and an error-prone outfield, were wallowing in the National League cellar 11 games out in mid-July. But Stallings had finally convinced most of his players that they couldn't lose because he was using counteracting whammies on all jinxes. Amazingly, the Braves started winning and, in one of the most stunning turn-arounds in baseball history, captured the pennant and the World Series.

AL SIMMONS
Outfielder · Philadelphia, AL · 1932

When it came to superstitions, the naked truth was that Hall of Famer Al Simmons believed in them.

After leading the American League in hitting with an eye-popping .390 batting average in 1931, the Philadelphia Athletics outfielder slipped into a terrible batting slump the following year. He tried everything to snap out of it, but nothing worked.

One day, after going hitless in five at-bats, he walked out of the clubhouse shower in deep thought. Standing nude and wet in front of his locker, he unthinkingly put on his hat.

His teammates broke out in laughter at the sight of the sopping wet slugger wearing nothing but a fedora. Simmons didn't find it at all funny. He quickly dressed and left the clubhouse without saying a word.

The next day, Simmons busted out of his batting doldrums by going 4-for-4. After the game, he stepped out of the shower, walked wet and naked to his locker, and put on his hat. And he continued the ritual the rest of the year. Having finally found his "barings," he finished with a batting average of .322.

WILLIAM "BILLY GOAT" SIANIS
Fan · Chicago, NL · October 6, 1945

No fan has left such a lasting curse on a team as William "Billy Goat" Sianis. Miffed that the Chicago Cubs refused to let his pet goat watch a World Series game at Wrigley Field, Sianis put a hex on the Cubs that they would never win a championship.

The curse has remained ever since (through the 2011 season).

In 1943, Sianis, a Greek immigrant who owned the Lincoln Tavern near Chicago Stadium, rescued a goat that had fallen off a truck. He kept the goat and named him Murphy. Although Murphy lived in a pen behind the tavern, the pet often wandered into the bar, where it begged swigs of beer from the patrons. Meanwhile, Sianis grew a goatee, gave himself the nickname Billy Goat, renamed his bar the Billy Goat Tavern, and took his goat around town for publicity.

As a loyal Cubs fan, Sianis was thrilled when Chicago won the pennant and faced the Detroit Tigers in the 1945 World Series. With the Cubs up two games to one, he paid $7.20 for two tickets to Game 4 at Wrigley Field—one for himself and one for Murphy. Sianis thought the goat would bring his favorite team good luck.

Before the game, Sianis paraded Murphy outside the ballpark with his pet wearing a sign that said, "We Got Detroit's Goat." But as game-time neared, the ushers refused to let him take Murphy into the stands because the ballpark banned animals. According to the tavern's own historical account, this is what happened next:

Outraged by the ban, Sianis appealed to Cubs owner P. K. Wrigley who, after listening to him, told the ushers, "Let Billy in, but not the goat."

"Why not the goat?" Sianis asked.

"Because the goat stinks," Wrigley replied.

Sianis was so upset that he threw his arms up and exclaimed, "The Cubs ain't gonna win no more! The Cubs will never win a World Series so long as the goat is not allowed in Wrigley Field." Having officially cursed the team, he tied up Murphy to a post in a parking lot and

Sianis's goat getting the boot   CHICAGO TRIBUNE

then went into the ballpark to watch Chicago lose 4–1. The Cubs then dropped two of the next three games and lost the Series.

Sianis, according to the tavern's account, promptly sent Wrigley a telegram that said, "Who stinks now?"

It was the last time the Cubs, who had not won a World Series since 1908, even appeared in the Fall Classic.

UNIFORM NO. 15
Detroit, AL · 1948–1950

Pain and suffering—and near tragedy—plagued any Detroit Tigers player who, between 1948 and 1950, dared to wear No. 15.

Relief pitcher Johnny Gorsica was the first Tiger to fall victim to the uniform number from hell. After compiling a 2–0 record in 1947, the seven-year veteran donned No. 15. He immediately suffered arm problems and was promptly released. Gorsica never pitched in the Majors again.

Before the start of the 1948 season, fellow hurler Art Houtteman was the next Tiger to put on the jinxed number. Houtteman, coming off a fine 7-2 season in 1947, was looking forward to a great year. Instead, he lived a pitcher's nightmare—by losing his first eight games.

By June, Houtteman was desperate to switch uniform numbers with any willing teammate. At first, he couldn't find a taker because, as fellow pitcher Dizzy Trout told him, "That number's no good."

However, George Kell, Tigers third baseman and team captain, scoffed at the thought the uniform number was jinxed. "I'll switch numbers with you, Art," said Kell. "I don't believe in all that stuff about bad luck numbers." So Kell swapped his No. 21 for Houtteman's No. 15.

The hurler finally recorded his first victory of the season after the number switch. But Kell wasn't so fortunate. During a game against the New York Yankees, a line drive off the bat of Joe DiMaggio smashed into Kell's jaw and sidelined the Tiger for the final month of the season. The skeptic turned into a believer in the black-cloud powers of No. 15 and refused to wear it again. "Too much tough luck goes with it," said Kell. "I don't want any part of it."

At spring training the following year, Houtteman gave Kell back his old uniform number and put in a request for a new number. To his shock, the pitcher was handed his old No. 15. He put up a tremendous howl until the club offered to give him a different number. But because new uniforms weren't going to be ready for two weeks, he reluctantly agreed to wear No. 15 temporarily.

Nine days later, Houtteman lay close to death in a Florida hospital with a fractured skull after a collision between his convertible and a tractor-trailer. He survived the near fatal accident and returned to the mound two months later—but with a different uniform number.

Tigers first baseman Paul Campbell, a five-year Major Leaguer, was the next player foolish enough to wear No. 15. Campbell didn't have it long. He was sold to a minor league club early in the season and never played in the bigs again.

To end the curse of No 15, team trainer Jack Homel packed the uniform in an old trunk. By the time the number was worn again years later, its alleged evil powers had vanished.

KEVIN RHOMBERG
Outfielder · Cleveland, AL · 1982–1984

Superstition was literally a touchy subject for Cleveland Indians reserve outfielder Kevin Rhomberg.

He believed that if anyone touched him, he had to touch that person back—a peculiarity that some would say was a compulsion that made him a favorite target for practical jokes.

"He wouldn't let anyone touch him last," said Milt Thompson, a 13-year National League veteran who played against Rhomberg in winter ball. "Sometimes his teammates would gang up on him and then run in different directions. He'd go crazy trying to touch them all back."

Cleveland teammate Rick Sutcliffe once reached under a bathroom stall to touch Rhomberg on the toe. Not knowing whom the culprit was, Rhomberg went around the clubhouse and touched each player.

Another teammate, pitcher Bert Blyleven, once touched Rhomberg while they were together in a car. Then at the next stoplight, Blyleven bolted from the car and ran off. According to the Associated Press, Rhomberg's wife, Denise, pleaded with Blyleven. "Let him touch you or he won't sleep all night." Blyleven did.

Rhomberg, a player with a touchy superstition

If Rhomberg was tagged out while running the bases, he'd wait until the end of the inning and then, as the teams were trading sides, he would chase down the player who'd touched him.

As word spread in the Majors about his weird superstition, "it seemed like half the American League tried to touch him," said former teammate Rick Manning. An umpire once halted play during a game in New York to tell Yankees players to stop touching Rhomberg.

"The fans got into the act too," Manning recalled. "They sent Rhomberg letters saying, 'You touched my letter—I got you last.' So he'd write back so he could be last." Rhomberg would write, "This constitutes a touch."

In the minor leagues, Brook Jacoby once tagged Rhomberg with a ball and threw it out of the stadium. Rhomberg spent two hours looking for the ball before finding it.

During a winter game in Venezuela, Rhomberg was at bat when his teammate, Chicago Cubs infielder Danny Rohn, ran up behind him, touched him on the back, and dashed into the clubhouse to hide. "He looked for me for two hours," Rohn recalled in the *Seattle Times*. "I was hiding under desks, in the shower, the bathroom. He couldn't find me."

But Rhomberg had a plan for the touch-back. He was staying in the same hotel as Rohn. So Rhomberg got up at 3:30 a.m. and knocked on Rohn's door. When the sleepy player opened it, Rhomberg touched Rohn's hand and ran off.

Asked to explain his superstition, Rhomberg said at the time, "I don't know why I do it. I've been doing it since I was a kid."

MIKE CUELLAR
Pitcher · Baltimore, AL · 1969–1976

When Mike Cuellar pitched for the Baltimore Orioles, he was the most superstitious pitcher in baseball.

His every move on and off the diamond involved a series of never-changing rituals. The four-time 20-game winner was convinced that his strange routines had given him a special, favorable rapport with Lady Luck.

On his way to the mound, he leaped over the top dugout step and avoided the foul line—a superstition practiced by many players. But after each inning, he walked into the dugout, placed his glove on the "lucky end" of the bench, stopped at the water cooler for a drink, then retreated to the runway for a cigarette. He kept smoking until the first

Orioles hitter was retired—whether it was 30 seconds or 30 minutes later. Then he tossed the cigarette away, returned to the dugout, picked up his glove, and sat down in a special place on the bench. If Baltimore manager Earl Weaver inadvertently was sitting on that spot, Cuellar would make him move.

Whenever the Orioles catcher made the last out of the inning, Cuellar wouldn't budge from the bench until the catcher had put on his shin guards. Once on the mound, the pitcher wouldn't allow anybody to throw him the ball to start his warm-up tosses. He had to pick it up off the ground, circle the mound, and then walk up to it from the second base side before he was ready to warm up.

Long aware of Cuellar's eccentricities, Cleveland Indians outfielder Alex Johnson devilishly tried to disrupt the hurler's rigid routine during a game on May 26, 1972, in Baltimore. After catching a fly for the last out of the third inning, Johnson slowly carried the ball back to the infield. Timing his arrival with Cuellar's approach to the mound, Johnson tossed the ball to the Orioles pitcher. Cuellar ducked just in time and let the ball roll free. Helpfully, the bat boy retrieved it and threw it to the pitcher. Once more, Cuellar dodged the tossed ball, which dribbled toward first base. Momentarily forgetting his teammate's superstition, Orioles first baseman Boog Powell threw the ball squarely at Cuellar, who was forced to catch it in self-defense.

Convinced the ball had been tainted, Cuellar flipped it to plate umpire Bill Haller and asked for a new one. The ump obliged and threw the desired replacement to the mound. Again, Cuellar sidestepped the toss. The new baseball trickled dead near second baseman Bobby Grich, who finally showed the proper respect for his pitcher's superstitious beliefs. Gently, Grich rolled the ball to the mound. After it came to a complete rest, Cuellar picked it up, satisfied now that no evil spirits had invaded his place of business.

In the next inning, Alex Johnson again caught a third-out fly ball and sought a repeat performance as he returned to the infield, ball in hand. Johnson's intended victim would have no part of it, however, and remained in the Baltimore dugout until his Cleveland tormentor lobbed the ball to Powell. This time Powell rolled the ball to the mound. Only then did the hurler walk back onto the field.

Cuellar had a few other rituals. The night before he pitched, he always ate Chinese food. On days he was slated to start, he arrived in the clubhouse dressed from head to toe in blue—blue shirt, blue tie, blue suit, blue socks, and blue shoes. He also drove to the ballpark in a blue car.

He always wore the same Orioles cap when he pitched. On the morning of September 6, 1974, hours before he was scheduled to start in Cleveland, Cuellar realized he had left his lucky hat back in Baltimore and refused to pitch without it. So the team secretary arranged for a courier to put it on the next flight to Cleveland. The hat arrived just minutes before game time.

Feeling confident now that he had his lucky hat, Cuellar threw a complete-game five-hit shutout.

MATT ANDERSON BOBBLEHEAD
Detroit, AL · 2002

When Detroit completed a three-game sweep of the Texas Rangers on Matt Anderson Bobblehead Day on May 19, 2002, the Tigers bullpen crew came to the conclusion that the doll of their fellow reliever possessed some sort of supernatural power that would bring them good fortune.

That's because during the series, they had placed the bobblehead between the team's two bullpen mounds at Detroit's Comerica Park. The relievers had done their part to preserve the three victories against the team that had swept them a week earlier.

So with their good luck charm in place, the Tigers went on and took three straight from the visiting Cleveland Indians.

After a disappointing road trip—in which the bobblehead had been left behind—the Tigers returned home. On June 3, they faced the first-place Boston Red Sox. With their treasured Matt Anderson bobblehead doll to inspire them, three Detroit relievers combined to shut out Boston for six and a third innings in a 7–6 come-from-behind victory.

In the bottom of the first inning the following day, Tigers leadoff batter Ramon Santiago blasted a home run over the wall in right-center field to tie the game at 1-all. That should have been a good thing. But it wasn't—at least not to the Detroit bullpen corps. The ball landed right on top of their favorite bobblehead and broke it.

According to Danny Knobler of Booth Newspapers, the relievers went into a panic. "They called the dugout and asked for a trainer," Knobler was told by Tigers manager Luis Pujols.

Horrified that their lucky bobblehead was seriously injured, the relievers fell apart. Four of them combined to give up six runs on eight hits in six and a third innings in a 10–5 beating. After the game, Detroit's bullpen coach, Todd Maulding, told Knobler that the bobblehead was given some ice to treat the injury. Declared Maulding, "He's okay."

But the Matt Anderson bobblehead doll wasn't okay . . . and neither were the Detroit Tigers. They dropped the next six games. As if that wasn't bad enough, Matt Anderson—the pitcher, not the bobblehead— ended up on the 60-day disabled list.

ANGER MISMANAGEMENT

For the Most Hotheaded Meltdowns of All Time,
The Baseball Hall of Shame™ Inducts:

BURLEIGH GRIMES
Pitcher · New York, AL · June 18, 1934

New York Yankees hurler Burleigh Grimes was such a hothead that he once threw a beanball at the on-deck hitter!

Batters trembled just looking at Grimes. Nicknamed "Ol' Stubblebeard," he didn't shave before games because his thick whiskers blackened his glowering face, which he felt made him look more intimidating. But he didn't need facial hair to strike fear into batters.

The menacing right-hander believed he owned the inside part of the plate and any hitter foolish enough to trespass in his space would face a duster. Grimes, who hit 101 batters in his 19-year career (mostly with Brooklyn and Pittsburgh), once nailed six batters in a two-inning span.

One hit batsman who doesn't show up in the stats is fellow Hall of Famer Goose Goslin.

In a game against the visiting Detroit Tigers, Grimes came on to pitch in the sixth inning with the Yankees ahead 5–4. He gave

Ol' Stubblebeard pitching a fit   NATIONAL BASEBALL HALL OF FAME LIBRARY

up a screaming line drive single to Goslin but otherwise held the Tigers in check until the ninth inning when they scored two runs to win 6–5.

While warming up in the final frame, the volatile pitcher noticed that Goslin was swinging his bat in the on-deck circle while intently watching Grimes's delivery—much too intently as far as the hurler was concerned. On his next warm-up throw, the terrible-tempered Grimes low-bridged the Tigers slugger with a fastball.

"Goose was so eager to get back up there and bat that he was inching out of the batter's circle," Grimes explained after the game. "So I let him have it."

FRANK LACORTE
Pitcher · Houston, NL · May 26, 1982

Burned up over a lousy pitching performance, Frank LaCorte stalked off the mound and into the clubhouse and torched his uniform.

In a home game against the Montreal Expos, the Houston Astros relief pitcher came on to start the 10th inning of a scoreless tie. But after a groundout, he loaded the bases on three walks. LaCorte, who had yet to win a game that year, was summarily yanked. By the time LaCorte plopped down in front of his locker, his reliever, George Cappuzzello, gave up a run-producing sacrifice fly and a three-run home run for a 4–0 Astros defeat.

Because LaCorte was charged with the loss, he was flaming mad and had to do something to vent his rage. After several previous poor outings, he had destroyed the clubhouse trash cans and broken teammates' bats. This time he stripped off his uniform, pulled out a book of matches, and set fire to his jersey.

Slumped over the charred remains, LaCorte told reporters, "That jersey took a long time to burn. It took a lot of matches. It doesn't burn easily but it burns long."

Then he requested a new number from the club. He didn't want number 31 anymore because he was tired of running up so many 3-and-1 counts. He received a new number, 27, and a new jersey—along with a $250 fine for burning his old uniform.

The new number didn't help much. LaCorte won only once all year.

DAVID CONE
Pitcher · New York, NL · April 30, 1990

New York Mets hurler David Cone was so caught up in a squabble with an umpire that he didn't hear his own teammates' warning shouts that runners were scoring at will behind his back.

Cone, too caught up in pleading his case

Cone's fury erupted in the bottom of the fourth inning in a game against the host Atlanta Braves, who were winning 2–1. The Braves had runners Dale Murphy on second and Ernie Whitt on first with two out. Mark Lemke hit a grounder that first baseman Mike Marshall went for but couldn't reach. Second baseman Gregg Jefferies fielded the ball and tossed it to Cone who had raced over to cover first. Although it was a close play, the pitcher thought the runner was out and the inning was over.

However, umpire Charlie Williams called Lemke safe, claiming Cone hadn't touched the base. Cone exploded and launched into a lengthy tirade.

Murphy, who had reached third, noticed that Cone's back was to him and began sneaking down the line and then broke for home. Other Mets hollered at Cone to no avail.

Whitt, meanwhile, had gone to second and then on to third. Seeing Cone still pitching a fit with Williams, Whitt bolted for home.

Jefferies, whose shouts went unheeded, ran over to Cone, yelled at him (see photo), then grabbed him and tried to turn him around.

But the angry hurler was oblivious to everyone but Williams—until the ump mockingly told him, "While you're arguing, another run just scored."

Cone finally regained control of himself, but it was much too late. The Mets never recovered from his two-run outburst and lost 7–4.

"I just snapped," Cone admitted after the game.

Said miffed Mets manager Davey Johnson, "I've seen some strange things in my life in baseball, but this is up there on top of the list."

CHARLIE MOORE
Catcher · Milwaukee, AL
September 30, 1973, and July 19, 1978

Twice Milwaukee Brewers catcher Charlie Moore let his temper get the best of him . . . and twice his team came out the worst for it.

On the final day of the 1973 season, his rookie year, the visiting Brewers led the Boston Red Sox 2–1 in the bottom of the eighth inning at Fenway Park. But Boston had runners Tommy Harper on third and Danny Cater on first with one out. Ben Oglivie then lofted a fly to center fielder Bob Coluccio, who caught the ball and threw it home. Moore snared the ball and tagged the sliding Harper, but plate umpire Bill Kunkel called the runner safe.

Moore leaped to his feet and slammed the ball down in a fit of rage. Then he laid into Kunkel with a string of invectives. Unfortunately, Moore never bothered to call time-out and was oblivious to the ball, which was now rolling aimlessly toward the Brewers dugout.

Meanwhile, Cater had tagged up from first after the catch and scrambled to second, then to third, and kept on motoring to the plate. Cater crossed home with the winning run before Moore realized that he had forgotten to call time. The Brewers lost 3–2.

Apparently, Moore didn't learn his lesson. Five years later he committed a similar boiling-mad blunder in another game with the Red Sox, this time in Milwaukee.

In the top of the seventh inning of a 2–2 deadlock, Boston had runners George Scott on second and Butch Hobson on first with two out. Batter Frank Duffy singled to left fielder Ben Oglivie (who was now with the Brewers) as Scott raced for home. Oglivie fired the ball to Moore, who thought he had the plate blocked, but umpire Rich Garcia called Scott safe.

Moore jumped up and charged Garcia, vigorously protesting the call. But once again, Moore forgot to call time-out. In the heat of the debate, he wasn't aware that the ball squirted out of his glove. Hobson, who had scooted to third on the hit, kept right on running, and crossed the plate unchallenged with the fourth run of the inning. Boston went on to win 8–2.

Moore faced the music with the press after the game. "I thought I still had the ball in my glove," he said. "The ball must have fallen out when I jumped up to argue with the ump. It was different than the time in 1973. Then, I actually threw the ball down. This time I thought I had the ball." Both his meltdowns led to the same finish—a maddening defeat.

GEORGE BRETT
Third Baseman · Kansas City, AL · July 24, 1983

Most umpires would agree that Kansas City Royals superstar George Brett was an incredibly nice player who treated them with dignity and respect . . . except for the time he tried to maul one.

Captured on videotape for all to see for generations, Brett went postal in the infamous Pine Tar Bat Incident. And he wasn't the only one who was furious. Before the epic dispute was finally resolved 25 days later, players, managers, owners, umpires, fans, and even a judge were, at one point or another, all royally ticked off.

Trying to protect a 4–3 lead, New York Yankees relief specialist Rich Gossage was brought in to pitch to Brett in the top of the ninth inning with one on and two out. Fans at Yankee Stadium gasped when Brett smashed a breathtaking two-run blast to put Kansas City up 5–4. Then the fun began.

Yankees manager Billy Martin sprinted from the dugout, rule book righteously in hand. He pointed out to the umpires that the pine tar on Brett's bat exceeded the 18-inch-long limit. So they measured the bat. In the Royals dugout, Brett's teammate Frank White told him the umps would probably call Brett out and negate the home run.

Recalled Brett, "I told Frank, 'If they call me out for using too much pine tar, I'll run out there and kill one of those SOBs.' As soon as I said that, [plate umpire] Tim McClelland, who stands 6'6" and weighs 250, looks for me in the dugout and says 'You're out.'"

Brett burst out of the dugout like an enraged bull bent on mangling McClelland. Never before had Brett been so stark raving mad. Umpiring crew chief Joe Brinkman intercepted Brett and held him around the neck to keep him from attacking McClelland. Brett broke free from Brinkman's chokehold only to be tackled by the other umpires. Back on his feet and restrained by umps and his manager Dick Howser, Brett blistered McClelland with every epithet he knew. (The video has become a favorite for lip readers.)

"I'm a very competitive person and I don't like to lose," Brett said years later. "To do something that I considered extraordinary—hitting a home run against Goose Gossage—in an extraordinary place like Yankee Stadium just kind of magnified my emotions, and as a result I went a little ballistic."

Because the home run was disallowed and Brett was called out, the game was over and the Yankees won 4–3. Or so it seemed.

The Royals were incredulous that Brett had hit an apparent game-losing homer. "Broadway wouldn't buy that script," groused Howser, who protested the game. "It wouldn't last past opening night, it's so unbelievable."

Four days later, American League president Lee MacPhail upheld the protest, declaring that although the pine tar was technically illegal,

Brett going postal　　　　　　　　　　　　　　© BETTMANN/CORBIS

it didn't violate "the spirit of the rules" nor did it help Brett's home run. Because the homer counted after all, the game had to be continued with two out in the ninth inning and the Royals ahead 5–4.

Now it was the Yankees' turn to howl. Snarled owner George Steinbrenner, "It sure tests our faith in our leadership." And in a typical veiled threat, Steinbrenner added, "I wouldn't want to be Lee MacPhail living in New York."

Martin griped that he had never heard about the rules being "spiritual" and suggested that the rulebook "is only good for when you go deer hunting and run out of toilet paper."

The completion of the suspended game was set for August 18. The Yankees then crassly announced they would charge regular admission for the game—and that brought an angry group of fans steaming into court. Two suits were filed claiming that the extra charge was illegal. A judge issued an injunction prohibiting the mini-game. Or so it seemed.

The fiasco made it all the way up to the Appellate Division of the New York Supreme Court where Justice Joseph P. Sullivan called a screeching halt to all the foolishness with perhaps the shortest ruling in legal history: Play ball!

The Yankees came sulking into the stadium still complaining. But few fans knew the players were there. The team didn't bother announcing that management had reconsidered, and fans with ticket stubs to the first game would be admitted without charge. Everyone else would have to pay $2.50 for the grandstand seats or $1 for the bleachers. Consequently, only about 1,200 fans showed up.

The completion required only nine minutes and 41 seconds. The Royals' Hal McRae struck out to end the top of the ninth and the Yankees went down in order in the bottom half. New York's Don Baylor said afterward that he was disgusted, adding, "If I had wanted to watch a soap opera, I'd have stayed home."

Brett says that although he's in the Hall of Fame, he'll always be known as the Pine Tar Guy. "I look back at it and laugh," he said. "I think it's the funniest thing that happened in my career. My son Jackson, every once in a while, will say, 'Dad, put in the movie where you hit the home run and you run out and you're real mad.'"

CHUCK KNOBLAUCH
Second Baseman · New York, AL · October 7, 1998

On a controversial play, New York Yankees second baseman Chuck Knoblauch blew his cool . . . and as a result, blew his team's chances for a postseason victory.

The host New York Yankees were tied 1–1 with the Cleveland Indians in the top of the 12th inning of Game 2 of the 1998 American League Championship Series at Yankee Stadium. With one out and Cleveland's Enrique Wilson on first base, Travis Fryman laid down a bunt toward first baseman Tino Martinez, who charged the ball. Knoblauch raced over to cover first but Martinez's throw hit Fryman in the back and the ball rolled behind Knoblauch.

Convinced that Fryman should have been called out for interference because he ran outside the baseline on the bunt attempt, Knoblauch ignored the live ball and lit into first base umpire John Shulock. Knoblauch pointed at the basepath and argued while Wilson rounded second. Knoblauch pointed at the basepath and argued while Wilson reached third. And Knoblauch pointed at the basepath and argued as Wilson sprinted for home.

The second baseman was so intent on debating the call that he failed to pick up the ball until it was too late. Wilson scored the go-ahead run and the Indians tacked on two more runs to win 4–1 and even the ALCS at a game apiece.

New Yorkers let Knoblauch know that a temper tantrum during a playoff game is a no-no. He was booed loudly by the hometown crowd when he came to bat in the bottom of the 12th inning. (He reached first on an error.) The New York papers slammed him with headlines calling him "Blauch Head" and "Chuck Brainlauch."

The next day, he faced the press and admitted, "I screwed up the play, and I feel terrible about that. I should have got the ball, regardless of what the outcome of the umpire's call was. I need to apologize to my teammates and my manager and the Yankees and all the Yankee fans. Bottom line, I screwed up the play."

Fortunately for Knoblauch, the Yankees went on to win the ALCS in six games—and nothing brings forgiveness faster than victories. But no one forgets. "He was yelling at the umpire, and you can't do that," said Yankees manager Joe Torre. "You have got to make the play and then go back and argue with the umpire."

OUT OF LEFT FIELD

For the Most Far-fetched Excuses of All Time
for Missing a Game or Blowing a Play,
The Baseball Hall of Shame™ Inducts:

JOSE CARDENAL
Outfielder · Chicago, NL · 1972–1976

Even if Jose Cardenal hadn't been a good outfielder and hitter, he'd have been worth keeping on the roster just for his wonderfully imaginative excuses for not wanting to play.

Cardenal played for eight teams during his lengthy career. He was the kind of player who, if he couldn't give 100 percent effort on the field, thought it best not to give any. So he often drove his managers crazy with his reasons why he belonged in the comfort of the dugout rather than out in the hot sun. He was especially exasperating during his stint with the Chicago Cubs.

When the team was training in Scottsdale, Arizona, in 1974, Cardenal asked to be scratched from the lineup of an exhibition game because of a cricket. "There was only one cricket in my room, but all night long it was driving me crazy," Cardenal recalled years later. "He was jumping all over the place and every time I tried to catch him, he would hop to another corner. I couldn't sleep at all and the next day I went to the ballpark and saw my name in the lineup. I went to [Cubs manager] Jim Marshall and said, 'Jim, last night, I had a bad night.' When he asked me what I meant, I said, 'There was a cricket in my room and I couldn't sleep. I didn't even get an hour of sleep, so I don't think I can play today.' Jim made a big deal about it with the media and I can laugh about it now, but in those years, people really gave me a hard time about it."

Cardenal took himself out of the lineup of another game because his left eye was stuck shut. Claiming he had a small infection, he told Marshall that his eyelid and eyelashes were stuck to his left eyeball. "My eyelashes were stuck together," Cardenal told a reporter at the time. "I couldn't see, so I couldn't play."

Sporting one of the game's biggest afros back then, Cardenal looked like he was sprouting Mickey Mouse ears under his batting helmet. He also liked to wear skin-tight uniform pants during an era when most players preferred the baggier look. And that led to one of Cardenal's craziest excuses for not playing. According to Fred Talbot, who pitched for five American League teams from 1963 to 1970, Cardenal once sat out three straight winter league games because he couldn't find pants that were tight enough around his legs.

LOU "THE MAD RUSSIAN" NOVIKOFF
Outfielder · Chicago, NL · 1941–1944

Chicago Cubs outfielder Lou "The Mad Russian" Novikoff had a problem. Anytime a ball was hit over his head during home games, he would back up only so far and go no farther. More often than not, the ball bounced off the wall and shot past him back toward the infield.

Why did he constantly give up on those catchable long drives? Because, as Novikoff explained to perplexed Chicago Cubs manager Charlie Grimm, he had an incredible fear of vines. That was a real problem considering he was playing in the outfield in the ivy-covered confines of Wrigley Field.

Novikoff, all wet over his fear of vines

CHICAGO TRIBUNE STAFF PHOTO
BY CY WOLF

Grimm tried everything he could think of to cure Novikoff of his phobia. The skipper brought in poisonous goldenrod to show the outfielder that the vines were not goldenrod. Grimm even rubbed the Wrigley vines all over his own face and hands and then chewed a few to prove they weren't poison ivy. But Novikoff never did get over his aversion to the vines. Consequently, a lot of balls sailed over his outstretched glove.

And if that excuse got a little weak, he had another cooked up to explain away his poor fielding (which a Chicago sportswriter described as "wrestling the ball to the ground"). Novikoff complained to Grimm, "I can't play in Wrigley because the left field line isn't straight like it is in other parks. It's crooked."

FLINT RHEM
Pitcher · St. Louis, NL · September 19, 1930

The St. Louis Cardinals were in Brooklyn for a crucial three-game series with the Dodgers (then known as the Robins) during a battle for the 1930 pennant. Because the teams were in a virtual tie for first place, the Cards were depending on their strong pitching staff, including hard-throwing—and hard-drinking—right-hander Flint Rhem.

Rhem, who was 10-8 at the time, was scheduled to start the second game, but he disappeared without a word of explanation. He was missing for two days, and the St. Louis management was beginning to fear the worst about their big hurler.

Then, just as suddenly as he vanished, Rhem showed up. There was a simple explanation for his disappearance, he reported. Gangsters had kidnapped him! Yes, gangsters from Brooklyn had snatched him right off the street in front of the Alamac Hotel. And not only that but they held him prisoner at gunpoint in a log cabin and forced him, totally against his will, to consume massive amounts of liquor! "They told me, 'We're going to get you drunk so you can't pitch against our Robins,'" Rhem claimed.

Of course there weren't any kidnappers and the log cabin was really a gin joint down the street from the team hotel. By the time Rhem had sobered up, the Cardinals had swept the series and were on their way to winning the pennant.

As for Rhem's excuse for his absence, St. Louis general manager Branch Rickey told reporters, "You couldn't disprove his story by the way he smelled."

BILLY LOES

Pitcher · Brooklyn, NL · October 6, 1952

Brooklyn Dodgers hurler Billy Loes was pitching more excuses than fastballs during the 1952 World Series.

He gave his best alibis concerning two plays that he botched in Game 6 against the New York Yankees. The Dodgers, who had a 3-games-to-2 lead, were up 1–0 entering the top of the seventh inning at Ebbets Field. Loes had pitched six shutout innings, but in the seventh, he gave up a leadoff homer to Yogi Berra followed by a single to Gene Woodling. When Loes went into his stretch, he accidentally dropped the ball, and the umps called a balk. Later, Loes claimed the ball squirted out of his hands because there was "too much spit on it."

He gave an even more outrageous excuse about the play that followed a strikeout and a pop-out in the seventh. With Woodling in scoring position at second, weak-hitting pitcher Vic Raschi hit an easy grounder back to the mound. Loes didn't get his glove down in time and the ball bounced off his knee for an RBI single. The Dodgers ended up losing 3–2. After the game, Loes gave this confounding excuse for missing the grounder: "I lost it in the sun."

Even before the Series began, Loes issued a different kind of excuse while trying to talk his way out of a touchy situation. Trouble erupted when a newspaper quoted him saying the Yankees would beat the Dodgers in six games. Because that wasn't the smartest thing to say about a team you're pitching for, Brooklyn manager Chuck Dressen read him the riot act for his careless statement. In his warped defense, Loes blamed the reporter. "I told him the Yankees would win it in seven," the pitcher said, "but he screwed it up and had me saying they would win it in six."

Well, at least Loes was right about one thing. The Yankees did win it in seven.

JESSE BARNES
Pitcher · New York, NL · 1922

Jesse Barnes came up with a phony excuse for missing a bed check, but it turned out great for him. He was perhaps the only curfew violator in baseball who made money because he *did* get nabbed for breaking the rules.

Barnes, then one of the New York Giants' best pitchers, just never could see why anyone should be in bed by midnight. So most every chance he got, he sneaked out for some late-night fun. More often than not, he made it back without anyone being the wiser. But occasionally, he was caught and fined by manager John McGraw.

During the 1922 season, McGraw snagged Barnes sneaking back to his room after curfew and fined him $100. "Next time I catch you, it'll be $200," snapped the manager.

A few weeks later in Philadelphia, Barnes partied until the wee hours of the morning. Rather than risk going through the lobby of the team's hotel, Barnes tried climbing the fire escape to his room. But he slipped and fell on one of the iron rungs and badly bruised his shins.

Later that morning, he walked into the clubhouse with a noticeable limp. McGraw stared at Barnes coldly and asked, "What happened to you?"

Barnes screwed up his face in pain and hobbled toward his locker. "I slipped on a cake of soap in the bathtub," he replied.

The answer was too glib to fool an old pro like the Little Napoleon. "Slipped on a cake of soap, huh? Well, that's pretty dumb. You're fined $200—and next time, don't use soap."

The following day the newspapers ran the story of Barnes's fine and his bogus excuse. One of the executives of a company that made rubber bath mats read the article and had a brainstorm. He phoned Barnes and offered to pay him $1,000 for a testimonial. Barnes agreed in a flash.

Within a week, an ad appeared in the papers showing a photo of the smiling pitcher with one leg over the tub. Underneath, the caption read, "If Jesse Barnes had used a NON-SKID BATH MAT, he wouldn't have slipped in his tub."

Thanks to his lie, Barnes walked, or rather limped, away with a tidy $800 profit.

TURNSTILE TURN-OFFS

For the Most Undignified Ballpark Promotions of All Time, The Baseball Hall of Shame™ Inducts:

CLEVELAND INDIANS' TEN-CENT BEER NIGHT
June 4, 1974

It probably wasn't the best promotion that the Cleveland Indians management ever conceived. Okay, it was by far the worst: Fans were offered all the beer they could guzzle at 10 cents a cup.

Was it any surprise that this idea turned into a colossal mistake that would drive one—or in this case, most everyone—to drink? The promotion was nothing more than an open invitation for fans, including under-aged teens slipping money to adults who could buy the beer for them, to get rip-roaring and raucously drunk and riot.

At first, management seemed pleased when more than 25,000 people—twice the usual crowd—showed up for the game against the Texas Rangers. Of course, some of them showed up already drunk or stoned, or both. Among them were those who smuggled in hundreds, if not thousands, of firecrackers, even though it was June 4, not July 4. And they brought in their pot. So by the early innings, the stadium was shrouded in a cloud of gunpowder and marijuana smoke.

As the drinking increased, the inhibitions diminished. A heavyset woman ran onto the Indians on-deck circle and bared her breasts to tremendous cheers. She tried to kiss umpire crew chief Nestor Chylak, but he wasn't in a smooching mood. In the fourth inning, a naked man ran onto the field and slid into second. In the next frame, two men jumped the wall and mooned the Rangers outfielders before being chased by stadium security.

The exhibitionists seemed to inspire the drunks to act more boisterously. When Texas pitcher Ferguson Jenkins was doubled over in pain after being hit in the stomach by a line drive, the sloshed crowd chanted, "Hit him again, hit him again, harder, harder!" And when Rangers manager Billy Martin came out to argue a call, they tossed cups—many still full of beer—at him. He responded by blowing kisses to them.

Midway through the game, the vendors couldn't keep up with the demand, so in the infinite wisdom of the Indians' management, fans were allowed to line up behind the outfield fences and have their cups filled directly from the beer trucks. With the same kind of thinking—or lack of it—management never thought to request additional police for the beer bash.

By now, mothers and fathers had scooped up their young and fled the ballpark as a constant barrage of beer, rubbish, and firecrackers rained down on the field between innings—and between dashes by an ever increasing number of streakers.

When firecrackers were bursting in the Rangers' bullpen, Chylak ordered both bullpens evacuated and told relievers they could get extra warm-up tosses on the mound.

In the ninth inning, the Indians rallied to tie the game 5–5 with the winning run on second base. But the team never had a chance to drive him in. A fan jumped from the outfield seats and knocked off the cap of Rangers right fielder Jeff Burroughs. That was the signal for all hell to break loose. Fueled by more than 60,000 10-ounce cups of beer, drunken fans poured onto the field, some surrounding Burroughs, trying to rip off his glove.

Ten-Cent Beer Night: boozers and losers RON KUNTZ

That's when Billy Martin grabbed a fungo bat and led a charge of Texas Rangers on a rescue mission only to be ambushed by hundreds of angry, soused fans wielding knives, chains, and pieces of stadium seats. Now it was the Indians' turn to rescue the rescuers. Armed with bats, Cleveland manager Ken Aspromonte and his players sprinted out of the dugout, joining forces with police who had finally showed up. They soon cleared a path of safety for both teams and the umpires.

Understandably, although some say belatedly, Chylak ordered the game forfeited to Texas. Nine people were arrested and seven were treated at nearby hospitals for minor injuries. Chylak, whose hand and head were bleeding from flying debris, called the fans "uncontrollable beasts."

So what had Indians management learned from the debacle? Team officials announced that at the three other planned Ten-Cent Beer Nights, fans would be restricted to only four cups apiece per night, no exceptions. American League president Lee MacPhail said that wouldn't be necessary because there would be no more such promotions.

WASHINGTON SENATORS' LADIES DAY
1897

It was a promotion ahead of its time. In 1897, the Washington Senators (a National League team that lasted only eight years) introduced Ladies Day to the nation's capital. To broaden the appeal of the game and to boost the box office take, the ball club invited women to attend free to learn more about the game. The ladies, it turned out, knew a whole lot more and acted a whole lot differently than management thought.

A mob of pushing, shouting, anything-but-ladylike guests filled the stands at Boundary Field (also known as National Park). They focused most of their attention on pitcher George "Winnie" Mercer, the city's heartthrob. His nickname came from "Winner" which was shortened to "Win," but the gals called him "Winnie." The boyishly handsome 5-foot, 7-inch, 140-pound hurler had piercing dark eyes and a smooth delivery both on and off the field that made women swoon.

In a game against the Cincinnati Reds, Mercer was dazzling on the mound to the delight of his adoring audience. But Mercer also happened to hate umpires as much as he loved the ladies—and the combination of the two in the same ballpark at the same time spelled trouble. The more he baited umpire Bill Carpenter, who was calling balls and strikes, the more the women squealed in glee. But after one heated rhubarb in the fifth inning over a ball that Mercer thought was a strike, Carpenter ejected the pitcher. The ladies were incensed and let loose with epithets that, under other circumstances, would have left them blushing.

They kept up their indignant uproar until the final out of the game, won by Cincinnati. Unable to restrain themselves any longer, the infuriated women charged onto the field. It was like girls gone wild, only instead of taking their clothes off, they were trying to strip the umpire. They surrounded Carpenter, battered him to the ground with their parasols, and ripped his clothing. With the help of some players, the beleaguered ump fought his way through the mob to the safety of the clubhouse. He was able to leave the ballpark only after putting on a disguise.

But the turmoil didn't subside. Angered by his escape, the women attacked the ballpark. They ripped out seats, broke windows and doors, and tore railings from their moorings before police quelled the disturbance.

No one dared hold another Ladies Day in Washington for years.

NEW YORK YANKEES' ARMY DAY
June 10, 1975

A thunderous 21-gun salute honoring the military created some embarrassing repercussions for the New York Yankees and the Army.

Barry Landers, Yankees promotions director, decided to celebrate the U.S. Army's 200th birthday by holding "Army Day" at Shea Stadium, where the team was playing during the renovation of Yankee Stadium.

Before a game with the California Angels, a battery from Brooklyn's Fort Hamilton positioned two 75 mm cannons on the warning track, facing the center field flag. The Army brass assured Landers that the paraffin in the cannons would flash harmlessly and burn out after flying about 20 feet over the fence and onto a grassy area beyond. The Army experts were probably the same ones who predicted the Vietnam War would last only a few months.

With an ear-splitting boom, the battery fired the first salute—and knocked down part of the fence. But rather than call a cease-fire, the soldier boys kept right on blasting away. The whole stadium filled with smoke and shook with earthquake force. Glass shattered in the stadium's exclusive enclosed Diamond Club, adding to the terror.

When the smoke cleared, 31,809 temporarily deaf fans saw a gaping hole in the center field fence. The cannoneers had blown away three fence panels and set fire to a fourth, which was quickly doused. The game was delayed while groundskeepers hurriedly covered the holes with plywood.

"I was the one who got the idea," a chagrined Landers recalled. "I was the one who got the blame, too." And he was the one who ended up with the nickname "Boom Boom."

Commenting on the promotion on his nightly TV newscast, Walter Cronkite told his viewers, "The final scores: Yankees 6, Angels 4; Army 21, Fence 0 . . . and that's the way it is . . ."

CHICAGO WHITE SOX'S DISCO DEMOLITION NIGHT
July 12, 1979

If ever there was a promotion that was off-key, it was Disco Demolition Night.

The event was dreamed up by popular Chicago disc jockey Steve Dahl, who, along with his legion of listeners, hated disco and its intrusion on the music scene. So he schemed with Mike Veeck, the son of ailing team owner Bill Veeck, to blow up a pile of disco records in center field between games of a twi-night doubleheader at Comiskey Park.

A real blast for disco-hating fans   © BETTMANN/CORBIS

Fans who brought a disco record for destruction at the ballpark were
charged 98 cents admission (as in 97.9 FM, the call numbers of Dahl's
radio station, WLUP).

Roland Hemond, general manager of the White Sox at the time,
recalled that Bill Veeck had checked himself out of the hospital that
day and showed up at the stadium unexpectedly. "I said, 'What are you
doing here?'" recalled Hemond in a *New York Times* article. "And Bill
said, 'I'm worried about this promotion. It could be catastrophic.'"

As it turned out, father knew best. Son Mike Veeck expected an
extra 5,000 fans to show up, which meant an attendance of 20,000 to
25,000. He woefully underestimated Chicago's level of disco loath-
ing, because more than 50,000 crammed into the stadium for the

doubleheader against the Detroit Tigers. In fact, when all the seats were taken, people on the outside brought ladders so thousands more could scale the walls to get in.

It took only a few innings before the fans noticed the striking resemblance between a record and a Frisbee. Flying records sailed through the air, causing a halt to the game several times to clear the discs off the field.

"They [the records] would slice around you and stick in the ground," recalled Rusty Staub, the Tigers designated hitter in the first game. "I've never seen anything so dangerous in my life. I begged the guys to put on their batting helmets."

After the Tigers won the first game 4–1, the rowdy fans were primed for the disco demolition ceremony. Dahl, dressed in army fatigues, went out to center field where the records had been piled and worked the crowd to chants of "Disco sucks!" Then a bosomy blonde "fire goddess" named Lorelei triggered the explosion. With a thunderous boom, thousands of records went up in flames, shooting hundreds of feet in the air.

To the fans, the blast looked like a signal to attack. While yellow-jacketed security guards had been sent outside the stadium to prevent people from crashing the gates, thousands of fans inside Comiskey Park surged out of the stands and ran wild over the field. They tore up the pitching rubber and scooped up the dirt. They stole the bases—literally—and dug up home plate. They dragged out the batting cage and trashed it. They burned banners and climbed foul poles.

Pleas over the public address system by Bill Veeck and broadcaster Harry Caray fell on deaf ears. Finally Veeck had no choice but to call the cops. A detachment of helmeted police cleared the field relatively quickly and made 50 arrests. At least six people suffered minor injuries.

Although the crowd was unruly, it was relatively nonviolent, recalled Mike Veeck. "The great thing was all the kids were stoned," he told the *New York Times*. "Had we had drunks to deal with, then we would have had some trouble. The kids were really docile."

But they had damaged the field. As luck would have it, Nestor Chylak, the supervisor of umpires, happened to be at Disco Demolition Night. He also had been the chief umpire at Cleveland's disastrous 10-Cent

Beer Night five years earlier. After Chylak met with the umpires, Bill Veeck and Tigers manager Sparky Anderson, the White Sox forfeited the second game.

When asked about that night 30 years later, Hemond told the *New York Times*, "It was a great promotion. We're still talking about it today."

NEW YORK GIANTS' SCRAP METAL DAY
September 26, 1942

The New York Giants held a "Scrap Metal Day" to help the war effort—but ended up fighting a losing battle at the ballpark.

For the last day of the 1942 regular season, kids were admitted to the Polo Grounds free if they brought in scrap metal, which would be transformed into new uses by America's armed forces during World War II. More than 11,000 youngsters responded by piling up 56 tons of scrap outside the stadium before a doubleheader against the visiting Boston Braves.

The kids behaved through the first game, won by the Giants 6–4, and most of the nightcap. But in the bottom of the eighth inning, with New York ahead 5–2, the young fans tumbled out of the stands, streamed onto the field, and engulfed the Braves, who were trying to take their positions.

Umpires Ziggy Sears and Tommy Dunn were swallowed in the maelstrom—a hopeless, tangled mass of kids running helter-skelter all over the field. Having fought his way to the Giants dugout, Sears asked for an announcement stating that the game would be forfeited if the field was not cleared. But the announcement couldn't be heard above the din.

Police, ushers, and grounds crew could not move the wild mob off the field. Although the Braves claimed they wanted to keep playing, Sears ordered the game forfeited to Boston.

It would have taken a whole battalion to round up the rampaging youngsters. But most of the battalions were overseas with a much bigger fight on their hands.

HOUSTON'S "BREAK THE JINX NIGHT"
September 3, 1962

When an expansion team found itself in danger of setting an all-time record for futility, it tried to change its luck with a day of mysticism, magic, and superstition, including a bizarre ceremony that featured a witch doctor.

In their debut year, the Houston Colt .45s (who later became the Astros) were on their way to becoming the first team in the modern era ever to lose an entire season series to an opposing club. They had dropped their first 15 games against the Philadelphia Phillies.

For its final three-game homestand with the Phillies, which included a twi-night doubleheader, the team publicized the bad news record and scheduled a "Break the Jinx Night" for the twin-bill.

The front office hired Dr. Mesabubu, a fictitious witch doctor from the equally fictitious Wauwautua tribe, to hex the Phillies. Before batting practice, he climbed a ladder in front of the Philadelphia dugout and spewed his mumbo jumbo. Shortly before the game, the witch doctor—decked out in head dress and skins—performed a ceremonial dance that freaked out a couple of Phillies who were strong believers in the occult. They refused to leave the bench until the witch doctor left the field.

As a backup to the shaman, Houston management brought in Joe Btfsplk—the human version of the bad-luck-attracting character in the "Li'l Abner" comic strip. Joe went out to the bullpen and put a double whammy on Philadelphia starting pitcher Art Mahaffey during his pre-game warm-up. Houston also had ex-prizefighter Kid Dugan, who was known for his devastating stare, to put a spell on the Phillies.

Then, for extra juju, Colt .45 fans were given half off the ticket price if they brought jinx-breakers to the ballpark. People brought four-leaf clovers, rabbits' feet, horseshoes, lucky old shoes, and black cats. Even the owner of the team, Roy Hofheinz, got into the act. He wore a beaded headpiece from Thailand that was supposed to bring good luck.

The efforts of the crowd, Dr. Mesabubu, Joe Bftstlk, and Kid Dugan worked like a charm—against the home team. Houston lost both games,

3–2 (a complete game four-hitter by Mahaffey) and 5–3, making the streak 0-17 against the Phillies.

The next day, with only one shot left to crush the curse, the Colt .45s avoided total humiliation by beating Philadelphia 4–1.

ATLANTA BRAVES' FOURTH OF JULY CELEBRATION
July 5, 1985

The Atlanta Braves' Independence Day fireworks show lit up more than just the sky. It sparked a blaze of alarm from neighbors who thought they were under attack.

Perhaps it had something to do with the time. Braves management thoughtlessly set off the booming Fourth of July pyrotechnic display at *4:01 a.m. on July 5.*

In all fairness, the Braves didn't plan on triggering the fireworks at such a wee hour of the morning. The team had promised the 44,947 fans who arrived at Atlanta-Fulton County Stadium a spectacular sky show after the night game with the New York Mets. But, unfortunately, the game went on and on and on.

It turned into a record-setting marathon featuring an 84-minute rain delay at the start of the game and another 41-minute interruption in the third inning. Making this a long night's journey into day was the game itself, a 19-inning affair that lasted six hours and 10 minutes before the Mets won 16–13.

When the game mercifully ended at 3:55 a.m.—the latest finish in Major League history at the time—only about 8,000 hardy souls were still on hand. True to their word, Braves officials went ahead with the fireworks without any regard for the thousands of unsuspecting people who were sleeping peacefully in their homes near the stadium. Rather than give the survivors of the marathon a free ticket to the next night game and shoot off the fireworks at that time, management sent the bombs bursting in air at 4:01 a.m.

While the fans were oohing and aahing over the boomers, instant terror swept through the minds of the Braves' rousted neighbors. One startled citizen dialed 911 and shrieked, "We're being bombed!"

"Lord, there were a few wild minutes there when we thought we had a mini-panic on our hands," recalled Captain C.V. Forrester, of the Atlanta Public Safety Department. "The first thing that was heard was this huge explosion that must have knocked everybody out of bed. People were running out into the streets, some were rushing into our precinct office, and others were jamming our phone lines. Most of the neighborhood thought the Civil War had started all over again. I doubt if anyone went back to bed after that."

CHICAGO WHITE SOX'S AL SMITH NIGHT
August 26, 1959

Al Smith should have played under an assumed name when his team offered free admission—in his honor—to anyone named Smith.

That's because Al Smith Night turned into Al Smith Nightmare.

From the moment Smith donned a White Sox uniform in 1958, the Chicago fans didn't like him. They were upset over the trade that brought the left fielder from the Cleveland Indians in exchange for their longtime hero Minnie Minoso. It didn't help matters any that Smith was hampered by a bad ankle and hit only .252 in his first year with the White Sox while Minoso hit .302 for the Indians. During the following year, when Chicago was battling for its first pennant in 40 years, Smith's average had sunk to .232.

So team owner Bill Veeck decided to help Smith win over the fans by staging a special Al Smith Night at Comiskey Park. Everyone named Smith was admitted into the left field seats for free, just by showing some kind of identification.

The idea was grand, but the results weren't. Sure, Veeck had the fans *behind* Smith, but that didn't necessarily mean they were *for* him. Throughout the game, most of the 27,750 spectators, including 5,253

Smiths who got in free, booed Smith unmercifully. The besieged left fielder could have silenced the crowd and maybe even have won them over if only he had played well. Alas, he didn't.

In the game, pitting the first-place White Sox against the seventh-place Boston Red Sox, Smith grounded into a force play with a runner on second in the second inning, singled in the fourth, and struck out with a runner on first in the sixth.

In the top of the seventh inning with Chicago clinging to a 2–1 lead, Boston had the tying run on second with no outs when Vic Wertz drove the ball to deep left-center field. Smith caught up with the ball—then dropped it for an error, right in front of all the Smiths. His flub paved the way for a four-run outburst, including two unearned runs, that vaulted the Red Sox ahead 5–2.

To cap off Al Smith Night, Smith came to bat in the bottom of the eighth inning with two on and one out. He had the perfect opportunity to atone for his less than acceptable play and turn the jeers into cheers. But it was not to be. He popped out to the third baseman, and the White Sox went on to lose 7–6.

Smith later said he had a premonition that the night might not go the way he had hoped. Before the game, he went out to the lower left field stands to sign autographs for fans named Smith. "I saw my milkman that night," Smith recalled. "He was a Polish fellow. So I said, 'How the hell did you get out here?' He said he got hold of somebody's tax bill that had the name of Smith on it. I told him, 'Well, you be my bodyguard out here tonight. I might need one.'"

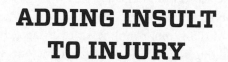

ADDING INSULT
TO INJURY

For the Most Bizarre Diamond Mishaps of All Time, The Baseball Hall of Shame™ Inducts:

GLENALLEN HILL
Outfielder · Toronto, AL · July 6, 1990

Toronto Blue Jays outfielder Glenallen Hill sleepwalked his way right onto the disabled list—after a horrific nightmare about spiders.

Hill, who suffered from arachnophobia (an extreme fear of spiders), went to bed at his home only to have a frighteningly realistic nightmare that huge, poisonous spiders were attacking him. While still in his sleep, Hill bolted out of bed to fight off the spiders that were crawling everywhere in his mind—on the walls, the ceiling, the floors, and on him. Panic-stricken, Hill fled toward the stairway and crashed into two glass coffee tables, smashing one of them.

So desperate was he to escape the spiders that Hill crawled on all fours right over sharp, broken shards of glass. When he finally woke up, he was relieved to discover that it was just a terrible dream. But he was also shocked to see that he was bleeding from head to toe.

The broken glass lacerated his feet, arms, and elbows. His face was bruised and bleeding because he had smacked his head on a table during his blind rush to get away from the creepy crawlies.

The severe cuts on his feet forced Hill to use crutches for a couple of days. In fact, he was so sliced up that the Blue Jays put him on the 15-day disabled list.

He managed to recover nicely from his sleepwalking injuries. But it took him a little longer to get over the ribbing he received from teammates and bench jockeys who kept calling him "Spider-Man."

JOEL ZUMAYA
Pitcher · Detroit, AL · October 10, 2006

Detroit Tigers' flame-throwing relief pitcher Joel Zumaya struck the wrong chord when he had to sit out the 2006 American League Championship Series because of an injury to his pitching hand—from playing too much of the popular video game Guitar Hero.

At the end of the regular season, the 22-year old rookie right-hander was suffering from inflammation in his right wrist and forearm. When he went to the Tigers training staff about the injury, they were perplexed because the cause of the pain wasn't consistent with his powerful throwing motion.

After making him recall everything he did on and off the field in the previous days that might have led to the discomfort, the staff discovered that Zumaya was all but addicted to Guitar Hero. The PlayStation 2 video game came with a guitar-shaped controller modeled after a black Gibson SG guitar. Zumaya would simulate playing an electric guitar while performing popular songs by rock stars from the Red Hot Chili Peppers to Ozzy Osbourne. Zumaya admitted that he sometimes got carried away, spending hours riffing on his virtual guitar.

Detroit management ordered him to quit playing the game. After sitting out the ALCS, in which the Tigers swept the Oakland Athletics in four games, Zumaya recovered from his injury. In the World Series, which the St. Louis Cardinals won four games to one, Zumaya pitched pain-free in three games, giving up one hit and one run in three innings.

Although he curtailed his Guitar Hero playing, Zumaya didn't lose his love for good guitar rock. His entrance music the following season was Jimi Hendrix's "Voodoo Child."

RON LUCIANO
Umpire, AL · June 1, 1971

Ron Luciano looked more like Hulk Hogan than an umpire when he flattened New York Yankees shortstop Gene Michael and put him out of action for several days.

Luciano, one of the most flamboyant arbiters to ever don the blue, was umpiring at second base in a game between the visiting Oakland Athletics and the Yankees. In the top of the ninth inning with the A's ahead 5–2, Oakland's Joe Rudi singled and got the sign to steal.

On the pitch, Rudi took off for second, Michael ran over to cover the base, and Luciano rambled into position to make the call. However, catcher Thurman Munson's peg was wide toward the first base side of the bag.

Michael, Rudi, the ball, and 220 pounds of charging umpire arrived at second at about the same time. Michael caught the throw as Rudi slid safely beneath him. In his own inimitable style, Luciano gave a Broadway performance as he theatrically spread his hands signaling safe. But one man was out—Gene Michael.

The shortstop sailed through the air just as the ump was giving the safe sign. Luciano's battering-ram forearm and elbow slammed into Michael's head and laid him out flat. "One minute Gene flashed by me, and the next minute he was out for the count," recalled Luciano. "I mean, I nailed him good."

When Michael was revived several minutes later, he was too woozy to stand and had to be carried off the field on a stretcher. Michael was rushed by ambulance to the hospital where he was treated for mouth

Luciano, a big hit in more ways than one   © BETTMAN/CORBIS

lacerations and a severe case of whiplash. He was fitted with a neck brace and ordered to sit out for a few days.

"I didn't know what happened," Michael recalled. "I got hit, then my head started hurting. I couldn't figure it out."

When he returned to the Yankees lineup, Michael saw that Luciano was once again the second base umpire. So Michael took up his position at deep short—as far away as he could get from Ron "The Hit Man" Luciano.

FREDDIE FITZSIMMONS
Pitcher · New York, NL · March 26, 1927

During spring training in Miami, chubby Freddie Fitzsimmons had survived the oppressive heat, the wind sprints, and the exercise workouts. But in 1927, there was one thing that got the better of the New York Giants pitching star—his rocking chair.

One balmy evening after eating a big meal, Fitzsimmons settled into a rocking chair on the front porch of the club's hotel and chatted with teammates Rogers Hornsby and Bill Terry. During a lull in the conversation, Fitzsimmons dozed off, prompting Terry and Hornsby to chuckle at the sight of the snoring, rotund pitcher still rocking in his sleep.

Suddenly, Fitzsimmons awoke with a bloodcurdling yell. His companions thought he was reacting to a nightmare, but when they saw him grimace in pain and hold his pitching hand, they knew what had happened. While Fitzsimmons was asleep, his right hand had slipped off his lap and got caught underneath the low-seated rocker. His fingers were flattened under the weight of his 190-pound body.

Although his fingers weren't broken, they were so injured that he couldn't get a proper grip on the baseball and missed several April starts for the Giants. It was a crucial injury because he had been the team's best pitcher the year before with a 14-10 record and an impressive 2.88 ERA. Although he pitched well once he returned to the starting rotation, the Giants couldn't overcome his early-season absence. They finished third, only two games out.

"When he rocked on his hand, we laughed at first," recalled Terry. "But there weren't many of us laughing about it when the season was over."

CHRIS COGHLAN
Left Fielder · Florida, NL · July 25, 2010

A congratulatory shaving cream pie in the face of the day's hero left a bad taste for the Florida Marlins and put their young star outfielder, Chris Coghlan, on the disabled list.

What made it so bizarre was that Coghlan wasn't getting the pie, he was delivering it.

In a home game against the Atlanta Braves, Florida's Wes Helms smacked a bases-loaded single in the bottom of the 11th inning for a thrilling 5–4 victory. It was the fourth walk-off hit for the Marlins during their 10-game homestand.

As was the custom on the team, every time there was a walk-off hit, the hero would get nailed with a full plate of shaving cream in the face, usually while being interviewed on live television. So Coghlan, the reigning National League Rookie of the Year, took it upon himself to deliver the celebratory pie to Helms, who at 35 was the oldest Marlin on the roster.

Grabbing a can of shaving cream that was kept behind the Marlins dugout just for this purpose, Coghlan loaded up a towel and crept up behind Helms, who was being interviewed live on TV near the on-deck circle. After he leaped up on Helms's back to deliver the pie in the face, Coghlan landed awkwardly on his left leg. An MRI the following day revealed that he had a torn meniscus in his left knee that required season-ending surgery.

Florida manager Edwin Rodriguez banned any more pie celebrations. "If you ever get injured, you want to do it while you're out there competing, not when you're celebrating," Coghlan told reporters at the time. "Emotions get the best of you, you're excited. There's nothing wrong with that but be a little smarter when you're celebrating a win."

Helms told the *Palm Beach Post* that pie celebrations were getting out of hand. "You hate for this to be the cancellation of the celebration, but you can't take celebrations too far. Each time you celebrate, it seems like it gets more and more exciting and guys get more and more into it."

Despite sitting out the rest of the season from his injury, Coghlan told the *New York Times* the following year that he still wanted his teammates to celebrate. "You don't want to just walk around like a robot and act like you don't care," he said. "'Oh, we hit a walk-off and came from behind. I guess that's a good job. Let's high-five each other.' There's a lot of emotion, a lot of passion in this game. You have to let those play out and be smart."

As for the ban on pie celebrations, he vowed, "I'll pie everybody if we win the World Series."

DENNY HOCKING
Infielder-Outfielder · Minnesota, AL
September 2, 2001, and October 6, 2002

It was agonizingly obvious that Minnesota Twins utility player Denny Hocking didn't know how to celebrate big wins without getting hurt.

During a tie game in 2001 against the visiting Anaheim Angels, Hocking was called on to pinch-hit in the bottom of the ninth inning. He responded by going deep in a walk-off that vaulted the Twins to a 5–4 victory. As he reached home plate, Hocking was mobbed by his joyous teammates, who pounded him on the head. During the celebration, someone accidentally slammed the bill of Hocking's batting helmet smack in Hocking's face, breaking his nose. Just two months earlier, he had cracked his nose in Oakland while breaking up a double play.

After the game, Hocking—whose nostrils were plugged with cotton—said he didn't know who had busted his schnozz, "but I'm gonna look at the tape and [mess] somebody up!"

Hocking, who was grinning over the first walk-off homer of his career, added, "I just hope my nose doesn't stay crooked. Hopefully I can do this again, get mobbed and get my nose pushed back the other way. But if the price of hitting a game-winning home run and winning a series is getting my nose re-broken, I'll take it."

If Hocking didn't fully appreciate how hazardous celebrations could be, he definitely learned it the following year.

In the fifth and deciding game of the 2002 American League Division Series, the visiting Twins beat the Oakland Athletics 5–4. Hocking got two hits, drove in a run, and caught the ball for the final out to help send the Twins into the American League Championship Series against the Angels, a team he cheered for as a teenager.

Moments after beating Oakland, Hocking joined his teammates in a celebratory pileup near the mound. While Hocking was somewhere near the bottom of the raucous heap, an overly enthusiastic teammate who was jumping up and down stepped on Hocking's right hand. The player's metal spikes split the nail on Hocking's middle finger. The injury to his hand was serious enough to knock him out of the entire ALCS, which the Twins lost.

"I'm not good at celebrating," Hocking said. "I like the whole celebration concept. I just haven't perfected it."

SHERRY MAGEE
Left Fielder · Philadelphia, NL · September 13, 1908

Philadelphia Phillies slugger Sherry Magee was in a deep sleep, dreaming of chasing a fly ball, when he leaped out of an open third-story window.

Miraculously, Magee, a chronic sleepwalker, survived without any broken bones or internal injuries. He blamed it all on the late-night snack he had of green grapes and ham sandwiches.

In its account of the bizarre incident, the *Philadelphia Inquirer* reported: "From a third-story window of the Junction Hotel, Magee, with a shriek that he was after a high flyer, jumped more than 12 feet to the roof of a stable below. Had the roof not stopped his fall, he would have been killed upon the stone pavement of the hotel yard.

"As it was, the player proved to be only slightly injured. The physicians at the German Hospital could not find a broken bone and, after an examination, sent Magee back to his hotel.

"'I'll be back in the game in three or four days,' declared the ballplayer.

"Dr. John Boger says that the ballplayer had been working under mental strain for some time. He was completely absorbed in the race of the Phillies for the pennant, working like a beaver and wanting everybody else to do likewise. [Philadelphia finished the season in fourth place.]

"His wife, who was asleep in the same room, was awakened by excited cries from the ballplayer: 'Get together, come on . . . We've got 'em now.'

"Mrs. Magee went to procure some water. As she was returning with a pitcher, she saw her husband spring out of the bed with a wild leap and make for the window. She screamed and fell in her haste to catch Magee in time.

"The ballplayer was after a high flyer in his sleep. In his mind's eye, he saw it soaring just beyond the open window. With a frenzied leap and one arm raised high in the air, he jumped through the open window.

"Mrs. Magee stumbled over to the window and looked out. About 12 feet below, upon the roof of the stable, was the form of her husband in a heap. Everybody in the hotel was aroused. All expected to find the ballplayer dead or dying. 'Not a broken bone,' said the doctor. 'Just shaken up and bruised a bit.'

"'It was one of the most exciting games I ever played, even though I was asleep,' Magee declared. 'I was going after a high flyer. Why, even when I jumped from the bed, I thought I was simply jumping a fence that seemed, somehow, to have grown up near left field.

"'I guess the grapes and ham sandwiches caused the trouble. They never did agree with me.'"

GREG HARRIS
Pitcher · Texas, AL · August 17, 1987

Texas Rangers right-hander Greg Harris was scratched from several starts after he was stricken by the most dreaded ailment known to pitchers—sunflower seed elbow.

Harris was sitting in the dugout during a game against the visiting Kansas City Royals. He began playfully flicking sunflower seeds at a friend who was sitting in a box seat nearby. "I held them in my left hand and flicked them with my middle finger on my right hand," Harris recalled. "I was getting a few of them up past the first aisle."

Soon afterward, Harris's right elbow began to swell and hurt so badly that he couldn't throw. He had no choice but to rest his arm through several scheduled starts over the next three weeks. "I know," he said sheepishly. "It sounds ridiculous."

ABOUT THE AUTHORS

BRUCE NASH, president of Nash Entertainment, is the creator and producer of more than 80 television series and specials, including *Before They Were Stars, Magic's Biggest Secrets Finally Revealed, Meet My Folks,* and *Who Wants to Be a Superhero?* His *Modern Marvels* series is one of cable's longest-running programs, with more than 500 one-hour episodes.

On the sports front, Nash created and produced the critically acclaimed series *Amazing Sports Stories,* which was nominated for four Sports Emmys.

His company is headquartered in Hollywood, California.

ALLAN ZULLO has written more than 100 nonfiction books on such subjects as sports, the supernatural, history, animals, war, survival, and heroism. His latest books are *Heroes of 9/11* and *Titanic: Young Survivors.*

Among his many sports books are *When Bad Things Happen to Good Golfers, Golf Is a Funny Game,* and *March to Madness.* He writes two best-selling series for Scholastic, *Haunted Kids* and *Ten True Tales,* and produces boxed daily page calendars for Andrews McMeel, including the popular *Butter My Butt and Call Me a Biscuit.*

Zullo lives in Fairview, North Carolina.